Knowledge Diplomacy

Michael P. Ryan

Knowledge Diplomacy

Global Competition and the
Politics of Intellectual Property

BROOKINGS INSTITUTION PRESS
Washington, D.C.

Copyright © 1998 by

THE BROOKINGS INSTITUTION
1775 Massachusetts Avenue, N.W.
Washington, D.C. 20036

Library of Congress Cataloging-in-Publication Data

Ryan, Michael P. (Michael Patrick), 1960—
    Knowledge diplomacy : global competition and the politics of
    intellectual property / Michael P. Ryan.
        p.   cm.
    Includes index.
    ISBN 0-8157-7654-3 (cloth)
    ISBN 0-8157-7653-5 (pbk.)
    1. Intellectual property—United States. 2. Intellectual property
(International law) 3. Technological innovations—Law and
legislation—United States. 4. Patent laws and legislation—
United States. 5. Copyright—United States. 6. United States
Intellectual Property Organization. I. Title.
KF2979.R93 1998
346.7304′8—dc21   98-8966
                                                                                                    CIP

9 8 7 6 5 4 3 2 1

The paper used in this publication meets the minimum requirements of
the American National Standard for Information Sciences—Permanence
of Paper for Printed Library Materials, ANSI Z39.48-1984

Typeset in Times Roman

Composition by AlphaWebTech
Mechanicsville, Maryland

Printed by R.R. Donnelley and Sons Co.
Harrisonburg, Virginia

THE BROOKINGS INSTITUTION

The Brookings Institution is an independent organization devoted to nonpartisan research, education, and publication in economics, government, foreign policy, and the social sciences generally. Its principal purposes are to aid in the development of sound public policies and to promote public understanding of issues of national importance.

The Institution was founded on December 8, 1927, to merge the activities of the Institute for Government Research, founded in 1916, the Institute of Economics, founded in 1922, and the Robert Brookings Graduate School of Economics and Government, founded in 1924.

The Board of Trustees is responsible for the general administration of the Institution, while the immediate direction of the policies, program, and staff is vested in the President, assisted by an advisory committee of the officers and staff. The by-laws of the Institution state: "It is the function of the Trustees to make possible the conduct of scientific research, and publication, under the most favorable conditions, and to safeguard the independence of the research staff in pursuit of their studies and in the publication of the result of such studies. It is not a part of their function to determine, control, or influence the conduct of particular investigations or the conclusions reached."

The President bears final responsibility for the decision to publish a manuscript as a Brookings book. In reaching his judgment on competence, accuracy, and objectivity of each study, the President is advised by the director of the appropriate research program and weighs the views of a panel of expert outside readers who report to him in confidence on the quality of the work. Publication of a work signifies that it is deemed a competent treatment worthy of public consideration but does not imply endorsement of conclusions or recommendations.

The Institution maintains its position of neutrality on issues of public policy in order to safeguard the intellectual freedom of the staff. Hence interpretations or conclusions in Brookings publications should be understood to be solely those of the authors and should not be attributed to the Institution, to its trustees, officers, or other staff members, or to the organizations that support its research.

Foreword

IN THE PAST two decades, the protection of intellectual property has become one of the most important concerns of international economic negotiation. As goods and services have increasingly depended on patents, copyrights, and trademarks to maintain their competitiveness in world markets, trade negotiators have participated in bilateral, regional, and multilateral forums to achieve stronger protections through multilateral treaties and the efforts of international organizations. As a result, the harmonization of national laws and policies protecting intellectual property has become a key element in the "deep integration" of international economic policy.

For the average citizen, however, the idea of intellectual property and the laws governing patents, trade secrets, trademarks, and copyrights are little understood. In this study Michael Ryan explains contemporary changes in the international law and governmental policy regarding intellectual property protection by using an analytic framework that draws from the economics of industrial organization, organizational sociology, educational psychology, and political science. He shows that changes in international intellectual property policy have been the product of learning by everyone involved.

The bilateral and multilateral treaties reached in the 1990s and the strengthening of national and international institutions will influence global competition in chemicals, pharmaceuticals, agricultural products, information technology, computer software, information and publishing, and music and film entertainment well into the next century. The changes will also influence economics and politics around the world, especially in developing countries. These new developments, the author argues, will be increasingly reflected in a general refocusing from a diplomacy that liberalized merchandise trade principles after World War II to a "knowledge diplomacy" that is guiding institutionalization of information-market liberalization, product and service regulation, and the harmonization of national standards.

The author is grateful to Dr. Arpad Bogsch, director general of the World Intellectual Property Organization, for opening the organization to him for this study, Albert Tramposch for arranging interviews with senior WIPO staff, the WIPO library for its help with archival information, and the many staff members who generously gave of their time to meet with him. The staffs at the libraries of the U.S. Court of Appeals for the Federal Circuit and at the U.S. Patent and Trademark Office were also helpful. Some one hundred members of the Washington and Geneva intellectual property policy communities provided information for the study. The attendees of the World Bank's TechNet seminar, to whom the author presented a paper derived from the project, made useful comments. Finally, for interesting discussions he thanks the participants in his 1994–96 Georgetown University intellectual property seminars.

For financial support received during the four years of research that went into this study, the author gratefully acknowledges the Center for International Business Education at the University of Michigan, the Center for International Business Education and Research at Georgetown University, the Landegger Program in International Business Diplomacy at the Georgetown University School of Foreign Service, and the IBM Corporation. For final research and writing of the study, the Center for Law, Economics, and Politics at the Brookings Institution gratefully acknowledges support received from Pfizer Corporation, Pharmaceutical Research and Manufacturers of America, and Wyeth-Ayerst International, Inc.

James Schneider edited the manuscript, Cynthia Iglesias and Helen Kim verified its factual content, Sally Martin proofread the pages, and Mary Mortenson compiled the index.

The views expressed in this book are those of the author and should not be ascribed to any of the persons or organizations acknowledged above, or to the trustees, officers, or staff members of the Brookings Institution.

Michael H. Armacost
President

Washington, D.C.
March 1998

Contents

ONE

Introduction and Framework
for Analysis

THE OFFICE of the U.S. Trade Representative insisted in Punta del Este, Uruguay, in 1986 that protecting intellectual property rights be on the agenda for the GATT Uruguay Round of multilateral trade negotiations, although in truth few people at the USTR knew much about patents, copyrights, trade secrets, or trademarks. Yet by the time the Uruguay Round negotiators met in Montreal in 1990 to take stock of their efforts, the institutionalization of intellectual property rights had become one of the highest trade-related priorities of the U.S. government. When the final agreements were signed in Marrakesh in 1994, the Agreement on Trade-Related Aspects of Intellectual Property Rights (TRIPS) institutionalized the international laws of intellectual property rights, an achievement important not only for the U.S. national interest but for the future of innovation and expression in the world economy.

TRIPS is potentially the most important legal advance for the world trading system since the establishment of the General Agreement on Tariffs and Trade (GATT) in 1947. Postwar diplomats conducted an "industrial diplomacy" that institutionalized global trade in manufactures, offering machinists and mill hands incentives to make products for a whole world of consumers. Now post–cold war diplomats are conducting a "knowledge diplomacy" that is institutionalizing trade in products of invention and expression, offering innovators the incentive to make their products for the global market. The negotiation of TRIPS is a response to developing countries' growing production of and trade in innovation and expression

1

products. Through the global institutionalization of the law, the agreement aims to stimulate more trade in these products.

The international intellectual property regime has been largely the handiwork of the industrialized countries, just as the "state power," realist school of international relations predicts.[1] In the past ten years the negotiations on intellectual property rights in the multilateral TRIPS and trilateral North American Free Trade Agreement (NAFTA) were conducted by a U.S. government representing a hegemonic power in innovation and expression-based global markets. According to the National Science Foundation, U.S.-based capabilities are superior or equal to those of Europe and Japan in environmental monitoring and assessment, computing, communications, biotechnology, materials, avionics and controls, and other critical technologies.[2] In 1992 some 45 percent of all industrial R&D in the industrialized countries was carried out in the United States. U.S.-based inventors earned about 45 percent of patents granted by the U.S. Patent Office and 25 percent of those granted by the European Patent Office.[3]

The same NSF study found that technology products accounted for 17 to 19 percent of all U.S. imports and exports from 1990 to 1994 and that exports far exceeded imports. Exports of computer software doubled, and computer-integrated manufacturing equipment yielded a big surplus during these same years. U.S.-based firms are the world's largest exporters of products in biotechnology, life sciences, advanced materials, aerospace, weapons technology, and nuclear technologies. U.S. multinational manufacturing enterprises increasingly transfer intellectual property internationally through the industrial processes that they sell abroad. Exports, as measured by royalties and licensing fees, amounted to about $27 billion in 1995, while imports amounted to only $6.3 billion. At least $20 billion of the exports are transactions between U.S. firms and their foreign affiliates, thus the protection of the intellectual property in the foreign market is of concern to these U.S.-based companies.[4]

1. Kindleberger (1973); Gilpin (1981); Krasner (1976).
2. National Science Board (1996, p. 6–5).
3. General Electric, IBM, AT&T, RCA, and Hitachi were the top five U.S. patent earners in 1983; IBM, Toshiba, Canon, Eastman Kodak, and General Electric were the top five in 1993. National Science Board (1996, pp. 6-16, 6-19, 6-20). IBM, Canon, NEC, and Motorola were the top in 1997. Liebovich (1998, p. A10).
4. Coleman (1997, pp. 23–25).

Complex Interdependence of Intellectual Property Diplomacy

Hegemonic power pretty much explains how the United States imposed its will on Mexico over intellectual property rights in the NAFTA negotiations. But state power offers only a superficial explanation of the multilateral diplomacy concerning intellectual property rights that has been conducted in the 1980s and 1990s. U.S. power explains neither the demand for international institutions to protect intellectual property nor their characteristics nor how they have changed. Followers of the complex interdependence school of international relations have commented, "Power over outcomes will be conferred by *organizationally* dependent capabilities, such as voting power, ability to form coalitions, and control of elite networks."[5] International regimes, it is said,

affect the costs of transactions. The value of a potential agreement to its prospective participants will depend, in part, on how consistent it is with principles of legitimacy emobodied in international regimes. Transactions that violate these principles will be costly. Regimes also affect bureaucratic costs of transactions: successful regimes organize issue-areas so that productive linkages (those that facilitate agreements consistent with principles of the regime) are facilitated, while destructive linkages and bargains that are inconsistent with regime principles are discouraged.[6]

State power, interests, and goals are thus mediated by the principles, norms, procedures, and rules of international regimes, the "principles, norms, rules, and decisionmaking procedures around which actor expectations converge in a given issue area."[7] Explanatory emphasis in the tradition of complex-interdependence research is placed on technical information and ideology and an international diplomacy involving not only the states themselves, but multinational corporations, nongovernmental organizations, the secretariats at international governmental organizations,[8] and transnational epistemic communities, bodies of professionals with expertise in given subjects.[9] Noting that most public international law is based on

5. Keohane and Nye (1977, p. 55).
6. Keohane (1984, p. 92).
7. Krasner (1983, p. 1).
8. Young (1983, pp. 106–12; 1989, pp. 95–103); Lipson (1985); Aggarwal (1985); and Crawford and Lenway (1985).
9. P. Haas (1992). The idea of an epistemic community was foreshadowed by research such as that of Jacobson and Stein (1966).

treaties, scholars argue that an international regime is typically based on the codified rules of treaties among states and usually associated with an international governmental organization (IGO).[10] The outcomes of the international intellectual property diplomacy were mediated by international regimes for intellectual property and trade.

Global Competition of Intellectual Property–Based Industries

My study, following the research tradition of complex interdependence within international relations, begins in chapters two and three with an analysis of industry structure. Patents, trade secrets, and copyrights are very important to some industries and of little importance to others, thus an explanation of international diplomacy and institutional change involving intellectual property begins with the study of the nature of competition in industries based on intellectual property. Structural analysis of industries, commonly known as the Harvard Business School method and rooted in the economics of industrial organization, investigates industry competition through the study of rivalry among competitor firms, bargaining relationships with buyers and suppliers, substitute products and services, and potential new entrants to competition.[11] The sources of competitive advantage are analyzed by investigating the nature of rivalry within the industry, including the number of firms and their market shares, the pace of growth in the industry, the extent of product or service differentiation, and the barriers to entry and exit. The analysis of entry barriers examines variables such as product differentiation and brand identification, capital requirements, access to distribution channels, scale economies, learning and experience curves, government regulation, and proprietary product knowledge or technology. It is the last of these that is of special interest to the study of competition based on intellectual property and its policy diplomacy.

The costs of product development in the innovation and expression industries are high. Filmmaking, music producing, and research-oriented pharmaceuticals manufacturing are risky businesses that survive with three hits out of ten at bats; competitors who thrive do so with home runs. That is, competition in industry sectors is better measured by slugging percentage

10. Aggarwal (1985, p. 20); and Henkin and others(1980, pp. 36–113).
11. Porter (1980).

than by batting average. Seven out of ten music CDs fail to turn a profit; seven out of ten films fail to turn a profit. An average of one commercially viable drug emerges from every 4,000 to 10,000 compounds screened in a development process that may involve ten years of testing and clinical trials for efficacy and safety. One film such as *Jurassic Park* or a music CD such as *Jagged Little Pill* pays a lot of bills at an entertainment company, just as one Norvasc heart drug does at a pharmaceutical maker.

But if the costs of development are high, the costs of product imitation (or outright theft) may be relatively low, a circumstance that economists call the *appropriability problem*. A book, music compact disc, or movie video can be appropriated cheaply; a pharmaceutical product faces human and financial barriers to market entry that are higher but not different in kind. The institutions of patent and copyright attempt to resolve the appropriability problem by conferring limited periods of exclusivity to stimulate people to risk investing in product development.

In the United States a nexus of the market and institutions to protect intellectual property rights encourages these risky businesses to grow and prosper. The nexus comprises a large population of wealthy consumers, risk-taking capital markets, mobile labor markets, world-leading university research and know-how institutions (including firms' organizational and managerial skills), enforceable contracts, and intellectual property rights. It is important to emphasize that these industries succeed in certain countries and not in others only in part because of patent and copyright institutions, for it takes the full range of the market-institution nexus to establish the conditions for success. As a matter of business strategy, it then takes assembling the right competences in product development, production, and marketing to be a winner.

Intellectual property–intensive industries share the appropriability problem, but business strategies to combat piracy vary. On the one hand, producers of information technology use intellectual property protections extensively because such software is more subject than hardware to inexpensive appropriation. On the other hand, microprocessor plants costing $1 billion or more are themselves strong barriers to illegal appropriation of intellectual property. Information technology also tends to be a business of systems that requires technologies and products made by many competitors who are also collaborators through cross-licensing relationships. Blatant piracy of intellectual property is bad business strategy. When the regime to prevent the piracy of intellectual property is weak, making licensing strategies difficult to maintain, technology strategists tend to seek control through the purchase of equity in the partner.[12] Vertical integration, especially the establishment of equity-related manufacturing capabilities, is an additional nonlegal means to protect intellectual property.[13] Weak intellectual property regimes also challenge the business strategies of copyright-dependent industries, which rely on licensing to distribute products.

Policy Purposes of Intellectual Property Institutions

Patents and copyrights were devised by the Venetians to stimulate innovation and expression in a city-state that was losing its trade hegemony in the eastern Mediterranian and with it the capacity to compete with Florence and other city-states. The institutions gradually spread northward, developing certain distinctive characteristics in France, Germany, and England. The authoritarian French government came to view patents and copyrights as royal favors to be bestowed at whim. Eighteenth-century French revolutionaries established instead that they were "natural rights" of the creative process of innovation and expression and were not to be subject to government intervention other than ratification. Early seventeenth-century English reformers reacted to the perversion of the patent and copyright into royal monopolies by codifying into law that these were rights bestowed by government to stimulate innovation and expression. Thus the institutions in England kept to the original Venetian intent.

The framers of the U.S. Constitution rejected the French assumptions in favor of the British, and laws regarding patents and copyrights were promulgated by the new Congress during George Washington's first presidential term through the leadership of Thomas Jefferson on patents and Noah Webster on copyrights. The aim of U.S. intellectual property policy has always been to promote public welfare; private property rights have been the means toward that end.

From its beginning the basic contract between the innovator and society has been that, rather than safeguarding the know-how of the innovation through the darkness of trade secrets, the innovator discloses the know-how in exchange for a limited period of exclusivity to produce and authorize to produce. Disclosure is fundamental to the patent institution and has gradually made the major patent offices of the world enormous treasure troves

12. Oxley (1997).
13. Pisano (1991).

of technological knowledge. The institution has evolved other features to ensure that a proper balance is struck between encouraging an innovator and ensuring public access to the product. Among these features are rules regarding the scope of patentability, the demand that the innovation possess an "inventive step" or be "novel" and "nonobvious" to one skilled in the art, and the condition that it be useful or have "utility." Rules and procedures have also been developed in the industrialized countries to settle the inevitable disputes between competing innovators. Together these measures have built a patent institution that stimulates innovation without leading to monopoly behavior.

Similarly, U.S. copyright law has been written to stimulate expression to the benefit of the public welfare. The limited period of exclusivity has gradually lengthened so that it now approaches two lifetimes and is narrowly defined to cover only the expression of a work, not the underlying ideas. A copyright cannot, for example, be obtained for a story plot or deductive argument. Of course, this principle is easier to lay down than to apply, so the courts have elaborated analytic frameworks and tests to define what precisely is "fair use" and what is infringement of a copyrighted work.

There can be cases of copyright fair use or infringement that are close legal calls, but outright infringement has always been the greater challenge for artists. Venice provided that unauthorized copies of a work be seized and burned and instituted criminal penalties to deter pirates. These principles have been carried forth in the copyright institution in contemporary industrialized countries, but there is less certainty in legal codification and little vigor in enforcement in developing countries, where pirated products often account for more than 90 percent of total sales. Nevertheless, developing countries have more often acknowledged the utility of copyright than of patents. The institutional histories of patent and copyright, characterized by the philosophical tension between *natural property rights* and *public welfare–enhancing incentives for risky investment,* evolve in developing countries such that policymakers tend to confer legitimacy on copyright because it appears to protect the "moral rights" of local authors. But they tend to deny the legitimacy of patents because these appear to protect the "economic rights" of foreign inventors.

Business Interest Mobilization in the United States

Complex interdependence in research erases the traditional boundary between domestic and foreign policies; the research tradition emphasizes transnational coalitions, and above all, the way in which domestic political forces determine patterns of international cooperation.[14] According to students of the "deep integration" era in which we live, the boundary between international and domestic politics is no longer distinguishable.[15] Thus chapter four shows that U.S. patent and copyright business interest groups drove trade-related intellectual property policy in the 1980s and 1990s, although the diplomacy was conducted on their behalf by the U.S. executive branch. Pharmaceutical makers and the copyright industries, the sectors most vulnerable to piracy because of their relatively low barriers to entry, were the strongest of these interest groups. Other sectors, such as makers of semiconductors and information technology hardware, have maintained an active interest in intellectual property policy, but because of their relatively higher entry barriers, they have not been active in resorting to international diplomacy and promoting institutional change.

Conventional wisdom has it that business lobbying activity is explained by analysis of the economic sources of a firm's competitiveness. However, although the international trade policy preferences of firms and their advocacy activities are usefully explained with reference to their economic interests, supplemented by analysis of institutional relationships and economic interests,[16] it may be best to say that business interests mobilize to advocate for changes in trade policy to contribute to their global business strategies and that may mean according to a logic of strategic intent regarding goals rather than according to interests measurable at a given time.[17] For example, the pharmaceutical interests, unlike the copyright interests, did not advocate stronger intellectual property laws based on claims of huge piracy losses in developing countries. Instead they urged U.S. action based on their opportunities and potential for future foreign investments and sales.

The concerns of business are nevertheless often expressed by groups that may be ad hoc, short-term committees or coalitions or may be deeply institutionalized, long-term industry associations.[18] An interest group is most effective when its leaders focus on an objective, design appropriate

---

14. Haggard and Simmons (1987). See also Lawrence (1996).
15. Lawrence (1996, p. 8).
16. Aharoni (1966); and Goodman (1987).
17. On economic interests see Aggarwal, Keohane, and Yoffie (1987); Milner (1988); and Milner and Yoffie (1989). On the combination of institutional relationships and economic interests see Martin (1995). On the logic of "strategic intent" regarding goals see Hamel and Prahalad (1985, 1993).
18. Olson (1965).

strategies to achieve it, encourage committed membership, recruit capable staff, and raise enough money to fund the group's activities.[19] Put another way, interest-group organization is relatively difficult to do. Indeed, one study of business-government trade policy interaction in the 1970s found that U.S. lobbying groups were generally ill managed, underfunded, and ineffective in influencing Congress.[20] But the industries based on intellectual property demonstrated in the 1980s and 1990s an impressive capacity to push their interests in Washington and Geneva. The Intellectual Property Committee and International Intellectual Property Alliance have been well managed, well staffed, well funded, and effective.

Issues of public policy may remain defined merely as conditions that require no special government action until they are defined as problems by policymakers. As one policymaker remarked, "Conditions become defined as problems when we come to believe that we should do something about them."[21] This redefinition may be achieved through advocacy made persuasive by the market and the political power of the industry sector making the demand on the political system.[22] In democracies, business enterprises "are taller and richer than the rest of us and have rights that we do not have. Their political impact differs from and dwarfs that of the ordinary citizen."[23] Both the patent and the copyright interests, led by chief executives of pharmaceutical manufacturers, entertainment producers, and software providers, have effectively leveraged their market positions to encourage policymakers to wield U.S. economic power abroad on their behalf.

The industries that demanded U.S. policymakers protect intellectual property rights are world competitive and major contributors to the U.S. economy. American research-based pharmaceutical makers maintain an impressive share of a global market that exceeded $37 billion in 1989.[24] The U.S. chemical industry accounts for nearly a quarter of global chemical production, far more than Japan, Germany, or France, and produces a significant trade surplus for the U.S. balance of payments.

In 1994 filmmaking, musical composition and performance, writing, and software creation contributed 3.78 percent of U.S. GDP.[25] Industries related

---

19. Walker (1991); and Wilson (1995).
20. Bauer, Pool, and Dexter (1972).
21. Kingdon (1984, p. 115).
22. Kingdon (1984, p. 54).
23. Lindblom (1977, p. 5).
24. International Trade Commission (1991).
25. Siwek and Mosteller (1996, p. 1).

to filmmaking, music, publishing, and software creation brought the total to 5.72 percent of GDP. The copyright industries grew at an average annual rate almost double that of the economy as a whole from 1977 to 1994. In 1994 they employed 3.1 million people, and 2.8 million worked in related industries. By 1995 foreign sales grew to more than 10 percent of all sales by the U.S. copyright industries; they ranked behind only motor vehicles–auto parts and agricultural products.

The lack of patent protection, especially for pharmaceutical products, and the weakly institutionalized copyright protection in developing countries motivated U.S. business interests to mobilize for a major private-public initiative to reform world intellectual property institutions as a way to reform the institutions of the developing countries. Beginning in the early 1980s the patent interests designed an investment-related multilateral strategy lobbied by their CEOs within the forum of the Advisory Committee on Trade Policy and Negotiation. About the same time, although separately, the copyright interests designed an antipiracy, bilateral strategy based on "countable indicators" of piracy losses in developing countries (and in industrialized countries, where problems persist). These indicators, statistical evidence put together by the group and its consultants, successfully redefined a policy issue into a policy problem.[26]

The USTR's Intellectual Property Diplomacy

When the target of business interest advocacy is the U.S. executive and when the issue is trade-related intellectual property policy, the Office of the U.S. Trade Representative is the agent for the president. The USTR has been most responsive to the petitions of globally competitive industry sectors; it will act aggressively in their behalf through bilateral, regional, and multilateral diplomacy, but with special regard for the overriding U.S. commitment to the GATT-WTO trade institution.[27] The USTR's behavior has been consistent with its mission of serving a president who has been at once chief foreign policymaker, intergovernmental competitor with Congress for policy leadership, and domestic politician in need of interest group allies himself.

26. Kingdon (1984, p. 98).
27. Ryan (1995a, 1995b).

Caught in the vortex of trade deficits and trade conflict with Japan, the president and executive branch grasped the political utility of advocating on behalf of some of America's most globally competitive industries. The mobilization of the patent interests led the USTR to urge the GATT membership to include intellectual property protection on the agenda of the Uruguay Round negotiations. The mobilization of the copyright interests led Congress to amend the 1974 Trade Act's section 301 in 1984 to declare that failure to protect intellectual property was an unfair trade barrier that could provoke U.S. retaliation. In 1988 the copyright mobilization led, through another amendment to section 301, to the institutionalization of intellectual property rights as a regular, annual issue for surveillance and action.

The U.S. Trade Representative conducted aggressive bilateral diplomacy to seek reforms in developing countries, punctuating the commitment with the threatened loss of Generalized System of Preferences tariff advantages. The patent and copyright interests converged as the Uruguay Round began, although not without some testy USTR-mediated meetings. Both interests have learned from each other and have been pursuing bilateral and multilateral tracks simultaneously in the 1990s, but their interests diverge as often as they converge.

Chapter 4 studies the capacity of the Office of the U.S. Trade Representative to learn about intellectual property law and policy. The organization's competencies in the mid-1980s reflected its focus on real property—manufactured goods, raw materials, and agricultural commodities—not intellectual property. Responsibility for leading U.S. negotiation delegations composed of representatives from the U.S. Patent and Trademark Office and the Copyright Office demanded that the agencies acquire new skills and awareness of international trade politics and institutions. USTR staff demonstrated the capacity for quick-study, on-the-job learning, and the organization recruited new staff to contribute to its intellectual property competency.

Trade-Related Intellectual Property Diplomacy within GATT

International law pertaining to patents, trade secrets, copyrights, industrial designs, and trademarks has been more than a century in the making, owing to a series of treaties promulgated late in the nineteenth century and amended during the twentieth century to adapt to changing technologies and patterns of competition. During most of its history, international law of intellectual property existed apart from international law of real property trade: the former institutionalized government intervention into markets while the latter institutionalized government withdrawal from markets. The diplomacy of intellectual property rights was conducted by obscure administrators at the World Intellectual Property Organization (WIPO) and its predecessors; trade diplomacy was conducted by high-profile trade and economic ministers at the GATT forum. But in the Uruguay Round negotiations the two issues met to establish minimum standards of protection of intellectual property rights under authority of reformed treaties.

When U.S. business people and government representatives called for new international intellectual property laws, the governments of developing countries wanted no part of the reforms. From the standpoint of U.S. business interests and policymakers, the way out of the standoff depended on understanding the interaction of states in multilateral negotiations. The diplomacy of writing international law occurs on two levels: states bargain with their own domestic groups even as they bargain with other states. Bargaining at the domestic level may require addressing new domestic groups and issues, making domestic concessions, and even redefining the importance of issues in the minds of policymakers, legislators, and domestic groups.[28] Thus, the key to getting agreement is getting the right mix of issues on the table so that previously unrelated issues can be linked.[29] A negotiator offers something important to an opposing negotiator in order to receive a concession that the opposing negotiator would not otherwise be willing to offer. Linkage-bargain diplomacy can achieve treaties in diplomatically and politically difficult areas in which agreement would otherwise be elusive.

Because the international regime establishes the forum for international governmental organizations and the rules that govern multilateral negotiations to write international law, the creation of new international intellectual property law would need to be moved from the function-specific WIPO forum with its one-nation, one-vote decisionmaking to the GATT forum with its economic power-based decisionmaking. U.S. trade diplomats speculated that linkage bargaining in the GATT forum could achieve unprecedented multilateral intellectual property agreement: the developing countries would get reductions in tariffs on apparel and agriculture, and the

28. Friman (1993); and Schoppa (1993).
29. Hoekman (1989); Tollison and Willett (1989); and Sebenius (1983).

industrialized countries would get universal minimum standards of intellectual property protection as well as the relaxation of restrictions on foreign direct investment.[30] When the TRIPS agreement was finally achieved as part of the Uruguay Round package, it appeared that linkage-bargain diplomacy explained the outcome and that making international intellectual property law would from that time forward be by way of linkage bargaining.

Linkage bargaining in the Uruguay Round worked because U.S. negotiators demanded that agreements had to be accepted in their totality, a position with force because the final Uruguay Round package included agreements establishing the World Trade Organization and the Dispute Settlement Understanding. Within the context of the TRIPS agreement, the Dispute Settlement Understanding offered countries some respite from the threat of U.S. trade sanctions under authority of the section 301 policy. The threat loomed larged in the minds of developing country policymakers, who had little to fear from a European Community lukewarm on TRIPS but much to fear from a USTR that had initiated actions over intellectual property against Korea and Brazil in 1985 to get them to the table and pursued an aggressive bilateral trade diplomacy throughout the eight years of the Uruguay Round to keep them at the table.

However, closer examination of TRIPS diplomacy reveals that function-specific intellectual property diplomacy within WIPO was not dead. Functionalism proposes that specialists crucially help international cooperation through their technical knowledge.[31] Linkage bargaining in the Uruguay Round only worked because there was a draft TRIPS agreement on the table as the final bargains were being struck. Under the leadership of the TRIPS negotiation chair, the GATT Secretariat culled ideas from the negotiators and offered a Draft Composite Text that was the basis of the compromise final agreements.

Organizational Learning and Change at WIPO

The World Intellectual Property Organization confronted its need for major change in the 1970s, and its experience has been turbulent in the 1980s and 1990s. The 1974 agreement to become a UN agency turned the

---

30. Rubin and Graham (1984); and Hufbauer and Schott (1985, pp. 73–75).
31. Jacobson (1984, pp. 62–67).

organization from a club of patent-wealthy, industrialized countries into a potentially universal IGO including many developing countries that needed considerable help establishing patent systems. The Patent Cooperation Treaty of 1978 required WIPO to administer international patent applications of multinational corporations, a task that would ultimately result in its recruitment of scores of new employees skilled in reviewing patent applications and the creation of an administrative structure to manage processes unlike those that had been traditional at the organization. TRIPS encroached on WIPO's position as the forum for creating international intellectual property rules and meant that WIPO had to expand greatly the scope of its teaching regarding the purpose, implementation, and enforcement of intellectual property policy to help developing countries meet their TRIPS obligations. Presuming that IGOs exist because they accumulate and manage knowledge better than global markets do, WIPO's organizational capacity to learn explains its capacity to adapt.

According to educational psychologists, learning depends on cognition, the learner's ability to process information, and motivation.[32] Cognition and motivation are interdependent and dynamic: cognition depends on the existence of appropriate cognitive structures and learning strategies; cognitive structures and learning strategies relate to personality and motivation characteristics. Individual learning relates to, but is not identical to, organizational learning. Organizations are more than collected individuals, and organizational learning is more than collected individual learning.[33] An organization is learning when it is "encoding inferences from history into routines that guide behavior," where "routines" are rules, norms, procedures, beliefs, paradigms, and codes.[34] Perhaps fundamental to organizational learning is that it depends on the investment of adequate resources.[35] But organizational learning also depends on organizational climate and culture. Organizational climate comprises size, structure, complexity, reward structure, and leadership style. When the environment is turbulent, leadership style can be decisive in promoting organizational responsiveness, and having a team leader appears to be the best style for turbulent times.[36] Leadership is very much about articulating a vision for the organi-

---

32. Corno and Snow (1986); and Pintrich and others (1986).
33. Kim (1993).
34. Levitt and March (1988).
35. Mohr (1969).
36. Guskin and Bassis (1985).

zation and acquiring the organizational competencies to realize it, in effect stretching the organization to meet new demands and challenges.[37]

It has become conventional wisdom that hierarchical bureaucracy can effectively carry out administrative routines and perform repetitive tasks but is slow to improve procedures even when change is necessary. Organizations that are steeply hierarchical tend to be unresponsive to new challenges and slow to change. Flatter organizational structures can be much more responsive and flexible. Furthermore, according to theory, organizational learning requires motivated staff and rewards, including financial compensation, opportunities for career advancement, and recognition, that are part of a climate contributing to motivation. Learning in organizations depends on intelligence from outside the organization, which entails gathering, processing, interpreting, and communicating the technical and political information needed and is difficult for organizations to do. The organization must encourage the acquisition of information not only through recruiting new staff,[38] but also by encouraging their professional staff to join professional associations and become members of transnational "epistemic communities.[39] These communities are valuable for their enormous pools of information and their capacities to acquire and generate more.

Bringing valuable intelligence into an organization, however, is only the beginning for organizational learning, because the information must be acted upon and come to be part of the life of the organization. Organizational learning thus involves governance structures and practices in which "hierarchy, specialization, and centralization are major sources of distortion and blockage of intelligence."[40] Poor communication leads to distrust, suspicion, information hoarding, and lack of involvement, while organizational learning depends on reward systems that encourage information sharing, teaching, and mentoring.[41] Furthermore, horizontal flows of information are crucial to organizational learning.

Organizational culture, in contrast to organizational climate, refers to values, attitudes, appreciation systems, behavior patterns, local knowledge: "the way we do things around here."[42] Culture facilitates socialization and

37. Hamel and Prahalad (1993).
38. Simon (1991); and von Hippel (1987).
39. P. Haas (1992, pp. 187–224); and E. Haas (1990, pp. 21, 41).
40. Wilensky (1967, p. 42).
42. Pucik (1988).
42. Schein (1984); and Wilkins and Ouchi (1983).

is important in recruiting and selecting new members. Sociologists have found that a strong, externally oriented culture of achievement, which tends to create high satisfaction, strong performance, and healthy innovation, is the most effective and may be the best learner.[43] Organizational learning depends on shared mental models that encourage the integration of new knowledge into organizational routines. Shared mental models, or shared world views, begin with recruitment, because new staff with educational preparations, career paths, and attitudes resembling those of existing staff facilitate their integration into the organization. Shared world views are the product of socialization within the organization and the essence of its culture.

This study finds that WIPO possesses distinctive organizational characteristics of climate and culture that have encouraged learning and adaptation. It has learned in a process that is both top-down and bottom-up. Leadership at the resource-rich organization designed a flexible secretariat with a flat organizational structure with staff members who belong to transnational professional communities, share world views, communicate through institutionalized internal mechanisms, are characterized by orientation toward achievement, and are motivated. As idea generator, organizer, and diplomat the director general led the organization's adaptation, and professional staff acquired new skills related to their roles as teachers about intellectual property policy and administration and intermediaries in international intellectual property law negotiations.

TRIPS Implementation and Development

The implementation of TRIPS offers the potential for increased innovation and expression activity in developing countries and is an unprecedented initiative of judiciary building in the third world by the industrialized world. But the support of domestic coalitions in developing countries for the "shallow integration," nondiscrimination, and border measure trade reduction program of GATT in the second half of the twentieth century remains unconsolidated, while support for the new "deep integration" global regulatory and policy harmonization program of the WTO is weak.[44] TRIPS implementation by developing countries in the coming years will

---

43. Litwin and Stringer (1968).
44. Haggard (1995).

challenge ideas about economic development strategy and enforcement capacity and the judiciary. Implementation will occur in a context very different from the one that existed when TRIPS negotiations were begun in 1986. Industrializing countries are increasingly participating in the world economy through deliberately open, liberal policies. The economic development strategy of import substitution has clearly failed, and the debt crisis of the 1980s and the export-oriented success of some Asian countries has motivated policymakers in developing countries to rethink their ideas about what makes successful development strategies. During the TRIPS negotiations, policymakers began to see that investment, trade, and technology transfer were discouraged by weak enforcement of intellectual property rights and thus that indigenous innovation and expression activity might be better encouraged by protection than piracy of intellectual property. Thus, the ideology of development strategy is changing with respect to intellectual property, but changing at different rates from country to country. TRIPS implementation faces considerable opposition within national governments and from domestic interest groups in developing countries.

Intellectual property trade and commercial competition imposes on states an enforcement problem qualitatively different from that imposed by financial capital flows and real property trade. Enforcement of policies regarding financial assets and trade are essentially problems of a central government's power and its capacity to control its borders. Enforcement of intellectual property rights depends on a government's capacity to enforce policies at local levels. The essence of the state is its capacity to make and enforce policy, and TRIPS poses an enforcement challenge that may help developing countries better institutionalize the capacity to enforce intellectual property rights by reforming their judiciaries. The demands made in TRIPS for the reform of national courts and judicial procedures and the public administration of enforcement are unprecedented as a matter of public international law.

Communication Revolution and Intellectual Property

Even as the TRIPS negotations were grinding along, a communication revolution was occurring, born of the spectacular rise in the use of the Internet, telephony deregulation that increased providers, and an important breakthrough in digital compression technologies that is increasing channel capacity and may foment a digital convergence of communication media.

The Internet offers a powerful new medium by which to distribute copyrighted materials. It also, however, offers the prospect of piracy of digitized music, films, and software downloaded over and over again with no loss of quality. The digital communication revolution challenges conventionl institutions of intellectual property such as copyright to adapt to new technological capabilities and commercial behaviors. It also challenges recent practices such as the assignment of domain names (electronic addresses) to adapt to the global reach of the Internet.

Interests and policy preferences in the United States and internationally have fallen into four basic groups: producers of copyrighted entertainment, information, and software content; users of copyrighted content, including libraries, governments, and universities; on-line and communication service providers, the deliverers of content; and makers of hardware. Content producers intended to ensure their ownership rights, users to ensure access, communication service deliverers to ensure delivery free of liability for user piracy, and hardware makers to ensure equipment production free of similarly being held liable for piracy by users. Ownership, access, and piracy all look different depending on the point of view.

Two treaties were negotiated and signed at the 1996 Geneva Diplomatic Conference under the auspices of WIPO. The agreements attempt to preserve the intent of the intellectual property policy of expression: confer exclusive rights of authorship and distribution to provide incentives for risky investment while maintaining the public's access to information and expression. However, the final texts omitted crucial issues, so the conference only begins the process of creating new rules regarding communication technology change and copyright.

That function-specific lawmaking happened at all in the WIPO forum after the conclusion of linkage-bargaining TRIPS lawmaking indicates a need to choose forums with purpose. Function-specific diplomacy contributes learning capacity to making international law: specialists at an international governmental organization form the core of a subnational and transnational community that shares the knowledge needed for learning to adapt law to changing technologies and market conditions. Linkage-bargain diplomacy contributes multiple policy issues to such lawmaking. Trade negotiators have at their disposal a panoply of matters on which to offer concessions that benefit affected domestic groups and pave the way to new law. Function-specific diplomacy is the law creation mill; linkage-bargain diplomacy fixes the breakdowns. Because making international intellectual property law is both function-specific and linkage-bargain diplomacy, policymakers will in the future exploit the capabilities of both the WIPO and WTO forums. They will consider the forums' bargaining rules and technical expertise when planning multilateral negotiations. Given the importance of learning and technical knowledge to successful lawmaking, they need to put as much consideration into secretariat knowledge-support capabilities as into forum decisionmaking procedures when planning multilateral negotiations for international rule creation.

Research Considerations

The research in this book is based when possible on written evidence. However, I carried out some one hundred interviews with government, public organization, and industry sources that yielded information available nowhere else. Because practitioners must advocate and negotiate without stating publicly exactly what their goals are and because they move from public sector to private sector and back, their comments are neither cited nor quoted. I designed an interview protocol that was administered to each person interviewed. Question selection varied according to the information and experience of the person and the dynamic of the meeting.[45] Interviewees were asked questions regarding their behavior, characteristics, tasks, and goals and the characteristics, culture, and climate of their organizations.

My analysis draws from the structure of competition in industries dependent on intellectual property right. In its rooting in international diplomacy and institutional change, the book follows in a tradition of research in political economy regarding foreign direct investment and policy regarding real property.[46] It is thereby a significant departure from previous studies of GATT trade diplomacy, which ignored the behavior of companies and industries.[47] The study applies theory from political science, international relations, organizational sociology, and educational psychology to the study of the international political economy of intellectual property rights and presents a dynamic, learning-based explanation of decisionmaking and decisions made. As applied to the issue of intellectual property rights, it is comprehensive because it integrates discussion of innovative patent and

---

45. Dexter (1970).
46. Gilpin (1975); Lipson (1985); and Moran (1985).
47. Preeg (1970); and Winham (1983).

trade secret–intensive competition and expressive copyright-intensive competition.

The study makes only occasional reference to the trademark institution because it is not so internationally controversial as the other institutions of intellectual property. Most developing countries quickly grasp the utility of trademarks even if they tolerate some pirating and counterfeiting. Indeed, once conceding the inevitability of TRIPS negotiations, the developing countries called for the sole agenda issue to be trademark counterfeiting. The International Anticounterfeiting Coalition and a few other interests in the United States advocate to ensure that trademark is taken up by U.S. policymakers bilaterally, regionally, and multilaterally.

Institutions learn and adapt rules and practices because of the teaching of functional specialists, but effective learning also depends on the capacity to integrate the discrete facts and concepts of the specialist into a coherent whole. This book aims to provide that whole with respect to the international diplomacy of institutional change in protecting intellectual property rights.

TWO

Patents for Technological Innovation

THOMAS EDISON earned his first patent for an invention that allowed members of a legislature to vote simultaneously.[1] Demonstrating his invention to congressional leaders, he tried to sell them on the improved efficiency it offered over the slow roll-call, manual voting system then in use. But they did not buy it, explaining that their way might be inefficient but it allowed a lot of vote changing, horse trading, and log rolling, which was what the legislative process was all about. Edison learned a lesson he never forgot: customer needs and preferences guide invention. He adapted his vote counter into a stock ticker and promptly sold it to Kidder Peabody, which, unlike Congress, valued efficiency. Edison was considered one of the best chemists and metallurgists of his day, but the great commercial success of his patented inventions equally depended on his determination to anticipate customer needs, manufacture, and market. The patent rewarded Edison for the "90 percent perspiration, 10 percent inspiration" of his inventive genius.

The patent institution was established by the medieval Venetian state, which articulated the basic features of the law today: spur innovation through the incentive of limited-time exclusivity by demanding the demonstration to the public of a working model and promising to seize and destroy counterfeit products. Patent rights arise because inventing is an expensive process and costs must be recouped to provide incentives to invest. If others

1. Baldwin (1995, pp. 46–48).

can cheaply appropriate an inventor's innovation, calling it their own without having invested time and energy in it, investments in innovation will not be made.

Free markets tend to underproduce innovation because of this "appropriability problem," thus government intervenes into the market to provide a period of exclusive distribution rights as an incentive to invest in innovation. However, government demands of the innovator a quid pro quo for the granting of a patent: As a matter of business strategy, inventors must not safeguard the invention through the darkness of trade secret protection, but rather must disclose how the invention works and in return receive a limited period of exclusive control to produce and license for production. Furthermore, in order to promote the public's interest in the prevention of monopolies from arising through the patent institution, government policymakers attempt to define concepts of inventiveness, scope, and duration of patent to strike a careful balance between exclusivity and competition as incentives to innovate and distribute.

In the contemporary world economy, research-based chemical and pharmaceutical companies are the most dependent on the patent as a matter of competitive advantage, for their chemical products can be relatively easily pirated by unscrupulous competitors unburdened by the investment in research and development (including ten years of clinical trials for safety and efficacy in the case of pharmaceuticals). Patents are earned in the industrialized countries through a public administrative procedure, and claims of infringement are settled in the courts and, when foreign imported goods are at issue in the United States, under the section 337 process administered by the U.S. International Trade Commission.

Evolution of the Patent Institution

Property rights, which are specified in western legal tradition as early as the Roman law of the sixth century B.C., were granted for exclusive use of mines and natural resources as early as 1200 A.D. These rights are the antecedents of the patent institution.[2] In medieval European towns, craftspeople organized into occupation-based guilds to look out for their common interests. The guilds monopolized trade and artistic activities,

2. Kelly (1992, pp. 76, 35).

establishing prices, standards, and import restrictions. But individual masters aggressively competed with each other. To identify their handiwork, they marked their products with the antecedent of the modern trademark.

In the fifteenth century the Venetian state, an economic oligarchy with the "great aim . . . to secure a monopoly of the Eastern trade on which the prosperity of Venice rested," sought to introduce innovations that would weaken the monopoly strangleholds that the guilds held on local technologies and so to compete with the other Italian city-states.[3] Increasingly short of cash yet still long in aspirations and valuing new inventions for the benefits they introduced to work and life, Venice announced a "worldwide" competition for the best new design for a water mill, pledging that the winner would be rewarded with the privilege of either producing his design himself or authorizing its production "exclusively for life."[4] An important rule of the competition was that that a working model be built and demonstrated; mere drawings were not enough. In 1460 Jacobus de Valperga, a German, won the competition and received his patent, the first to be granted in Venice. The state provided that infringement of his patent would result in a fine and the burning of the offending construction.[5]

The Venetians apparently got the idea of the patent from Florence, which had issued the first known patent to Fillippo Brunellesci in 1421. The preamble states clearly the institutional purpose:

> Considering that the admirable Filippo Brunelleschi, a man of the most perspicacious intellect, industry and invention, a citizen of Florence, has invented some machine or kind of ship, by means of which he thinks he can easily, at any time, bring in any merchandise and load on the river Arno and on any other river or water, for less money than usual, and with several other benefits to merchants and others; and that he refuses to make such machine available to the public, in order that the fruit of his genius and skill may not be reaped by another without his will and consent; and that, if he enjoyed some perogative concerning this, he would open up what he is hiding, and would disclose it to all: And desiring that this matter, so witheld and hidden without fruit, shall be brought to the light, to be profit of both to said Filippo and to our whole country and others; and that some privilege be created for said Filippo, as hereafter described, so that he may be

3. Strayer and Munro (1970, p. 526). See also Prager (1944, p. 714).
4. Kaufer (1989, p. 3).
5. Bugbee (1967, p. 21).

animated more fervently to even higher pursuits, and stimulated to more subtle investigations.[6]

The preamble therefore illustrates a motivating force behind the patent: that trade secrets be turned into publicly available benefits and thus encourage innovation.

The patent to Fillipo was granted for three years, although he had not demonstrated then that his invention would work.

The Florentine practice of granting patents stopped due to a combination of guild and Medici politics, but Venice institutionalized the right of patent in 1474 in a statute that contained all the main features of contemporary patent law, including requirements that the device be novel, be actually constructed ("reduced to practice" in modern jargon), and be made public. It also required that it be examined (although the examination was rather informal), that there be term limits to exclusive rights, and that there be remedies for infringement. Finally, the Venetian statute declared that the inventor must teach others how the invention worked and be granted exclusivity in return.

The patent institution gradually spread northward as Venetian artisans looked for better markets. Patents were granted in France, Germany, and England beginning in the 1540s and 1550s.[7] As often as not, however, absolutist governments distorted the patent into a royal reward for favorites. The purpose of these monopolies was "to enrich the king or the state, as well as the grantee, at the expense of the community."[8] The practice became so corrupt under Queen Elizabeth I and her successors that Parliament passed the Statute of Monopolies in 1623, establishing that an invention must be a new invention in England, that the applicant for patent be the first to invent it, and that the term of patent be limited to fourteen years, a period twice the length of the seven-year apprenticeship and deemed long enough to protect the know-how of the master.[9] Thus the purpose of these English reforms was to make the patent add to public wealth.

The inventor . . . creates something new which the community did not possess before and adds to the choice of goods available to the public. The patent monopoly does not prevent any member of the public from

---

6. Bugbee (1967, p. 17).
7. Prager (1944, pp. 722–33).
8. Meinhardt (1946, p. 22).
9. Kaufer (1989, p. 6).

continuing any manufacture or trade he exercised before the grant of the patent. The patent monopoly protects only articles having qualities which were not present in articles previously on the market.[10]

The statute employed the phrase "letters patent," which means "open letters," to notify all that the know-how contained in the patent would not be sealed but would be exposed to view with the Great Seal of the Realm at the bottom.[11]

Lyons, France, the eighteenth-century textile manufacturing center, also relied on the patent to promote manufacturing innovation and the state itself. The first design patent statute, established by the silk manufacturing guild to encourage creativity within its ranks, was enacted in 1711.[12] And for the first time a patent was rationalized on the basis that design inventions were the "property" of the designer and that rights were inherent in such property of mind. This was a significant development. Although Venice and Florence had established the patent to foster more innovation and technological dynamism, they had never conferred a "natural" right on an inventor. They had only conferred a contractual right: teach others about your invention and you will be rewarded with a limited period of exclusivity. The French policy, motivated by the desire to oppose state monopoly power, introduced a wholly new rationale. But intellectual property as natural right would create problems for the institution as its logical extensions were derived.

British settlers in the New World brought the English patent practice with them, writing laws in Massachusetts (1641), Connecticut (1672), and South Carolina (1691). The framers of the Constitution provided that patent law in the United States be made exclusively by the federal government: Article I, section 8, states, "The Congress shall have the power . . . to promote the progress of science and useful arts, by securing for limited times to authors and inventors the exclusive right to their respective writings and discoveries."

Article I makes no mention of property. The words, rather, are "progress," "limited Times," and "exclusive rights." Thomas Jefferson, who would become the first patent administrator by virtue of being the first secretary of state, set the course for the U.S. patent institution. As the primary author of the 1793 Patent Act, he adopted a social and economic

---

10. Meinhardt (1946, p. 23).
11. Meinhardt (1946, p. 35).
12. Prager (1944, pp. 727–33),

rationale for patents rather than a natural rights rationale. The patent system was needed for the public good, to induce and reward invention that was made available to the public. It was not needed to protect the "intellectual property" of the individual. Jefferson purposely employed the language that the applicant for a patent must signify "a desire for *obtaining* an exclusive" property right.[13] Keeping the knowledge a darkly held secret was a legitimate option, but if the inventor wanted the benefits the public offered through the patent, he was obligated to contribute to public know-how. Jefferson established that under U.S. law the inventor enters into a contract with the public: he teaches others how the invention works, and the government grants limited exclusivity as a reward for introducing it into the marketplace.

Patents and Technological Innovation

Patent rights arise to solve the appropriability problem: invention is expensive and costs must be recouped to provide incentives for the investment.[14] "If a firm could not recover the costs of invention because the resulting information were available to all, then we could expect a much lower and indeed suboptimal level of innovation."[15] The patent institution aims to encourage the introduction of new products and processes into the marketplace to benefit the public and propel economic growth. It is an intervention by government to correct a deficiency of unregulated markets, which if left to themselves tend to underproduce innovation. And as the Australian patent commissioner said, "The temporary monopoly is justified on the grounds that if it had not been for the inventor who devised and disclosed the improvement, nobody would have been able to use it at that or any other time since its existence, and the manner of production may have remained unknown."[16] Advocates of research-based pharmaceutical companies emphasize this point when they contend that the costs to society of untreated diseases should be considered in policy discussions regarding the patent institution.

13. Prager (1944, p. 742).
14. Garud (1994).
15. Dam (1994, p. 247).
16. Smith (1989, p. 12).

Patents matter most to competition in industry sectors characterized by high costs of research, development, and innovation but relatively low (or acceptably low) costs of imitation. In the contemporary economy, the research-based pharmaceutical maker and the manufacturer of fine chemicals best exemplify this pattern of competition.[17] The pharmaceutical companies earn more patents each year—15 percent of all U.S. patents—from the Patent and Trademark Office than any other industry, and the chemical companies rank second.[18] Producers of bulk chemicals and over-the-counter drugs owe their competitive advantages in the main to manufacturing and marketing capabilities. Producers of memory chips, microprocessors, computer hardware, and industrial electronics owe some of their competitive advantages to intellectual property created by R&D but in greater measure to manufacturing and marketing capabilities. The information technology hardware makers are active users of the patent institution, but because manufacturing and marketing competencies establish substantial barriers to market entry by would-be competitors, the patent institution is generally less critical to their competitive advantage.

The chemical industry's dependence on patents is rooted in its history and structure. At least since the mid-nineteenth century it has depended on innovative products: coal tar dyes, explosives, synthetic fibers. In turn the English, French, German, and American industries thrived. These competitors were growing within an environment that was offering good patent protection, adequate financing, sophisticated chemical science education, and capable management. During the 1920s, mergers, acquisitions, and failures resulted in market consolidation in the United States, Germany, Great Britain, and Switzerland—the modern global chemical industry was taking shape. Until the 1974 oil shock the chemical industry was the world's largest and fastest growing industrial sector.

The chemical industry, maker of soaps and detergents, synthetic fibers, pharmaceuticals, paints, adhesives, and automobile tires as well as intermediate products that are essential to the agricultural, construction, manufacturing, and service industries, requires heavy investment in equipment and

17. Mansfield (1986) found in survey research of ten industry sectors that pharmaceutical and chemical makers placed higher priorities on adequate intellectual property protection than did other sectors. For example, electronics and transporation product makers less frequently cited intellectual property as critical to new product development. My judgment regarding patent dependency differs from Mansfield's conclusions to reflect high-technology markets of the late 1990s rather than the mid-1980s when he conducted the research.

18. Rapp and Rozek (1990, p. 86).

R&D.[19] Gross capital stocks per employee were $197,000 in 1992, a level twice that of U.S. manufacturing as a whole, and total capital investment in the same year was $23 billion.[20] Investment demands are high in both the basic commodity chemicals and the fine, high-technology chemicals. Yet competitive advantage in commodity chemicals rests on manufacturing scale economies; competitive advantage in high-technology chemicals rests on proprietary product and process technology. In 1992 the U.S. chemical industry spent $14 billion on R&D, and in 1993 the federal government spent $950 million on primarily university-based chemical research.

U.S. companies such as Amoco, Chevron, Dow Chemical, and DuPont produce 70,000 chemical products, own more than 12,000 production facilities in the United States, and operate more than 2,800 facilities in foreign countries.[21] The manufacturing sector buys nearly a third of this chemical production and the chemical industry itself buys about a quarter. The remainder is taken by nonmanufacturing firms and consumers. The world's largest chemical makers are based in Europe: Bayer, Hoechst, BASF, and ICI are the top four in revenue; UniLever, Royal Dutch Shell, Elf Aquitaine, Akzo, and Solvay are in the top twenty as are some pharmaceutical companies based in Switzerland, the United Kingdom, and France.

Compliance with environmental regulatory standards now offers the overwhelming rationale for capital investment in chemical R&D. Environmental, health, and safety regulations govern the release, disposal, transportation, workplace exposure, and use of chemical products, and these regulatory costs are offering competitive opportunities for research-based chemical makers. Environmentalism in the United States and Europe and increasingly in other parts of the world has shifted competitive advantage to manufacturers with cleaner products and services.

Chemical companies are major patent recipients, but more than any other industry, the pharmaceutical industry emphasizes the importance of patents to new product development. Pharmaceutical companies, traditionally suppliers of bulk chemicals to pharmacists who compounded finished drugs themselves for their customers, have since World War II become manufacturers and distributors of finished products to pharmacies and hospitals.[22] The Federal Food, Drug, and Cosmetic Act of 1962 fundamentally changed

19. Chemical Manufacturers Association (1995, p. 7).
20. Brennan and Long (1994, p. 2).
21. American Chemical Society (1994).
22. Pharmaceutical Research and Manufacturers of America (1997, p. 11).

the business by demanding "effectiveness" through a clinical trial-based approval process meant to protect consumers. Because the FDA approval process takes ten to twelve years, new drug therapies enter the market carrying substantial development costs. The 1962 Drug Act led the industry to divide into its present structure of manufacturers and innovators: the manufacturers produce over-the-counter drugs for retail distribution to consumers directly; the innovators produce ethical drugs for distribution to pharmacies and hospitals, which distribute to consumers after receiving a physician's prescription. The sources of competitive advantage in the over-the-counter drug business are manufacturing and distribution capabilities; the sources of competitive advantage in the ethical drug business are R&D capabilities as well as manufacturing and distribution capabilities. Ethical drug makers in the late 1970s invested about 12 percent of sales into the R&D of laboratory studies, clinical trials, and regulatory approval.

Drug innovators in the 1970s believed that they were being squeezed by the FDA approval process, which shortened their patent protection from the legislated seventeen years to an effective five to seven years. The 1962 FDA Act resulted in relative declines in U.S. R&D expenditures, new drug introductions, and global sales.[23] To achieve effective patent protection in the United States, they lobbied for the Drug Price Competition and Patent Term Restoration Act of 1984, which extended by five years the patent term for any product subject to regulatory approval (up to an effective fourteen-year term). As a matter of policy, the 1984 Drug Act also simplified the FDA approval process for generic producers by no longer requiring full clinical trials for a proposed generic drug and setting a 180-day decision deadline, thus encouraging competing generic products soon after patent expiration. The 1984 Drug Act invigorated both the innovator-makers and the generic manufacturers.

Making research-based pharmaceuticals is a risky business. Six to ten drugs under patent earn much of the income of large, research-based pharmaceutical makers in any given year. The timeline for pharmaceutical R&D is one to two years research of concept and discovery of active substance; two to three years of preclinical trials with animals, including toxicity tests, investigation of main side effects, analysis of stability of active substance, testing regarding absorption, subchronic toxicity, and reproduction toxicity; three to four years of clinical trials with humans

23. Wheaton (1986, p. 19).

concerning efficacy, toxicity, and safety; and two to three years of product documentation and registration, FDA review, and marketing launch. After ten to twelve years of this development, only 1 of the 4,000 to 10,000 discovered compounds is marketable, burdening the typical new drug with about $350 million in investment costs.[24]

Choice in pharmaceutical research and development is typically driven by market forces—where health problems are the greatest. Most of the major companies compete in the same areas: cardiovascular diseases, central nervous system disorders, infectious diseases, arthritis and inflammation, osteoporosis, allergy and dermatologic disorders, cancer, urogenital disorders, surgery and interventional problems. The Orphan Drug Act of 1984 offers tax credits for R&D into health problems that affect small numbers of people. Thus it is unusual when a drug under patent has a monopoly in the field.[25] Typically, multiple therapies are available, so a new drug is priced consistently with its competitors, though at a premium if its therapeutic value is demonstrably superior.[26] Thus, patents rarely grant monopolies, despite what pharmaceutical industry critics in both industrialized and developing countries often claim.

Private enterprises introduce about 93 percent of new drug therapies.[27] These drugs are the result of ever increasing R&D investment: ethical drug makers invested about 12 percent of sales into R&D in 1980, about 15 percent in 1985, and came close to 20 percent in 1995.[28] Their industry association predicts that R&D will exceed 21 percent of sales in 1997, thus the industry (or, at least some companies within the industry) has become even more research-oriented in the 1990s than in the 1980s. Pharmaceutical competition is global, but 80 percent of world production takes place in the United States, Europe, and Japan.

The importance of pharmaceuticals to the U.S. economy is not at all diminished by the recent global consolidation in the industry that has increased the presence of European-based companies in the United States.

---

24. Tufts University/Boston Consulting Group study cited in Pharmaceutical Research and Manufacturers of America (1996–97, p. 9).

25. Rapp and Rozek (1990, pp. 92–93).

26. Vagelos (1991, p. 4).

27. Harvey Bale, senior vice president, Pharmaceutical Research and Manufacturers of America, "Improving the Hemisphere's Health through Intellectual Property Protection," Washington, October 1995.

28. Pharmaceutical Research and Manufacturers of America (1997, p. 11).

The investments made by European firms aim to acquire the R&D, marketing, and management competencies of U.S. firms. In some cases they are intended to acquire the pioneering technological advances in bioengineering that are being carried out by newly big U.S. pharmaceutical makers such as Amgen, Chairon, and Genentech and by many as-yet small biotechnology start-up companies. A bioengineering revolution is under way and, more than merely making new products, biotech competitors are creating a new way of doing R&D.

In the 1990s the largest-grossing pharmaceutical makers have created through mergers, joint ventures, and alliances an increasingly Euro-American competition among Bristol-Myers Squibb, Glaxo Wellcome, Hoechst, Johnson & Johnson, Merck, Novartis (Ciba-Geigy plus Sandoz), Pfizer, Pharmacia & Upjohn, Roche, SmithKline Beecham, and Warner-Lambert. Pfizer is the competitor most single-mindedly devoted to research-based product development; the others engage in considerable generic, off-patent competition.[29] One-half of all new drugs introduced in the past fifty years have been introduced in the United States; another 30 percent have been introduced in Switzerland, Germany, and the United Kingdom.[30]

Japanese pharmaceutical makers are manufacturers, not innovators, and their R&D expenditures as a percentage of sales are less than 10 percent, which is akin to U.S.-based health products maker Warner-Lambert and below the levels spent by more research-dependent Merck and Pfizer.[31] Although more than 13 percent of world pharmaceutical exports were produced in the United States, less than 3 percent were produced in Japan. More than 40 percent of U.S. production is exported, but exports were about 6 percent of total sales in Japan.

Patent and Trade Secret Law

Patent and trade secret law are complementary public policy domains. The following sections summarize some basic principles, rules, and administrative practices.

29. Tanouye and others (1996, p. A1).
30. Vagelos (1991, p. 4).
31. Ballance, Pogay, and Forstner (1992, pp. 80–81).

Patent Law

"Whoever invents or discovers any new and useful process, machine, manufacture, or composition of matter, or any new and useful improvement thereof, may obtain a patent" under U.S. law.[32] The inventor must meet three basic requirements to be granted a patent: show that the invention passes the first inventorship test, the novelty and nonobviousness test, and the utility test. These tests were codified in the original 1793 patent statute; the nonobviousness test was codified in the 1952 Patent Act.

Initially, Thomas Jefferson, the patent administrator as well as secretary of state, personally examined the applications for novelty and usefulness. He scrutinized applications closely, for he thought that the Federalists had demanded language in the patent statute that made getting a patent too easy.[33] But when he became too busy with foreign policy duties, patents came to be granted upon simple registration.[34] (The Patent Office later established a $35.00 registration fee to deter frivolous applications).

However, discontent with the patent administration system—one measure of which was increased litigation between individuals with contesting claims—grew, and the process was reformed in 1836. A formalized examination system was established, a staff of technical experts recruited, and the real purpose of the patent policy restored. The number of patents granted declined sharply in the 1840s because of the new scrutiny the applications received (and because the patent numbers of the 1820s and 1830s had been inflated). The 1836 law was not significantly amended until the 1952 Patent Act, but the federal courts have established a substantial body of common-law interpretation.[35]

The first inventorship test demands that inventors demonstrate that they are true, original inventors. Who is the first inventor? The one who "first arrives at a complete conception of the inventive thought is entitled to recognition and reward, unless and until the interest of the public is compromised by his lack of diligence in demonstrating that his invention is capable of useful operation."[36] That is, the new invention, in the jargon of the specialist, must be "reduced to practice"; a patent is not granted based on mere experimentation. As the Supreme Court ruled in 1836 in *Reed* v.

32. *Patent Act*, 35 U.S.C., sec. 101.
33. Bedini (1990, p. 206).
34. Sokoloff (1988, p. 818).
35. Choate, Francis, and Collins (1987).
36. *Laas v. Scott* (1908), cited in Choate, Francis, and Collins (1987, p. 121).

Cutter: "An imperfect and incomplete invention, existing in mere theory or in intellectual notion, or in uncertain experiments, and not actually reduced to practice, and embodied in some distinct machinery, apparatus, manufacture, or composition of matter, is not, and indeed cannot be, patentable under our patent acts."[37] The demand in U.S. law that the patentee be the "original" inventor means in practice that many lawsuits, so-called interference suits, are filed to challenge the originality claims of others. Inventors may challenge a granted patent and, when they do, it is typically a claim either that they actually conceived the innovation first or that even though the patentees may have conceived first, they did not show "due diligence" (continuous R&D effort aimed at commercializtion) and thus lost the rights that come with being the first conceiver.

The novelty test demands that inventors demonstrate their invention is, according to the 1793 act, a "new and useful art, machine, manufacture, or composition of matter, or any new and useful improvement." The principle that has guided court-made policy is that of Jefferson: the purpose of the patent is to promote the public interest, and the public interest is served by bringing new products to public use, not by rewarding inventors who have already brought the product to the market. Thus, patent rights are lost once inventors surrender their inventions to public use or sale without filing for a patent. An inventor may, however, be able to get around this rule by showing that the purpose is to test and perfect the invention. The courts recognize experimentation as legitimate until the "experimental motive" is superceded by a "profit motive."[38] If the invention is already known, that is, exists as "prior art," it cannot be patentable and, according to section 102, that can mean it is already described in publication. The courts have also made clear that an inventor cannot receive a patent for a known invention for which someone found a new use.[39] For example, Dunlop Holdings sued Ram Golf for patent infringement for making an unusually durable golf ball, but Ram successfully argued that the product was prior art since DuPont had invented it for another purpose.[40]

Because establishing the appropriate threshold for novelty has been a problem for patent administration and the courts, the criterion of non-obviousness was added to help define novelty and make patentability

---

37. *Reed v. Cutter* (1836), 1 Story, 590.
38. *Watson v. Allen* (1958), 103 U.S.App.D.C. 5, 254 F.2d 342, 117 USPQ 68.
39. *Titanium Metals v. Banner* (1985), cited in Choate, Francis, and Collins (1987, p. 166).
40. *Dunlop Holdings v. Ram Golf* (1975), 524 F.2d 33, 188 USPQ 481.

clearer. Section 103 of the Patent Act of 1952 codified the court precedent that "if the differences between the subject matter sought to be patented and the prior art are such that the subject matter as a whole would have been obvious at the time the invention was made to a person having ordinary skill in the art," the invention is deemed "nonobvious" and is patentable. That decision is made by examining the scope and content of the prior art, the differences between the prior art and the claim at issue, and the level of ordinary skill in the art—all at the time of the patent application.[41]

Some critics have charged that the Patent Office has granted patents too loosely, and a few courts held in the first half of the twentieth century that a "flash of creative genius" was needed to earn a patent. But the Supreme Court ruled in 1966 that "creative genius" was too strict a criterion, for the 1952 act stated that a patent was justified "if the differences between the subject matter sought to be patented and the prior art are such that the subject matter as a whole would have been obvious at the time the invention was made to a person having ordinary skill in the art to which said subject matter pertains."

In place of the novelty and nonobviousness tests, European patent examiners and courts apply the "inventive-step" test, which is conceptually a somewhat different standard.[42] The inventive-step test asks: Does the item for which the patent is sought represent an advance or progress over the prior art? "Would a person having ordinary skill in the art have been able to pose the problem, solve it in the manner claimed, and foresee the result?" If yes to all, there is no inventive step. If no to any, there is an inventive step.

Under U.S. law, earning a patent, finally, depends on passing the utility test: Is the invention useful? The inventor can demonstrate the utility of the invention by convincing an examiner who has "ordinary skill in the art." This can be done by offering evidence from experiments, citing commercial success, or proving that another has attempted to copy the invention. It is typically an easy hurdle to clear.

In the United States, inventors file an application with the Patent and Trademark Office, a division of the Department of Commerce headed by a commissioner who carries the rank of assistant secretary and serves by appointment of the president and with the advice and consent of the Senate. Once the application has been filed, the inventor may notify (through

41. *Moore v. Wesbar Corp.* (1983), cited in Choate, Francis, and Collins (1987, p. 370).
42. Smith (1989, p. 35).

product packaging or advertising or any other means) competitors that it has a patent application pending, but competitors are free to act as they wish. Meanwhile the office

—receives and stamps the date of receiving;

—checks for compliance with filing procedures;

—classifies the application by subject matter and assigns it to the proper examining group;

—conducts a search of the prior art; and

—determines patentability.

The application remains confidential during the examination, a matter of great importance to the inventors. (Even the Freedom of Information Act cannot supersede the confidentiality demand.) Patent applications to the U.S. Patent and Trademark Office have more than doubled since the mid-1980s, and software and biotechnology applications have especially increased.

Because a patent confers exclusive right in the marketplace over a product or process, U.S. patent law demands full disclosure of the product or the process when the patent is granted. The policy is that the inventor enters into a contract with the public: the inventor receives limited exclusivity as a reward for skill and in return teaches others skilled in the art how to do it. The 1952 act demands that the inventor specify distinctly the claim: "The specification shall conclude with one or more claims particularly pointing out and distinctly claiming the subject matter which the applicant regards as his invention." Without precise specification, the patent could sweep broadly, granting wide monopoly power for an inventor. The specifications, however, are drafted for "one skilled in the art," not for just anyone.

Technology diffusion is institutionalized into a patent system through the publication of the patent search reports and the patent itself in an official gazette. An administrator at the European Patent Office in Munich estimates that "between 80 and 90 percent of technical knowledge is stored in the archives of the world's patent offices."[43] He further estimates that some 30 percent of all expenditures for the development of new technical processes and products are already known, contained in previous patent documentation, and could be saved if this treasure were better mined by technologists and engineers.

---

43. Zilliox in WIPO (1994a, p. 37).

An administrator at the World Intellectual Property Organization recommends the utility of state-of-the-art searches for the information they reveal regarding the state of technology in a given area, the level of R&D activity, the names of researchers working in a field, and the technological competencies of and R&D paths being taken by competitors. The searches can help an innovator protect itself against patent infringement liability, prepare for licensing negotiations, suggest R&D directions for the organization. A Digital Equipment patent attorney asserts that most of the information disclosed in patent documents is not revealed anywhere else and that, in frequent contrast to scientific and technical journal articles, the information is commercially valuable.[44]

A U.K. patent administrator has remarked that small and medium-sized firms are not only frequently ignorant of patent documentation as a technology source, but they are resistant to using it when told about it for fear that "it is too expensive and too complex." He tells of the Australian yacht team that was rumored in advance of the 1983 America's Cup race to possess a radically new hull design that would shake up the competition. Members of the press spent fruitless days and considerable money trying to find out about these rumors, never realizing that full, detailed descriptions of the hull design were on the shelves of the U.K. Science and Patent Library three months before the race. He also tells about the U.K. chemical company that was developing a new process that was plagued by unwanted sludge. A search through the patent office revealed that the company itself had solved the particular problem thirty years before and had patented the innovation, but the information had been lost to the organization through employee retirements.[45]

Uninformed policy discussants ask: Is a patent system necessary to stimulate innovation? Students of innovation assert that the interesting research and policy questions are how long ought the patent term be?[46] How ought "market" be defined if a patent has possibly become anticompetitive?[47] To best serve the interests of the public, what is the appropriate scope of the patent? "The scope of the claims of a patent determines the ability of competitors to produce substitutes without fear of infringement suits, and hence the real 'monopoly power' of the patent holder."[48] Scope involves the

44. Ronald Myrick in WIPO (1992, p. 180).
45. Michael Blackman in WIPO (1994a, pp. 75, 81–82).
46. Gallini (1992).
47. Organization for Economic Cooperation and Development (1989).
48. Merges and Nelson (1994, p. 1).

description offered in the patent application, and it has been the basic strategy of patent attorneys working on behalf of their clients to define the scope as broadly as possible. For example, as a matter of intellectual property strategy, a pharmaceutical maker submits a broad patent application when a compound is believed to be commercially valuable, then submits a narrower one for the precise compound that testing and trials prove to be marketable. At each step the attorney defines the scope of protection to be awarded patent as wide as possible. Patent examiners, for their part, seek to limit the patent scope so that the granted patent does not constrain competition. Definitions of patent scope are frequent sources of litigation because patent holders seek as much breadth of patent as they can get and competitors seek to narrow the patent scope as much as they can. To settle these disputes, U.S. courts employ the *doctrine of equivalents* and the *reverse doctrine of equivalents* as tools of analysis (see below).

A patent system may be said to be an *industrial policy* in the sense the term was used in American policy debates in the 1980s, that is, it is an intervention by the government into the marketplace.[49] "But, unlike most industrial policies, it creates property rights in order to allow a market system to function. And it chooses these technologies, not by a process of bureaucratic or political evaluation of which technologies are the most worthy of government support, but, rather, through a set of prior rules that creates a system determining when property rights will be created in inventions."[50]

Comparisons of National Patent Laws

In revolutionary France the idea of moral property resulted in a 1790 patent act that did not impose a time limit on the period of monopoly and abolished the examination system entirely. "Finally, in 1887, the highest court of France, with practically no reasoning at all, declared that there is no such thing as intellectual property."[51] The French had been bent on destroying an absolute government that arbitrarily granted monopolies, but policy lost sight of the innovation-stimulating purpose of patents and likely contributed to the relative technological and economic decline of France during the nineteenth century.

49. Graham (1992).
50. Dam (1994, p. 248).
51. Prager (1944, p. 735).

In contemporary Europe, national patent structures remain, but the European Patent Convention created a European Patent Office in Munich in 1978 that confers patents recognized throughout the European Union (except Denmark and Ireland). A 1989 protocol established that dispute settlement would take place in the Common Appeal Court.[52] Because the national patent systems survive while the Europewide system holds ever growing sway, patenting processes and dispute settlement are complicated.

Japanese patent policy was modeled in 1885 after German law. As in Europe, patents may be conferred to the innovator who is the first to file; the United States may award patents to the innovator who is the first to invent. An advantage of a first-to-file system is that it avoids the plentiful litigation over which inventor got the idea first. Proponents of the first-to-invent system contend that the opportunity for litigation allows small inventors to get their just reward for innovation even when they are in competition with big organizations, and even if it can lead to occasional bizarre examples of litigation such as the Hyatt microprocessor case. In 1990 Gilbert Hyatt, a little-known semiconductor engineer, received a patent for "single chip integrated circuit computer architecture," which potentially meant a royalty check for every microprocessor produced up to that time and all microprocessors produced subsequently. Other microprocessor pioneers alleged that engineers at Intel, Texas Instruments, and other companies had had the conception, but reducing it to practice was the elusive part. They claimed that the Patent Office awarded a patent to Hyatt for ideas that had not been reduced to practice.[53] It is debated in the United States whether the practice of first-to-invent serves the public interest, but the practice is rejected out of hand in Europe and Japan as American romanticism with the lone genius inventor model of innovation and seduction by lawyers specializing in intellectual property litigation.

The Japanese patent institution has had some important differences from the U.S. institution. The application for patent was traditionally laid open by the Japanese Patent Office for eighteen months of public scrutiny to offer the opportunity for opposition from third parties. But recent pressure from the United States resulted in 1994 in a Japanese policy change toward harmonization with U.S. Patent Office practice that the application be held in the tightest secrecy.[54] Regarding the scope of claim, Japanese policy has

---

52. Goyder (1993, p. 322).
53. Malone (1995, pp. 215–19).
54. USTR (1996, pp. 187–88).

demanded that applicants file very narrow, single application claims, whereas U.S. policy permits comparatively broader claims with sub-claims.[55] This difference makes patent counts a poor comparative measure of U.S. and Japanese innovativeness. The counting of patent claims is a better measure. Because U.S. patents have about 35 percent more claims imbedded within them than do Japanese patents, U.S.-based inventors in the electrical, chemical, and mechanical sectors have consistently earned more patented claims than have inventors from any other country.[56] But patent claims may be a better measure of commitment to innovativeness than to innovativeness itself, for they are a quantitative measure when a qualitative judgment is desired.[57]

Japanese Patent Office procedures have tended to discourage patent protection. The office has been considerably understaffed: it can take six or seven years to receive a patent in Japan, regardless of whether the name on the application is NEC or IBM, Toyota or Ford. Japanese procedures do not discriminate against foreign applicants.[58] In addition, the structure of the patent system has encouraged competitors to design around the patent through study of the know-how of the application, which was traditionally open for inspection and years from being granted anyway. Innovators license their technology early because the appropriability regime is relatively weak.

Japanese patent policy has been an element of a market-institution nexus that has produced magnificent process innovation in semiconductor manufacturing as well as in electronics more generally. However, it is a nexus that has yielded considerable incremental innovation but fewer technological revolutions than has the U.S. nexus. The U.S. patent system's application secrecy, broader scope, and quicker decisionmaking raises the question of whether an increase in Japanese radical innovation depends on patent reforms as well as other policy actions that foster more dynamism in capital and labor markets and know-how institutions. Japan-U.S. bilateral agreements have reformed the Japanese patent institution to quicken decisionmaking, broaden patent claims, and provide for application secrecy. But implementation of these reforms may take some time, for deeply institutionalized practices are slow to change.

55. Ordover (1991).
56. Tong and Frame (1994).
57. Narin, Noma, and Perry (1987).
58. Kotabe (1992).

Trade Secrets Law

A trade secret is information, "including a formula, pattern, compilation, program, device, method, technique, or process," that has commercial value to a business and that the business wants to keep secret from competitors and customers.[59] Trade secrets have been common to shaman-priests in preliterate societies, and the concept has been intellectually rooted in Western thought in respect for individual liberty, confidentiality of relationships, common morality, and fair competition.[60] The law of trade secrets grows more out of the concepts of contract and trust than of property, for information maintained as a trade secret may be legally safeguarded against misappropriation but not against independent discovery or accidental leakage.[61] "Firms carry information in a web of contractual relations and property rights."[62] They have information apart from the human capital of the individuals that make up the firm, and some of this information may be protectable under the laws of trade secret.

The law of trade secrets varies widely across industrialized countries and even within the United States. The U.S. Uniform Trade Secret Act has been adopted by just half the states, thus trade secret law differs conceptually and remedies depend on local laws. Nevertheless, business enterprises may, as a matter of corporate strategy, sometimes choose whether to apply for a patent for a formula or manufacturing process or hold the information secret.[63] Applying for a patent has a cost and will result in disclosure of the information paired with a limited term of exclusivity, but a trade secret can be held forever. The expected economic value may not justify patent protection, yet the risk of misappropriation is often substantial. And a patent eases negotiation of a licensing contract: "Disclosure of the secret imperils its value, yet the outsider cannot negotiate until he knows what the secret is."[64]

Disputes over trade secrets may arise between employers and (often former) employees or between competitors, sometimes when misappropriation or even espionage is alleged. When the dispute is between employers and employees, intellectual property law and labor law are at odds because

---

59. *Uniform Trade Secrets Act,* section 1(4).
60. Suchman (1989); and Paine (1991, p. 250).
61. Friedman, Landes, and Posner (1991).
62. Kitch (1980, p. 688).
63. Friedman, Landes, and Posner (1991,p. 62).
64. Kitch (1977, p. 278).

the presumption within intellectual property rights law is that the employer owns the rights to organizational knowledge and information while the presumption within labor law is that the employee owns the rights to his knowledge and skills. The line between organizational knowledge and individual knowledge is not easily drawn.[65]

When settling disputes courts attempt to balance among the rights of business enterprises to protect commercially valuable information, the rights of workers to earn a living, and the interest of the public in the gains from free labor markets. Common law in the United States generally employs six criteria when considering disputes over trade secrets:

—the extent to which information is known outside the claimant's enterprise;

—the extent to which information is known by employees within the enterprise;

—the extent of measures taken to guard the secrecy of the information;

—the value of the information to the enterpise and its competitors;

—the amount of information and the investment in collecting the information; and

—the ease or difficulty with which information could be properly acquired by others.

It is well-settled law that employees, when leaving a business enterprise, can take with them all skills that they learned but cannot make use of trade secrets. The burden is on the employer to demonstrate that the former employee exploited trade secrets.[66] An employment contract may impose limitations on the employee's freedom to go work for a competitor by including a "noncompete" clause. However, the terms of the contract must be "reasonable" in order to balance all the interests at stake.[67] Trade secrets must also be protected, through "reasonable efforts," against misappropriation by competitors. In a famous precedent-setting case, a competitor hired a photographer to take pictures from the air of a plant, concealed behind fencing and blinds, that was under construction by DuPont. The court concluded that DuPont had taken reasonable efforts to safeguard its trade secrets and that there were "proper means," such as independent research or reverse engineering of a product, by which trade secrets might be obtained,

65. Joseph Straus in WIPO (1992, p. 21).
66. *American Chain & Cable Company, Inc. v. Avery* (1964), 143 USPQ 126.
67. *Emery Industries, Inc. v. Cottier* (1978), 202 USPQ 829.

but taking pictures from the air was an improper means of obtaining business information.[68]

Infringement, Courts, and the International Trade Commission

Allegations of infringement occur often, and considerable resources are spent by business and government to determine when infringement has taken place and to apply appropriate remedies. Under the 1952 statute, infringement exists if "whoever without authority makes, uses, offers to sell, or sells any patented invention." Courts hold both direct infringers and those who contribute to infringement liable under the laws of tort. Infringement strikes at the heart of the patent institution, reducing the incentives to invest in innovation; yet designing around a patent, if conducted properly, contributes still more. In a practice that dates in U.S. common law at least to the 1850s, the courts have dealt with the following question: "When should an accused infringer be liable for patent infringement even though technically avoiding the literal language of the claims?"[69] Since the precedent-setting *Graver Tank* v. *Linde Air Products,* the courts have looked for evidence that the allegedly infringing product or process "performs substantially the same function in substantially the same way to obtain the same result." This idea is called the *equitable doctrine of equivalents,* and without it, said the court, patent protection would be rendered "hollow and useless."[70] The *Graver Tank* three-part test, which examines function, way, and result, is widely used by district courts, but in the 1990s the Court of Appeals for the Federal Circuit has been rendering decisions that aim to remove the inconsistencies across the federal courts, decisions that were affirmed by the Supreme Court in 1996–97.[71]

European courts have also dealt with the challenge of infringement and dispute settlement. Courts in the United Kingdom and Germany have led Europe in analyzing infringement, and the Dutch, Austrians, and Swiss have traditionally followed the direction of German courts.[72] Courts in the

---

68. *E. I. DuPont de Nemours and Co., Inc.* v. *Christopher,* 431 F2d 1082, 166 USPQ 421, *cert. denied* 400 U.S. 1024, 915. Cf. 581, 27 L.Ed. 2d 637 (1971)
69. Dunner and Jakes (1993, p. 857).
70. *Graver Tank & MFG Co.* v. *Linde Air Products Co.* (1950), 339 U.S. 605, 70 S.Ct. 854, 94 L.Ed. 1097.
71. Dunner and Jakes (1993, pp. 865–69); Rader (1997).
72. Cornish (1997, p. 2).

United Kingdom have emphasized the actual language of the patent claims, which has resulted in careful, wide-as-possible draftsmanship by counsels for the inventors. Courts in Germany, by contrast, have looked for the essence of the claim, going beyond the literal language. Although the U.K. and German courts tended to follow their historical institutional tendencies after the European patent harmonization period in the 1970s, there has been a gradual convergence in national tendencies. Japanese courts, which in the past applied a strict reading of patent claim language, increasingly are applying criteria akin to the doctrine of equivalents.[73]

In the United States, allegations of domestic infringement of patents may be litigated in federal courts or settled through such alternative means as arbitration or negotiation. Allegations of foreign infringement in the U.S. market may be settled through federal court litigation, by alternative means of dispute settlement, or under section 337 of the Tariff Act of 1930, a process administered by the International Trade Commission. U.S.-incorporated firms have choice of legal remedy when infringement by imported goods is at issue: they can file a complaint in a federal court under U.S. intellectual property laws or file a section 337 petition.

The section 337 procedure is similar to other U.S. procedures under policies for dealing with unfair trade practices. The 1974 Trade Act amended the policy in some important ways; the 1988 Trade Act further amended it.[74] Section 337 declares unlawful any unfair methods of competition and unfair acts in the importation or sales of articles, the threat or effect of which is to destroy or substantially injure an industry in the United States, prevent the establishment of such an industry, or restrain or monopolize trade and commerce. It goes on to declare unlawful the importation or sale of articles that infringe a valid and enforceable U.S. patent or registered copyright or are made, produced, processed, or mined under a process covered by a valid and enforceable U.S. patent. It is also unlawful to infringe a valid and enforceable U.S. registered trademark or a registered mask work of a semiconductor chip product.[75] The language of section 337 closely parallels that of section 5 of the Federal Trade Commission Act, so that the scope of section 337 has been compared with that of antitrust and unfair competition policy. Although the language of the statute is broad, a 1987 Government Accounting Office study found that 95 percent of all

73. Thomas (1996, p. 287).
74. Newman (1989).
75. Committee on Ways and Means (1989, p. 72).

section 337 cases involved intellectual property, and section 337 had de facto become a means of remedying foreign violations of intellectual property rights.[76]

Before the 1988 amendment, a petitioner had to demonstrate that unfair, infringing imports existed; that a domestic industry had been injured; and that the industry was "efficiently and economically operated." With the 1988 amendments a petitioner need only show that unfair, infringing imports exist and that the petitioner is a domestic industry. It no longer needs to demonstrate that it has been injured by the violation, because injury is presumed, and it need no longer demonstrate that it is a well-run industry, for that is seen to be irrelevant when the accused foreign trade behavior is unfair.

A study of all 276 section 337 cases brought between 1974 and 1987 showed that about half were withdrawn before a final ITC decision, and about 80 percent of all cases concerned patents.[77] A more recent study found that the number of cases peaked around 1983, though it could offer no explanation for the finding.[78] The study also found that companies from Canada and Japan were named less often than would be statistically predicted by the percentage of imports coming from them, that companies from Europe were named about as often as would be predicted, and Taiwanese and Korean companies were named more often. ITC final determinations to exclude intellectual property–based goods from import were most common in cases involving companies from Korea, Taiwan, and the Association of Southeast Asian Nations (ASEAN), while cases involving companies from the United Kingdom, Japan, and Germany were more likely to be negotiated and settled before the ITC final decision.

Section 337 cases generally appeared to have merit and were not being used as harassment tactics by U.S. firms, as often seems to happen in antidumping and countervailing duty cases. A recent study by economists reinforces these results. Analyzing firm-level data on section 337 actions between 1977 and 1990, the authors found that those requesting protection tended to invest significantly more in R&D and to spend more on advertising as a percentage of sales than other firms in their industries.[79] The

76. Newman (1989).
77. Feinberg (1988).
78. Mutti (1993).
79. Mutti and Yeung (1996).

researchers also found that the policy got results: petitioners who won had improved profits; competitors who lost had lower profits.

The choice of forum for fighting infringement can be important. One legal practitioner has argued that the conventional wisdom within the American bar is that courts are at their best when disputes are complex, exist in the present or past but are not "emerging," or when one litigant is significantly more powerful than another.[80] Courts are at their worst when technical expertise is needed and when the dispute is linked with other issues, is on-going, or requires immediate resolution. The author contends that conventional wisdom is right about the trade-offs required in intellectual property cases. The courts tend to offer fairness and completeness but are slow and expensive. The ITC cases are decided by technically proficient administrative law judges who work under time limits that usually bring cases to conclusion within a year but who cannot demand tort remedies.

Despite the favor of at least some members of the American bar, section 337 policy has been internationally controversial. As a result of a dispute between chemical makers Akzo and DuPont, the Europeans challenged the law before a GATT settlement panel in 1989 and won, arguing that the procedure violated the national treatment demanded by the GATT.[81] There was a choice of forum for legal remedy when a foreign import was charged with infringement (either before the courts or the ITC), but not if a domestic firm was charged with infringement (before the courts only). The section 337 procedure imposed time limits for a decision; the federal courts did not. Finally, the accused infringer could not file counterclaims in section 337 proceedings but could in federal court proceedings. Thus U.S. noncompliance with its obligations under the GATT were determined by the dispute settlement panel to be procedural not substantive.[82]

As a matter of maintaining good GATT relations, the United States accepted the panel report but stated that changes in U.S. policy would require an act of Congress and thus could only come after successful completion of the Trade-Related Intellectual Property negotiations (TRIPS) of the Uruguay Round. Proposals for resolution of the problem included either transferring all foreign and domestic patent and copyright disputes to the Court of International Trade or to some new Special Patent Court.

80. Finlayson (1987).
81. Pescatore, Davey, and Lowenfeld (1996, vol. II, pp. DD74/1-21).
82. Barons (1991); Brand (1990).

Reforms in U.S. implementation of section 337 incorporated into the Uruguay Round legislation are likely bring it into de facto, if not de jure, compliance with GATT rules by codifying that any holder of U.S. intellectual property rights may make use of the section 337 process.[83]

83. Schwartz (1995).

THREE

Copyright for Artistic and Informational Expression

COPYRIGHTS arose to encourage the expression of ideas. Because artistic and information products are expensive to produce yet inexpensive to pirate, the state intervenes to provide incentives for the investment so as to promote the public welfare. The result is that more products are created, adding to the public stock of expression and ideas. But the business of artistic and informational expression is risky because few expression products return profits. Competition has thus become concentrated among large film studios and music and publishing houses to minimize the risks through huge portfolios of products, some of which earn enough to subsidize the rest. Relative freedom of distribution is thus crucial to promoting public welfare through increased information and entertainment.

Because distribution capabilities are central in the copyright industries, infringement is debilitating if widespread. Infringement is thus deterred by the state through injunction and payment for damages. Adjudicators, however, are challenged to define infringing acts and distinguish them from fair use with precision so that the incentives to create expressions are balanced with free public access to ideas. Copyright dispute settlement and lawmaking have historically allowed the balance to shift to exclusivity at the cost of reduced public access and competition. Ideas are not protected by the copyright, merely their means of expression, and the idea-expression dichotomy is central to the institution of copyright. When, historically, the ideas have been protected by copyrights that are too broad in scope, the effect in the marketplace has been to reduce the incentives for new expres-

47

sion products. And because distribution capabilities are so essential to the business of expression, the rights of authors, song writers, and film directors to control of the final products are at odds with the rights of book publishers, music houses, and film studios. The laws of the United States and Europe differ regarding these "moral rights" of authors.

Evolution of the Copyright

Printing with movable type, almost certainly the invention of Johan Gutenberg of Mainz, was brought to Venice by printers from that city.[1] In 1469 the Venetian state granted a patent to John of Speyer for his printing technique.[2] The making of books, previously the work of the calligraphers' guild, developed quickly in educated, cosmopolitan, and wealthy Venice. In 1486 the state, aiming to offer incentives to authors, granted the first known copyright to a historian, Marc Antonio Sabellico, who was awarded exclusive rights to publish his works.[3] In the succeeding decade, scholars Aldus Manutius received a twenty-year copyright to print all Greek language books and Terracina received a twenty-five-year copyright to print all books written in the Arabic, Armenian, Moorish, and Indian languages.

The result of these broad copyrights was anticompetitive; the copyright was killing rather than invigorating the printing industry. In response, in 1517 the state issued a statute that revoked many of the copyrights and specified that only the author ought be granted exclusivity to publish. A statute of 1533 further provided that to receive a copyright a work must be a new work of the author that was registered for copyright within a year of creation. The typical copyright term was ten years; it was increased to twenty in 1560. A 1545 statute provided that infringing copies would be seized and burned. Thus the Venetian state tuned the copyright institution to encourage artistic and informational expression. But governments often become wary of information they do not control, and foreshadowing the future, in 1548 printers were forced into a state-controlled guild "for more convenient censorship." The copyright institution became stifled by the weight of church and state, and the once vital Venetian printing industry

---

1. Chamberlin (1965, pp. 161–62).
2. Prager (1944, p. 715).
3. Bugbee (1967, pp. 44–45).

collapsed.[4] The copyright thus came to matter little in Venice, but it was an important innovation in the history of Western letters.

As had the patent, the copyright migrated northward. Rights of copy were becoming institutionalized into the common law in seventeenth-century England and came to be codified by the Statute of Anne in 1710. The preamble to the statute recalls the Venetian rationale by stating that allowing a twenty-one-year period of exclusive author's rights to publish a new work was "for the Encouragement of learned Men to compose and write useful Books."[5]

A copyright statute appeared in Massachusetts in 1672; it was fashioned from the precedent of the English common law to become the model for similar laws passed in twelve of the states during the early 1780s.[6] The prime movers in the institutionalization of copyright were Thomas Paine and, especially, Noah Webster. Paine argued that the backward state of literature and the arts in the New World could not be improved without the adoption of the copyright, just as the backward state of technological innovation could not be improved without the adoption of the patent. Webster, who had written a new book of English grammar that was to be published in 1783, lobbied state by state in 1782—the Articles of Confederation had granted little power to the Congress of the Confederation—to get laws of copyright passed in New England. As a result, Connecticut granted sole rights of publication to authors of books, maps, and pamphlets for a fourteen-year term; the five other states wrote similar statutes within the year. Webster's book sold well, allowing him to begin compiling his dictionary, but his frustration with the tedious lobbying he had undertaken led him to work avidly toward a stronger national government that would, among other things, ensure a copyright statute covering all states.

Other intellectual leaders shared Webster's passion for institutionalizing the copyright. James Madison commented in notes to himself during the debate over the Constitution that "to secure to literary authors their copy rights for a limited time" was one of his enumerated roles for a new national congress.[7] In 1790 in one of its earliest sessions, Congress passed a copyright statute, but the law only protected domestic authors; it explicitly authorized the importation, reprinting, and selling, without license or roy-

---

4. Prager (1944, p. 720).
5. Bugbee (1967, p. 53).
6. Bugbee (1967, pp. 105–17).
7. Bugbee (1967, pp. 123–46).

alty, of foreign-authored works, thereby legitimizing book piracy. Newspapers regularly serialized English and French novels with neither permission nor royalty payments, and paperback book publishers gave American readers pirated editions of entire works.

By the 1840s the piracy incensed authors such as Charles Dickens, whose works were especially popular in the United States. (International copyright reciprocity had been accepted by France in 1810 and by England and Germany in 1837.) And in the 1880s Mark Twain, Walt Whitman, Louisa May Alcott, and other commercially successful American authors lobbied the Senate to accede to the 1886 Berne Convention and offer copyright reciprocity to foreign authors for, they explained, they were themselves popular in Europe but were extensively pirated. Their pleas did not succeed, but the large publishing houses—the Scribners, Houghtons, Lippincotts, Putnams—successfully lobbied Congress, which passed reciprocal copyrights in 1890 (America would not accede to the Berne Convention for another hundred years).[8]

Copyright and the Business of Expression

The purpose of the copyright under U.S. law is to protect the *expression* of ideas, not the ideas themselves. The policy aims to encourage new expressions of ideas, to spur creativity, which is considered a public good. The copyright is important to competition in these products because although the cost of creating a book, movie, song, ballet, lithograph, map, business directory, or computer software program is often high, the cost of reproducing it, whether by the creator or by those to whom he has made it available, is often low. In theory, contracts could achieve the same exclusive results as the copyright, but in practice the transaction costs of negotiation and enforcement would be too great, so the copyright is the necessary institutional innovation.[9] Without it, copying would reduce incentives to create and would ultimately circumscribe the variety of expression products available to consumers.[10] As with the patent, the copyright provides a fair market opportunity and the chance of commercial success to risky busi-

---

8. Lardner (1987a, p. 65).
9. Landes and Posner (1989, pp. 326, 330).
10. Johnson (1985).

nesses. This practical logic has long been understood: "The question of copyright has always been joined with that of commercial value."[11]

Writing a book, making a movie, producing an application software, or recording a music CD most often fails to bring a respectable return on investment even under an effective copyright system. The result is that firms organize in publishing, moviemaking, and software and music production so that they may create a portfolio of products that in total will turn a profit. It is not that Hollywood filmmaking, for example, is a risky business because even "small" films cost several million dollars to produce but because 60 to 70 percent of the films produced by U.S. studios are commercial failures.[12] Thus Hollywood studios are often subsidiaries of media companies: Buena Vista, Disney, and Touchstone (Walt Disney), Warner Brothers and New Line (Time Warner), Universal (Seagram), Twentieth Century Fox (News Corp.), Columbia Tristar (Sony), and Paramount (Viacom).

The half-dozen major Hollywood studios dominate production and distribution (representing some 90 percent of revenue) and, in the United States, another half dozen bring in about 50 percent of the theater revenue.[13] Yet between 30 and 45 percent of theatrical gross is earned outside the U.S. and Canada, and licensing to ancillary markets, including cable, broadcast television, and video release, brings in more revenue than does theatrical release. Even in smaller filmmaking markets, exclusive distribution under copyright is crucial to commercial success. For example, filmmaking in Japan dates to the turn of the century and had its golden age in the 1950s: incomes were rising, theaters were being rebuilt, and a half-dozen studios made some 500 films each year.[14] When television arrived in the 1960s, the industry was hard hit: several studios went bankrupt and the number of films produced dropped by half. The industry rebounded in the 1980s to make about 300 films each year, most of which are marketed on VCR tapes to families and mature audiences, while a handful of blockbusters are released in theaters to entertain free-spending young people. Video piracy in Japan was a major problem for both Japanese and Hollywood studios, but in the late 1980s the two industries cooperated to combat it and have done so successfully. Video piracy is now neglible in Japan.

11. Ginsburg (1990, p. 1866). Still, some legal theorists deducing from false premises have wondered about the purpose for copyright. See Breyer (1970).
12. Vogel (1994, pp. 27–33).
13. Vogel (1994, pp. 33–84).
14. Lent (1990, pp. 36–40).

The Hollywood film studio invests great sums in product development and advertising but the video can be copied with inexpensive equipment, which reduces final reproduction costs to a dollar or two. The music business has these same characteristics of expensive product development and advertising but inexpensive manufacture and easy piracy. A CD, priced at $13.00 in a retail store, carries less than $1.00 in manufacturing and packaging costs, about $1.00 in distribution costs, $1.00 to $2.00 in royalties to the performers and song writers. About $5.00 goes to the retailer. The music producers retain the remaining $5.00 to produce the music in the studio and market it through advertising, music videos, and concerts (which typically lose money).[15]

The economics of the music business are similar to that of filmmaking: 90 percent of music CDs and tapes do not return a profit.[16] For the individual performer or band, cutting an album is difficult, and the odds are heavily against going gold and making a fortune. The economics have not changed much since Tin Pan Alley days. Composers and songwriters toiled in some forty-five Tin Pan Alley popular song factories along West 28th Street in Manhattan early in this century, churning out music to be performed in vaudeville shows and selling 30 million copies of sheet music a year. But few songs and compositions really sang in listeners' ears: million sellers made up the bulk of annual sales, so few composers and song writers worked professionally for longer than a decade.[17] The publishers, to make a go of it, built up catalogs of music to be sold for live performance. The business of musical entertainment would ultimately change drastically because Edison invented the talking machine and founded the Edison Speaking Phonograph Company in 1878, but the fundamental economics of the business have endured whether the big seller was Broadway, Bing, or the Beatles.

As with the film business, the risks of doing business in musical products have become aggregated by a few big music producers—Warner, Sony, Philips, BMG (Bertelsmann), EMI, and Universal (Seagram)—that create portfolios of albums and recording artists under contract to get enough hits to keep the business going. This industry structure accounts for the copyright—authors' rights, performers' rights, and conflicts between producers

15. Burnett (1996, p. 2).
16. Vogel (1994, p. 143).
17. Sanjek (1996, pp. 32, 102).

and writers and performers. Three groups, ASCAP, BMI, and SESAC, are unions of performers and music writers.[18]

More akin to the music business than to filmmaking, publishing serves mass markets through disaggregated, highly segmented markets—fiction, nonfiction; mystery, romance; popular acclaim, critical acclaim; self-help, corporate management; comic book, textbook. While the film studio survives on its few hits and thrives on its blockbusters, the book publisher turns small profits here and big profits there within the same categories. "A cheap manuscript by a serious writer could earn a favorable return on the firm's investment no less successfully than an expensive book by a popular author."[19] Marketing strategies differ for each category in the publishing business. For example, fiction tends to sell only within its cultural and linguistic group, while science, technology, and medical works tend to be written in English and sell worldwide. But effective copyright protection is a crucial source of competitive advantage for all categories because investments are similarly large and piracy is easy.

Infringement, Fair Use, and Distribution Strategies

Like patent law, copyright law in the United States has been made both by Congress and the courts, and perhaps more by the courts because decades elapse between congressional passage of new copyright legislation. The Copyright Act of 1976 attempted to codify two hundred years of copyright common law, especially precedents set after the Copyright Act of 1909, but it did so in ways that allow continued force to the 1909 statute and the court-made law, which leaves a good deal of ambiguity in U.S. copyright law.[20]

According to section 102 of the 1976 act, "original works of authorship" may be copyrighted when they are "fixed in any tangible medium of expression." Thus the first test an expression product must pass is that it be original. For originality, the courts have ruled, "All that is needed to satisfy both the Constitution and the statute is that the 'author' contributed something more than 'merely trivial' variation, something recognizably 'his

---

18. For a detailed history of these societies, their bargaining over time with radio and television broadcasters, and their competition with each other, see Sanjek (1996).
19. Wexler (1997, p. 9).
20. Litman (1987, p. 858).

own.'"[21] Originality, "means little more than a prohibition of actual copying." The copyright originality test demands a considerably lower standard than the novelty and nonobviousness tests of patent law because ways of expression are being protected, not novel inventions. "The net effect of protection [of new ideas] would be to reduce the number of works created."[22] But the ease with which the legal hurdle can be cleared means that the copyright does not prevent someone from producing a similar work, as long as it is not directly copied.

Being "fixed in any tangible medium of expression, now known or later developed, from which they can be perceived, reproduced, or otherwise communicated, either directly or with the aid of a machine or device" included in 1976 at least the following: literary works; musical works, including any accompanying words; dramatic works, including any accompanying music; pantomimes and choreographic works; pictorial, graphic, and sculptural works; motion pictures and other audiovisual works; sound recordings; and architectural works.

The courts have established that all expression regardless of the content of the meaning may be copyrighted, even if someone finds the expression objectionable. For example, in one court case the film *Behind the Green Door* was claimed to be obscene and thus not copyrightable, but the court held that whether it was indeed obscene was irrelevant to its copyrightability: "all expression" means just that.[23] Because copyright is limited to expression, it does not apply to works that are solely utilitarian in character.

In the United States, copyrights are registered with the Copyright Office, a unit of the Library of Congress. Registration is nothing more than what the word implies; there is neither search nor examination in copyrighting as there is in awarding a patent. The owner of a copyright has the exclusive rights, according to the 1976 act's section 106, to reproduce the copyrighted work; prepare derivative works based on it; distribute it to the public by sale, lease, or lending; perform works publicly; and display works publicly. However, article 109 imposes an important limit by granting to the owner of a copy of a work the right to sell, display, or otherwise dispose of it in any way desired. If the copyright extended to sales of all copies of the original, the market for expression products would be far different than it is today—

---

21. *Alfred Bell & Co. v. Catalda Fine Arts, Inc.* (1951), cited in Joyce and others (1995, p. 66).
22. Landes and Posner (1989, p. 348).
23. *Mitchell Brothers Film Group v. Cinema Adult Theater* (1979), cited in Choate, Francis, and Collins (1987, p. 804).

indeed, if there was a market, because the result would likely be anti-competitive.

The creator of a work has relatively few rights as author separate from copy holder rights under U.S. law. Section 106 does, however, grant "the author of a work of visual art" the right to "claim authorship of that work, and to prevent the use of his or her name as the author of any work which he or she did not create . . . of visual art and in the event of a distortion, mutilation, or other modification of the work which would be prejudicial to his or her honor or reputation." Authors also possess some limited rights to prevent mutilation or distortion that would be prejudicial to their reputations, but the copyright law is primarily intended to get expressions into the marketplace of ideas, not to protect an author's reputation: it "relies on wrangling greed to promote the advancement of both creativity and profit."[24] So the law has evolved with the rights of publishers and corporations being given the greater priority. "The soil of American copyright doctrine has proved inhospitable to the growth of any body of doctrine, however designated, under which authors would be recognized as possessing inalienable personal rights in the works they labor to create."[25] The courts have implemented and Congress has ratified an approach that emphasizes keeping risky businesses thriving and expression vigorous.

Ownership of the copyright, according to section 201 of the 1976 act, "vests initially in the author or authors of the work." It is language that is deliberately qualified because the succeeding clause states that "in the case of a work made for hire, the employer and other person for whom the work was prepared is considered the author for purposes of this title, and, unless the parties have expressly agreed otherwise in a written instrument signed by them, owns all of the rights comprised in the copyright." This clause is known as the *work-made-for-hire doctrine,* and it was previously codified in the 1909 Copyright Act. The 1909 act established that "copyright ownership should go to the party in the better position to exploit the value of the disputed work by bringing it to the public's attention."[26] The 1976 act discriminates between work created while under employ and work made by commission, but the courts have generally ignored this distinction and returned to the 1909 concept.[27] The work-made-for-hire doctrine is the

24. Ginsburg (1990, p. 1866).
25. Jaszi in World Intellectual Property Organization (1990, p. 54).
26. Hardy (1988, p. 181).
27. Hardy (1988, p. 182).

source of much of the tension between writers and publishers, directors and studios, and performers and their record labels. Authors often believe that they are being exploited, and publishers believe that their organizational, marketing, and distributional efforts are underappreciated and undervalued. This area of copyright law intersects with employment law and ultimately rests on the bargaining leverage of authors and publishers.

Laws regarding authors' possession of exclusive distribution rights are modified by the law of communication, which is of increasing importance in an era of radical changes in communications technology, markets, and policies. The 1976 Copyright Act details copyright relationships between audiovisual works and broadcast stations and cable television distributors. Primary distribution by video broadcasters and cable television requires a contractual relationship; without it the copyright may well be infringed. So-called secondary transmissions of cable television by, for example, hotels to their guests are not infringing activities, and disputes that may arise concern payment for the service to the cable TV provider. Similarly, the transmission of sound recordings by radio requires a contractual relationship to avoid infringement of the copyright holder's exclusive right to distribute.

For policymakers, the challenge of copyright has always been to find the right balance between the creator's interest in the ownership of the expression and the public's interest in access to it.[28] The duration of copyright under U.S. law is the life of the creator plus fifty years, except in the case of anonymous works, which can be protected for the shorter of two periods: seventy-five years from the date of publication or one hundred years from the time of creation. The trend in the law has been to lengthen the term: in 1790 it was twenty-eight years, in 1831 forty-two years, in 1909 fifty-six years; and in 1976 life plus fifty years.[29] The duration of copyright is thus much longer than the patent, and although a monopoly is being granted, the effect is not so anticompetitive as it appears. Copyright is a limited monopoly because it is typically a monopoly of a product that has some or even many substitutes, which is why the blockbuster sells for the same price as the dud in the marketplace. Indeed, it is the blockbuster, not exclusivity, that keeps moviemaking going when consumers have such entertainment alternatives as sporting events and video games.

28. Landes and Posner (1989, p. 326).
29. Landes and Posner (1989, p. 363).

Striking the right ownership-access balance requires determining what precisely constitutes an infringement. The copyright holder's exclusive distribution rights are limited through the U.S. copyright doctrine of *fair use*. The purpose of the doctrine is to ensure that the balance between private and public interests does not shift so far to the creator that access to ideas is hindered. The courts have established a few rules of fair use: an owner of a copy is free to sell or dispose of it in any manner and may display the copy publicly. Exclusive rights to sound recording include reproduction, preparation of derivative works, and distribution, but are limited when the issue is public performance. Copyright holders to sound recordings have the exclusive right to perform the sound recording publicly only for digital audio transmissions. They cannot restrict the broadcast rights of educational, radio, and television programs to the recording. Furthermore, the copyright holder cannot restrict the right to parody the original. In a case against a Rick Dees song parody filed on behalf of Johnny Mathis, the court decided that the test ought to be market effect, and the proper way of considering the market effect is to determine whether the work steals the market from the original. The court decided that it was unlikely Rick Dees's parody had stolen any sales from Johnny Mathis's ballad.[30]

Without using the phrase *fair use,* section 108 of the 1976 act granted to libraries and educators the right to make a single or occasional copy—but explicitly not multiple copies—for archival and educational, but not commercial, purposes. It was this language that was cited when book and scholarly journal publishers successfully took Kinkos, a chain specializing in rapid copying and distribution of documents, to court for selling thousands of photocopied college course packs without paying royalties. Professional copy services and college bookstores now must seek permission, typically from the Copyright Clearance Center, and pay royalties for articles sold to students.

In an 1841 case Supreme Court Justice Joseph Story offered a four-part test, finally codified in section 107 of the 1976 act, to help decide what is fair use rather than infringement.

—What is the purpose or character of the use? Profit or nonprofit?

—What is the nature of the copyrighted work? Possesses an argument? Data sources?

---

30. *Fisher v. Dees* (1986), 794 F2d 432, 230 USPQ 421.

—What is the volume of quotation? A qualitative, not quantitative, judgment.

—What is the effect on the market? Must demonstrate harm or future harm.[31]

Fair use, as debated in *Harper & Row Publishers Inc.* v. *Nation Enterprise,* demonstrated the significance of concepts of copyright and fair use to information dissemination in America.[32] When former President Gerald Ford wrote his memoirs, he made a deal with Harper & Row to publish the book version, with *Reader's Digest* to publish an excerpt, and with *Time* magazine to publish an article-length excerpt. Someone stole the book manuscript and sold it to the publisher of *The Nation,* which excerpted some 300 words—passages related to the pardon of Richard Nixon—of a 200,000 word manuscript. Scooped by *The Nation, Time* witheld its payment to Harper & Row, which filed a copyright infringement suit against the publisher of *The Nation.*

The Federal Court of Appeals for the Second Circuit had argued that the primary character of *The Nation's* excerpt was "news reporting" and thus not an infringement.[33] But Supreme Court Justice Sandra Day O'Connor argued for the majority that copyright was the engine of free expression in America and that *The Nation* had indeed stolen from Harper and Row and created economic harm. Justice William Brennan, in a minority opinion supported by Justices Byron White and Thurgood Marshall, argued that the exceedingly narrow idea of fair use espoused by the majority gave Harper and Row an inappropriate monopoly over information important to the public interest. It would have been interesting had *The Nation* chosen to offer no quotations at all but only summaries of Ford's thoughts, for then the ideas not the expression of the ideas would have been at issue. As it was, Harper won and the Supreme Court placed greatest emphasis on the economic harm part of Justice Story's four-part test.

The Ford case amply demonstrates that one person's fair use is another's infringement. Section 501 of the 1976 act states that the "legal or beneficial owner of an exclusive right under a copyright is entitled . . . to institute an action" if infringement seems to have occurred. The action may result in injunctions, impoundment of the offending product, award of damages and

---

31. Information Infrastructure Task Force (1995, p. 75).
32. *Harper & Row Publishers Inc.* v. *Nation Enterprises* (1985), cited in Joyce and others (1995, pp. 842–54).
33. Coyne (1991, p. 497).

profits, and reimbursement of costs and attorney's fees. Under some circumstances, such as trafficking in counterfeit music or videos, criminal laws permit fines and prison terms. The 1976 act does not, however, define infringement, nor does it offer guidance about determining when it has happened.

The test the courts have come to use to determine infringement is to compare the two works in question and ask whether the ordinary person would find them "substantially similar." Would an ordinary observer recognize the accused works as having been pirated? One scholar proposes that the ordinary person ought not to decide and recommends that the patent law's expert person of "ordinary skill in the art" ought be the judge.[34] The phrase *substantially similar* is itself sufficiently ambiguous to afford a variety of court interpretations, and recent courts have been concentrating on the "total concept and feel of the original expression."[35] Some scholars and commentators critical of the ambiguity of "total concept and feel" have argued that the better test is an old one provided by *Arnstein* v. *Porter* (1946).[36] The case involved the composer Ira Arnstein, who brought legal charges of infringement against Cole Porter. The court demanded that a question be answered first and in the affirmative: Is there copying? To show copying, the petitioner had to show access to the original by the alleged infringer or similarity with the original or both. A direct copy with the original's copyright notice in place demands the conclusion that copying took place. Anything less requires building a case around similarities and common errors and access to the original. Even this standard, however, leaves some subjectivity, and close-call cases are readily identifiable.

Accidental infringements, actionable under patent law, are not actionable under copyright law for the very good reason that "what is infeasible for the Copyright Office is also infeasible for the author. He cannot read all the copyrighted literature in existence."[37] Where the similarities are substantial, weak evidence regarding access is sufficient. Where the differences are substantial, "the copyright owner will normally have to provide strong evidence of access to rebut the defense of independent creation."[38] If copying is determined to have occurred, a second question ought be asked:

34. Wiley (1991, p. 120).
35. Jaszi in World Intellectual Property Organization (1990, p. 58).
36. Latman (1990, p. 1191).
37. Landes and Posner (1989, p. 344).
38. Landes and Posner (1989, p. 347).

Is there improper appropriation? Is the appropriation legitimated by the fair use doctrine?

New distribution technologies challenge the meaning of infringement and of the copyright institution itself. Technological change in distribution challenges conventional corporate strategies of marketing even as it challenges copyright policymakers. A prominent example that is frequently cited to prove the thesis that the copyright owners do not embrace techno-logical change in distribution is the case Universal Studios filed against Sony. It merits review here because its facts illustrate the more generaliz-able situation that within these industries corporate intrests and strategies differ: some embrace new distribution media, some do not. In September 1976 an advertising firm wrote to the president of Universal Studios asking for a signature to allow a proposed newspaper advertisement to run nation-ally: "Now you don't have to miss *Kojak* because you're watching *Col-umbo* (or vice versa)." After an explanation, the ad was to conclude, "Betamax—It's a Sony." Because *Kojak* and *Columbo* were among Universal's most popular television shows and because they aired at the same time on different networks, the advertising firm thought the producer would be pleased that viewers could indeed watch both and advertisers could be encouraged to pay even more for advertising time.

According to a detailed *New Yorker* account, the Universal president's reaction was certainly not expected. He had a video tape recorder in his office for work, but not in his home for entertainment, and he had had no idea that Sony was introducing a home version. He asked himself, "Should Sony be able to sell this product? . . . This machine was made and marketed to copy copyrighted material. It's a copyright violation. It's got to be."[39] Although the 1976 Copyright Act was just being completed and did not directly address video cassette recorders, Universal's lawyers concluded that the fair use exceptions in the act referred to librarians and educators, not home TV-watchers. They believed Universal could build a good copy-right case against Sony.

Universal may, however, have had other reasons for considering a law-suit. The company not only made popular television programs but also such hit movies as *Jaws, The Sting,* and *American Graffiti. Jaws,* which cost only $9 million to make, brought in $175 million at the box office. In partnership with researchers at IBM, Universal had also been working for some years

---

39. Sidney Sheinberg as cited in Lardner (1987a, p. 45).

on a technology that used a laser beam to decipher a picture encoded on a plastic disk and played on a television set, a technology they were calling DiscoVision but that was not yet ready and had no consumer electronics manufacturers yet in place.[40] A week after receiving the letter, Universal's president told Sony's chairman that unless he withdrew the video recorder product, Universal would sue Sony for copyright infringement. The content of the conversation is disputed, as memories became fuzzy. Sony executives claimed their chairman argued that VCR tape technology was an interim product before a video disk system such as DiscoVision arrived; Universal executives recalled no such discussion. Whether or not the subject was discussed, apparently Sony thought Universal had reasons other than fighting copyright piracy for any lawsuit it might file on the issue.

In November 1976 Universal decided to go forward with a suit, which Walt Disney Productions agreed to join, charging that Sony's Betamax videocassette recorder would contribute to copyright infringement of its library of television programs and films ("contributory infringement" may be remedied under the tort laws just as may direct infringement).[41] Warner Brothers did not join but agreed to chip in some money, and the other major studios agreed to submit a friend of the court brief in support of Universal and Disney through the Motion Picture Association of America.[42] Disney's lawyers argued that the company had many classic animated movies in its vaults that they would re-release every twenty years or so to be seen by a new generation of children, a practice that would be threatened by VCR technology and would cause economic harm. In courtroom testimony Jack Valenti, president of the Motion Picture Association, called the VCR "a parasitical device" and pointed out that, facing the similar situation, the West German government had settled the matter by demanding that a royalty fee be paid on each VCR sold. Universal executives explained how risky the movie business was and how every opportunity for revenue had to be exploited to stay in business.

Sony's lawyers looked for analogy in the fair use common law and found it in the audio cassette recorder commonly used by consumers to tape music from the radio, a practice music companies did not like but that they had never challenged in court. Knowing that the issue of economic harm would be important to the court, they also noted that public broadcasting

40. Lardner (1987a, p. 47).
41. Lardner (1987a, 1987b); and Oddi (1989).
42. Lardner (1987a, p. 50).

children's show host Mr. Rogers, video sellers, publishers of magazines for video buffs, and others in the entertainment business liked the idea of the time shifting that Sony's VCR permitted. They argued that many copyright holders of entertainment material welcomed VCR technology and that ultimately there would be no economic harm—economic change yes, economic harm no. Finally, they argued that a product that possessed substantial noninfringing uses had never been determined to infringe under intellectual property law.

The federal district court ruled that VCR technology was fair use under U.S. copyright law, but the appeals court reversed the decision, unanimously determining that home taping was clearly infringement, that the 1976 act did not explicitly permit home taping, and that the Sony technology would likely affect the market for Universal and Disney, which was enough to show economic harm.[43] In *Universal* v. *Sony* the Supreme Court agreed with the original district court decision, concluding that time shifting of copyrighted programs by the consumer in the home was a "private, noncommercial" activity that produced no economic harm and was hence not substantial direct infringement. "Absent such direct infringement, there could not be contributory infringement by Sony." Yet the ruling was decided five to four and might better be seen not as a victory for VCR technology but "as a mere failure on the part of the copyright owners to prove substantial direct infringement."

Both the majority decision and the dissent were rooted in the analysis of economic harm. Neither the majority nor the minority addressed "why the burden should be placed upon the developer of technology to protect copyright owners from how and why that technology is used."[44] Put another way, the Supreme Court seems to have employed a static analysis of economic harm when a dynamic concept is needed if institutions are to encourage technological change. Technological change brings economic change, which harms some but benefits others, ultimately to the public benefit of greater economic growth.

In the end, Sony won the court battle but lost the market war as Matsushita's VCR technology standard prevailed in the marketplace. During the court battle 20th Century Fox commented that Disney and Universal had the wrong distribution strategy and that they should embrace VCR

43. Lardner (1987a, p. 68).
44. Oddi (1989, pp. 48, 49, 58).

technology and exploit it to the fullest.[45] Disney, after it came under new management, learned how to play under the new rules and made hundreds of millions of dollars from video rentals and sales of *The Little Mermaid*, *Beauty and the Beast*, *Aladdin*, and *The Lion King*, animated films especially conducive to big sales because children like to watch them over and over. Japanese electronics manufacturer Matsushita bought MCA Universal apparently for supposed content-medium synergies that, according to management consultants, producing both the film and music and the TVs, VCRs, and audio equipment were supposed to bring (which probably also included the business-government-law "synergy" that meant no more lawsuits from film or music companies accusing piracy). Matsushita, however, ultimately divested to focus on its core manufacturing business. Sony similarly acquired Hollywood film studio and music house content-making capabilities.

Thus the courts settled a crucial dispute regarding the impact of new technology on the copyright industries by permitting the survival of VCRs, and corporate strategy was never the same again in the film industry. However, they did not embrace new technology; they warily approved it. When the long-anticipated moment of the digital convergence of computing and communication arrived in the 1990s, threatening to revolutionize distribution yet again, the battles were refought in the courts, in Congress, and in Geneva (see chapter 8). The VCR case, with all its plots and subplots, probably predicts the present and future of Internet-based revolutionary change toward electronic commerce.

Moral Author's Rights and Institutional Alternatives

In contrast to the Anglo-American institutionalization of copyright, which developed with economic incentives toward public welfare–enhancing expression as the paramount policy goal, France and Germany (and Europe generally, as well as Japan) developed rights of authors and so-called neighboring rights rather than copyrights. The institution developed in response to the policy of an authoritarian state: "The central theme in the history of French printing is that of royal power and intervention. In

45. Lardner (1987b, p. 75).

an era when the country was torn by religious and civil war, the French government was concerned more with censorship of this dangerous new medium of communication than with securing the rights of creative individuals."[46] Preoccupation with breaking the government's hold on free expression encouraged policymakers to establish an institution with considerably different characteristics from American copyright. Under American law, once an author signs over the copyrights to a print publisher or a composer signs over the copyrights to a motion picture company, the creator has limited rights over the expression. But in Europe author's rights is premised on the "personality" or "intellectual" or "natural" or "moral" rights that are presumed to go with being the creator, including the right to publish the work (or not), to withdraw it, to be acknowledged as its creator, and perhaps most significantly, to preserve its integrity. The work is seen as an extension of a person's mind; it is a manifestation of a certain personality and is thus the natural property of its creator.[47]

French law presents the best example of systematic protection of the creative personality. The basic source of contemporary author's and neighboring rights is a 1957 law that provides that the rights of disclosure, attribution, retraction, and integrity are "perpetual, inalienable, and imprescriptable." The rights of disclosure and attribution are relatively uncontroversial in France (or in Europe or even in the United States), and the right of retraction creates so many commercial problems that it is probably a dead letter in French law.[48] But the right to maintain the integrity of the work has created controversy in the French marketplace and courts, and it is the right American publishers and entertainment companies most oppose. For example, a writer who sells a short story to a film studio maintains rights of integrity over the adaptation of the story into the screenplay and the final film product. The director maintains rights of integrity over the film product, including future editing and adaptation.

Because art and commerce may be directly at odds in some cases, the French institution has evolved to bring the law of contract into the matter. There are three general types of contracts between authors and producers: unconditional authorization to adapt, adaptation in the spirit and character of the original and without distortion, and no modification without the

46. Bugbee (1963, P. 48).
47. Gibbens (1989).
48. Damich (1988, pp. 4, 6, 23).

author's approval.[49] Creators (and their executors) have moral rights in Canada for fifty years after death, in Germany for seventy years after death, and in France forever. The harmonization of the institution of moral, personal rights of authors with the narrower copyright institution was one of the tasks of the negotiators in the Uruguay Round Trade-Related Intellectual Property talks (TRIPS), discussed in chapter 5.

49. Damich (1988, p. 15).

FOUR

Business Mobilization and U.S. Trade Diplomacy

AMERICAN businesses based on intellectual property mobilized in the early 1980s to institutionalize modern intellectual property rights laws and administrative practices in developing countries. The interests of some companies that depended on patents or copyrights were becoming increasingly global. They were aggressively producing and selling in emerging third world markets. But many governments in these countries did not have intellectual property rights laws to match those in the industrialized countries, and large-scale piracy of foreign intellectual property had become all too frequent. Patent-intensive companies confronted laws and dispute settlement procedures unsuitable for direct investment in manufacturing; copyright-intensive companies confronted customs offices, police, and courts that were neither able nor motivated to enforce copyrights even where the laws were on the books. The patent and copyright interests determined that large long-term initiatives would be needed to establish and enforce intellectual property laws in emerging markets. And because many of the policymakers and business leaders in these countries opposed such reforms, the effort would require the leveraging of U.S. government diplomacy.

Mobilizing Intellectual Property Interests

Early in the mobilization effort the corporate leaders were Pfizer and IBM, archetypes of globally ambitious, intellectual property–intensive companies.[1] In the late 1970s their chief executive officers devised a strategy to improve intellectual property protection internationally until American standards became the international norm, especially in developing countries. For Pfizer, one of the world's largest manufacturers of pharmaceuticals, the goal was significant reform of the Paris Convention so that there would be minimum standards for the protection of intellectual property worldwide (many countries especially rejected patent protection for pharmaceuticals). Pfizer took its initiative to the World Intellectual Property Organization, but WIPO was a UN agency with one-nation, one-vote decisionmaking, and the developing countries opposed the reforms. For IBM, maker of both computer hardware and software, the goals included patent treaty reform but emphasized full implementation by developing countries (and some industrialized countries) of copyrights under the Berne Convention. The company's priority was reform of the Berne Convention to explicitly recognize the copyrightability of software. Together, Pfizer and IBM fostered a strategy of multilateral diplomacy using the forum provided by the GATT's Advisory Committee on Trade Policy and Negotiation (ACTPN), on which their chief executive officers were represented.

Until the ACTPN was established by the 1974 Trade Act to institutionalize business input into U.S. trade policy and multilateral negotiations, American business traditionally influenced trade policy in an ad hoc manner.[2] After the Tokyo Round multilateral trade negotiations had been completed in 1979 and the agreements enacted into U.S. law, the ACTPN began to articulate advisory positions for the planned round of GATT multilateral negotiations, which became the Uruguay Round that began in 1986. Chaired by Pfizer CEO Edmund T. Pratt, the committee emphasized that the next round of negotiations needed to go beyond purely trade policy matters and focus on obstacles to investment. Policies of developing countries, the committee stated, were not conducive to manufacturing investment and licensing partnerships, and weak protection of intellectual property rights constituted an important part of the problem. The committee recommended that the Office of the U.S. Trade Representative create the post of assistant trade representative for investment, a position that was established in 1981.

The ACTPN's message was announced through the U.S. Council for International Business, a trade group affiliated with the International Cham-

---

1. Santoro and Paine (1995, pp. 9–10).
2. Bauer, Pool, and Dexter (1972); and Committee on Ways and Means (1989, p. 181).

ber of Commerce, as well as through business councils in various countries. Pfizer worked in Washington to multiply the committee's efforts and strengthen its capacity to influence the multilateral policy agenda by calling on the membership of the Pharmaceutical Manufacturers Association (later renamed the Pharmaceutical Research and Manufacturers of America) to put the protection of intellectual property high on its lobbying agenda. An ally was found in the Chemical Manufacturers Association, whose members were also concerned about investment environments and trade secret protection.

The ACTPN emphasized educating people in Congress and the executive branch, especially in the Office of the U.S. Trade Representative, about the importance of protecting intellectual property rights to facilitate investment in developing countries. The committee sponsored conferences and distributed books drawn from them to Washington policymakers. The conferences emphasized that American competitiveness in innovation-based industries was injured by policies of many developing countries that denied effective protection of patents and trade secrets, compelled outside companies to license production to local partners picked by the state, discouraged direct investment, and encouraged piracy of pharmaceutical and chemical products. As discussed in the next chapter, the strategy worked: the USTR agreed to expend the considerable diplomatic effort needed to put intellectual property on the GATT Uruguay Round agenda.

At the beginning of the Uruguay Round Pfizer's Pratt and IBM Chairman John Opel established the Intellectual Property Committee to coordinate their policy positions in the negotiations.[3] The original thirteen member companies were Pfizer, IBM, Merck, General Electric, DuPont, Warner Communications, Hewlett-Packard, Bristol-Myers, FMC Corporation, General Motors, Johnson & Johnson, Monsanto, and Rockwell International. The IPC has been a spokesman for intellectual property–based companies ever since, operating with a couple of professional staff members who coordinate the positions and activities of its members and lobby for their interests in Washington and Geneva.

While multilateral GATT diplomacy strategy was being articulated under the leadership of the ACTPN and IPC, copyright-dependent companies pursued a separate strategy to strengthen international copyright laws and in late 1984 created their own organization, the International Intellec-

---

3. Santoro and Paine (1995, p. 10).

tual Property Alliance (IIPA), to do it. The IIPA's members were the American Association of Publishers, Motion Picture Association of America, Recording Industry Association of America, American Film Marketing Association, National Music Publishers' Association, and Computer and Business Equipment Manufacturers Association (CBEMA). (The CBEMA later dropped out as its membership of computer hardware companies focused on business problems other than intellectual property; it is now known as the Information Technology Industry Council.) The Business Software Alliance, a consortium of the major software companies, and the Interactive Digital Software Association, a group of video game companies, have been active members of IIPA in recent years. Generally satisfied with the Berne Convention copyright protections as they applied to films, music, and books but dissatisfied with weak enforcement of the rules in developing countries, the copyright companies did not initially advocate a multilateral, GATT-based diplomatic effort; instead they favored bilateral negotiations.

The IIPA was established to advocate an agenda for the U.S. Trade Representative's section 301 intellectual property mandate, which Congress had codified in the 1984 Trade Act at the urging of the copyright creators. The formation of the organization and its bilateral focus was owing to piracy problems faced by the motion picture companies. The Motion Picture Association of America successfully lobbied for an amendment to the Caribbean Basin Initiative (CBI) that piracy of U.S. copyrighted products excludes a government from tariff benefits conferred by the U.S. Generalized System of Preferences (GSP). When American book publishers had a problem with Dominican Republic pirates copying and distributing books throughout the hemisphere, they sought to use the CBI in the same way the motion picture companies had done. Cooperation among entertainment and publishing companies led to language in the 1984 Trade Act that expanded the scope of section 301 of the 1974 Trade Act, the "unfair trade practices" policy that is managed by the USTR, to include failure to protect intellectual property in the list of unfair trade practices that could bring a USTR investigation and subsequent trade sanctions.[4]

The copyright industries believed that they needed to teach U.S. trade policymakers, who knew a great deal about trade in real property agricultural and manufactured goods but little about trade in intellectual property

---

4. Ryan (1995a).

goods, about the magnitude of the worldwide piracy of U.S.-owned copyrighted works. In 1985 the IIPA submitted to the USTR a white paper, "U.S. Government Trade Policy: Views of the Copyright Industry," and a report, *Piracy of U.S. Copyrighted Works in Ten Selected Countries*.[5] Synthesizing information provided by IIPA member associations, each of which was organizing ambitious antipiracy efforts around the world, the report presented country-by-country sales losses caused by piracy in film, music, computer software, and books. The numbers staggered policymakers: in the ten countries studied (Singapore, Taiwan, Indonesia, Korea, Philippines, Malaysia, Thailand, Brazil, Egypt, and Nigeria) losses were estimated at $1.3 billion.[6] The white paper recommended a bilateral diplomatic strategy based on aggressive use of section 301 investigation, negotiation, and (if necessary) the threat of sanctions against lax governments. The paper packed a political punch because of the magnitude of the losses, and the USTR responded by initiating a 301 investigation against Korea for copyright piracy (as well as patent and trademark institutional weaknesses). Countable indicators had turned a policy condition into a problem that policymakers believed merited being solved.

To institutionalize annual USTR measurement of copyright problems in each country and aggressive bilateral diplomacy to improve the situation, the IIPA and its members lobbied Congress to amend section 301 in the 1989 Trade Act. The USTR would be required to produce an annual report and announce its intellectual property diplomacy agenda for the next year— the so-called special 301 trade policy. The alliance prepared a comprehensive report in 1989 for the first special 301 report from the USTR that said improved enforcement efforts, especially in Singapore, had reduced piracy losses in the ten countries studied in 1985 to $645 million. Total losses nevertheless exceeded $1.3 billion due to growing problems in China, India, and Saudi Arabia.[7]

The IIPA has prepared an increasingly thick report for the USTR every year regarding copyright policy and piracy rates. During the late 1980s and 1990s the motion picture, music, book, and software associations and their member companies became more sophisticated in their ability to gather, collate, and disseminate information. Company and trade association representatives, organized by industry group, are now networked throughout the

5. International Intellectual Property Alliance (1985a, 1985b).
6. International Intellectual Property Alliance (1989, p. 1).
7. International Intellectual Property Alliance (1989, p. 1).

world to gather information regarding production and distribution of illegitimate products. The representatives investigate usage patterns to estimate the size of the local market. Because they know the exact amount of the legitimate product they are selling, the associations can provide piracy rates and estimated losses for each country. The piracy rates typically exceed 90 percent in many developing countries and approach 100 percent in countries such as Russia because no legitimate products are sold there. The IIPA then aggregates the trade association data for advocacy use. The organization estimated that piracy was responsible for more than $14 billion in total losses in 1995: $2.27 billion in the film industry, $1.3 billion in music, $7.2 billion in business application software, $3.8 billion in entertainment software, and $780 million in book publishing. For 1996, when fewer countries were covered, the IIPA estimated more than $10 billion in losses: $1.8 billion in the film industry,$1.2 billion in music, $3.8 billion in business application software, $3.1 billion in entertainment software, and $690 million in book publishing.[8]

Separate, complementary countable indicator advocacy has been carried out by Nintendo (the Japanese-based video game maker) since the early 1990s and the Software Publishers Association (SPA) since the mid-1990s.[9] Taking a page from the advocacy strategy of the copyright industries, the Pharmaceutical Research and Manufacturers of America each year contributes to the USTR country analyses of the patent policies and other regulatory situations its members find in developing countries and recommends priorities for action.

The USTR and Bilateral Trade Diplomacy

Because of the advocacy by the copyright-intensive businesses, in the Trade and Tariff Act of 1984 Congress declared that inadequate protection of intellectual property constitutes an "unreasonable" practice and authorized the president to take action, including the removal of tariff preferences or the application of other sanctions under the authority of section 301 of the 1974 Trade Act.

8. International Intellectual Property Alliance, *Special 301 Recommendations* (1997). I have rounded the data for presentation here.
9. Pharmaceutical Research and Manufacturers of America (1996); Software Publishers Association (1996); and Arter & Hadden (1996).

Intellectual property protection would be grafted onto existing section 301 policy structure and patterns of behavior. Beginning in the early 1980s, section 301 trade diplomacy confronted foreign trade barriers with a tough, aggressive strategy of rule- and power-oriented negotiation: the USTR was to demonstrate the legitimacy of the U.S. complaint by proving, when possible, that the barriers violated the international trade rules of the GATT and to demonstrate the U.S. commitment to compel foreign governments to change policy by threatening or actually deploying economic sanctions.[10]

The strategy achieved considerable success in opening foreign markets to American manufactures and agricultural products and encouraging greater compliance with GATT rules. The USTR favored the petitions that came from internationally competitive industries confronting GATT-noncompliant trade barriers, and the intellectual property interests calling for help certainly qualified as internationally competitive. However, because international treaties were considerably weaker in their demands on state patent and copyright policies than were the GATT agreements, the USTR could not demonstrate that these developing countries were violating public international law. The agency thus needed a new negotiation strategy.

But the use of section 301 for lack of effective intellectual property protection was a policy change more easily drafted by Congress than implemented by the Office of the U.S. Trade Representative because the agency knew little about intellectual property issues in 1984. The conduct of intellectual property diplomacy, then, called for organizational learning at the USTR. The USTR, a small organization of specialists, possessed no in-house knowledge regarding intellectual property competition and policy. Thus the U.S. Trade Representative placed intellectual property policy in the portfolio of the Assistant U.S. Trade Representative for Investment, who recruited an intellectual property lawyer to serve as deputy. The deputy for intellectual property would advise the USTR staff dealing with bilateral, regional, and multilateral diplomacy.

The 1984 amendment to section 301 was a mandate that the USTR defend U.S. intellectual property rights in the world economy. The agency selected South Korea as the first target of the new bilateral diplomacy. American pharmaceutical makers had complained that the Korean patent laws, in particular when applied to chemical compounds, foods, and medicinal products, protected only the specific process for making the product,

---

10. Ryan (1995a, 1995b).

not the product itself.[11] Because many pharmaceutical and chemical products can be readily manufactured using slightly different techniques, the protection was worthless. The American manufacturers further complained that the term of protection was only twelve years from the time of a patent's publication, and because in the pharmaceutical industry the development period from discovery to market approval takes ten to twelve years, the term was tantamount to no protection at all.

American pharmaceutical and chemical manufacturers also complained that Korean trademark law protected only products that had been licensed to a Korean firm in a joint venture. And some products such as pesticides were ineligible for trademark protection. Korean courts offered little hope of redress for trademark infringements because judges employed a "famous in Korea" test for trademarks, which meant that a trademark merited protection only if it was well known to Korean consumers. Thus products new to the Korean market but well known in other parts of the world were denied protection. The Pharmaceutical Manufacturers Association pointed out that this interpretation of trademark law violated the Paris Convention for protection of industrial property, a treaty to which Korea had acceded in 1980.

American pharmaceutical makers further complained that technology transfers to Korean importers and producers were contingent upon the approval of the Ministry of Finance, which, they asserted, regularly rejected imports if they involved right of monopoly sales, technology that the government believed to be obsolete or no longer world class, or licensing arrangements that might lead to "excessive competition" among domestic producers. Although a Korean law had changed policy that year so that importers of foreign technology would only have to report to, not seek the prior approval of, the Ministry of Finance, American industry urged the USTR to ensure that the de jure policy change would not be thwarted de facto by the ministry's power to review each notification and order an investigation.

The IIPA complained that Korean businesses were extensively pirating books, recordings, films and video cassettes, and computer software.[12] Korean copyright law offered little protection for foreign copyrights, it

11. Statement by Pfizer Inc., New York, June 14, 1985; and Pharmaceutical Manufacturers Association, public file 301-52, USTR, December 2, 1985.
12. Statement by International Intellectual Property Alliance, public file 301-52, USTR, December 2, 1985.

alleged, and American companies were losing $150 million annually as a result. And the losses were increasing each year as the markets grew and pirating proliferated. Korea was not a signatory to any treaty that would protect foreign copyright holders. The IIPA urged the USTR to pressure Seoul to pass a new copyright law and accede to international copyright agreements.

Bilateral U.S.-Korean discussions on intellectual property rights had been going on since 1983. The Korean government claimed it had not yet reached a level of economic development sufficient to make intellectual property protection a cost-effective government policy. In addition, strong domestic opposition to strengthening the laws hampered the government's negotiations.[13] Not only was book piracy a big business, but the government was especially sensitive to the political threat posed by college students who would protest loudly if curtailed pirating led to higher textbook prices. Korean pharmaceutical and chemical makers also opposed changes in the laws.

Because Korea's position had not wavered, the USTR decided that the threat of sanctions was needed to resolve the dispute. In fall 1985, the USTR initiated new negotiations under authority of section 301, which carried the implicit threat of trade sanctions if negotiations failed.[14] At the same time the USTR chose its goal of placing intellectual property rights on the GATT multilateral trade negotiation agenda, the objective being to provide stronger protections of intellectual property and secure developing-country accessions to the stronger agreements. Because developing countries had been united in their opposition to intellectual property negotiations in the GATT forum, the USTR determined that bilateral negotiations under the threat of section 301 sanctions could separate Korea from other developing-country opponents in the GATT and lead it to reform its policy. The negotiations with Korea were thus important in themselves for the expected change in Korean policy, but also important to the Uruguay Round negotiation strategy and as a precedent for bilateral and multilateral negotiations with other developing countries.

---

13. Gadbaw and Richards (1988, p. 276).
14. U.S. Trade Representative, *Section 301 Table of Cases*, "Brazil Informatics," 301-49, and "Korea Intellectual Property," 301-52, January 30, 1996. For additional information regarding the Brazil case see Bayard and Elliott (1994, pp. 187–208); regarding the Korea case see Ryan (1995b, pp. 114–19).

Korean government negotiators persisted for many months in claiming that the country's level of development remained too low to permit reform of intellectual property policies. USTR negotiators consolidated the intellectual property dispute with the dispute over market access to insurance services, then threatened loss of benefits under the Generalized System of Preferences and sanctions on Korean exports of footwear, tires, and electronics. In July 1986 the negotiators reached agreement.[15] The Korean government offered to submit a comprehensive copyright bill to its legislature and to "exert its best efforts to ensure that the legislation is enacted so as to become effective no later than July 1, 1987." It also agreed to accede to the Universal Copyright Convention and the Geneva Phonogram Convention within ninety days of the effective date of the new law, which would cover all the types of works enumerated in the UCC and would explicitly recognize copyright protection for computer software. The law would protect sound recordings for twenty years and publications for the life of the author plus fifty years.

The government also pledged to strengthen penalties against copyright infringement, although "such penalties will be consistent with the nature and severity of penalties for other offenses under Korean law." Simultaneously with the new copyright law, it would put in force a Computer Program Protection Law, which would afford protection for software consistent with that offered other works. In addition, the government agreed to "study the feasibility of extending protection to data bases as compilations," "study the feasibility of extending protection to semiconductor chips," and "study satellite telecasts and cable TV, with a view toward protecting them under the new copyright law."

Korea also committed itself to amend its law on patents for pharmaceutical and chemical products, pledging to introduce a bill by the end of September 1986 and to "exert its best efforts to secure enactment . . . by the end of 1986." The new legislation would protect patents for fifteen years from the date of publication of the application. The government also pledged to accede to the Budapest Treaty in 1987. The U.S. and Korean negotiators addressed the crucial issue of retroactive coverage of pharmaceutical and chemical patents by agreeing that "through administrative guidance" (bureaucratic not legislative action) the government would pro-

---

15. *International Trade Reporter* (July 23 1986); "Record of Understanding on Intellectual Property Rights," signed by Ambassador Kyung-Won Kim and Ambassador Clayton Yeutter, August 28, 1986.

hibit the manufacture and marketing of "certain products" that had been patented in the United States after January 1, 1980, but before the effective date of the new patent law. The treaty provided that the two countries would agree on the products to be covered by this provision before the effective date of the new law.

On trademarks the Korean government noted that in September 1985 the Ministry of Finance had promulgated guidelines prohibiting domestic firms from registering for trademarks identical to or resembling those owned by foreign firms, "regardless of whether the foreign mark is 'well known' in Korea." The guidelines had ended the export requirement practice on trademark licenses. The Koreans also amended the Foreign Capital Inducement Act to remove the technology inducement as a condition for accepting applications for trademark licenses.

The Korean government pledged to enforce intellectual property rights strictly and impose "effective penalties" against violations. It also agreed to make all administrative rules and regulations on intellectual property rights transparent to the public. The two sides agreed to consult through the Korea-U.S. Economic Consultation Trade Subgroup on implementation of the agreement. With the signing the USTR agreed to terminate its section 301 investigation.

In February 1987 the USTR announced that guidelines had been negotiated with the Korean government for implementing the treaty provisions on U.S. pharmaceutical and chemical patents that predated the new Korean patent law.[16] American companies could have process patents that were pending with the Korean patents administrators amended to include product patent claims. Pharmaceutical and chemical products patented in the United States between January 1, 1980, and July 1, 1987 (the effective date of the new patent law), but never sold on either the Korean or the U.S. market, would be manufactured or marketed by Korean firms only with the permission of the U.S. patent holder.

Despite the bilateral agreement, new intellectual property laws, and accessions to multilateral treaties, American pharmaceutical companies remained dissatisfied with Korea's record of compliance. Squibb and Bristol-Myers resubmitted section 301 complaints with the USTR in 1988, charging that Korean companies were pirating patented products, often with the help of a research center funded by the Korean government.

16. U.S. Trade Representative, *Federal Register*, 52-3369.

European companies voiced similar complaints to their governments. A British company that held the patent rights to the AIDS drug AZT cried foul when a South Korean pharmaceutical company doing only US$4 million in sales a year announced that it had independently developed AZT in less than a year. The *Far Eastern Economic Review* reported that officials of the Korean company admitted privately that they "may have taken development shortcuts."[17]

In June 1988 the USTR announced that in lieu of a new section 301 investigation into Korea's alleged violations of intellectual property rights, it would carry out a fact-finding study jointly with the Patent and Trademark Office.[18] The USTR took the action to permit the Korean government five months to resolve the problems over pharmaceuticals and threatened that if a settlement was not reached, it would reinitiate a section 301 case.[19] The agency, the American embassy in Seoul, and American industries continually monitored the situation. But according to the IIPA, extensive copyright violations persisted.[20] It discovered, for example, that Korean publishers had put $2 million worth of pirated textbooks on the country's college market in February 1988. Pirating of video cassettes, records, and computer software also continued unabated. Seoul's enforcement efforts appeared to be minimal. In May 1989, because of pressure from the IIPA, the USTR placed Korea (along with Brazil, India, Mexico, China, Saudi Arabia, Taiwan, and Thailand) on its inaugural priority watch list of violators of section 301 of the 1988 Trade Act.[21]

Under this renewed pressure a new agreement was negotiated between the United States and Korea. This time the Korean government created an interagency enforcement coordination task force and assigned special teams of police and prosecutors to it. The government submitted additional proposed reforms to the legislature and pledged to do reforms for semiconductor masks in 1992. By early 1990, patent compliance improved and the pirating of books and videos decreased. American diplomats learned that vigorous enforcement is the most crucial matter in building intellectual property institutions and that enforcement procedures must be specified in detail if effective change in protection is to occur. The 1986 bilateral

---

17. Clifford (1988), p. 48.
18. U.S. Trade Representative, *Federal Register*, 53-22758.
19. Clifford (1988, pp. 4–49.
20. International Intellectual Property Alliance (April 1989).
21. U.S. Trade Representative (1990, p. 133).

agreement with Korea simply had too much loose language.[22] American holders of intellectual property learned from the experience that they would have to monitor enforcement with vigilance, committing significant funding and numbers of personnel to the effort.

American trade negotiators also learned from bilateral negotiations held to improve copyright protection in Brazil that with neither the persuasion of international legal norms nor the threat of U.S. trade sanctions, changing foreign government policy is not easy. At the end of 1987, after more than two years of negotiations with U.S. trade representatives, the Brazilian legislature passed a copyright law, but was either unable or unwilling to enforce it.[23] The pharmaceutical industry filed a complaint over the lack of patent protection that led to fruitless negotiations and in October 1988 to imposition of sanctions by the USTR.[24] The Brazilians demanded a GATT dispute settlement panel to evaluate the legitimacy of the U.S. action. In 1988 the USTR also encouraged Brazil to extend copyright protection to computer software, but the Brazilian government was no better able to enforce an amended copyright law than previous versions.[25]

Special 301 and Intellectual Property Reform in China

The 1988 Omnibus Trade and Competitiveness Act mandates that the Office of the U.S. Trade Representative provide an annual report to Congress on unfair trade practices abroad, the so-called Special 301 provision. Within thirty days of releasing the *National Trade Estimates* at the end of April each year, the USTR must

identify those foreign countries that deny adequate and effective protection of intellectual property rights, or deny fair and equitable market access to United States persons that rely upon intellectual property protection, and those foreign countries . . . that are determined by the Trade Representative to be priority foreign countries that have the most onerous or egregious acts, policies, or practices.[26]

22. See the discussion of agreement drafting and compliance in Ryan (1995a, pp. 123–31).
23. Bayard and Elliott (1994, p. 189).
24. U.S. Trade Representative, *Section 301 Table of Cases*, Case 301-61 (January 30, 1996).
25. U.S. Trade Representative (1989, p. 4).
26. *Omnibus Trade and Competitiveness Act* (1988, sec. 1303) See Committee on Ways and Means (1989, p. 761).

Under Special 301 the agency lists the countries that are the most onerous or egregious offenders with which negotiations are being conducted under threat of retaliatory sanctions. It also announces a "priority watch" list of countries that may have sinned no less but are not the target of deadlined negotiations. In addition, it announces the countries in which intellectual property protection problems persist but that are not the subject of negotiations. This annual ranking in effect presents the USTR's diplomacy agenda for the year to follow.

The Special 301 announcement is the result of a business-government process initiated in February each year when the USTR calls for public comment. The IIPA, Pharmaceutical Research and Manufacturers of America (PhRMA), Software Publishers Association (SPA), and Nintendo (as well as the International Anticounterfeiting Coalition on behalf of trademark interests such as sport shoes, apparel, and toy manufacturers) submit detailed assessments of intellectual property policies and practices around the world and their recommendations for the USTR's Special 301 announcement. The USTR, a lean agency with a small staff, relies extensively on the information provided by these groups to arrive at its agenda.

For 1989 the priority offenders included Brazil, India, South Korea, Mexico, Saudi Arabia, Taiwan, and Thailand, but nowhere was the sense of urgency to initiate negotiations greater than it was with China. While negotiations were being conducted with the Koreans, American producers of books, films, music, and software were claiming that the absence of copyright protection in China was costing them $400 million a year in lost revenue.[27] More than a million copies of Collier Macmillan's basic English textbook had been reproduced without a penny paid in royalties. Shoppers on "Silicon Street" in Beijing bought computer hardware from pushcart vendors who threw in the software free. Two dozen compact disk and laser disk factories in southern China were illegally producing an estimated 50 million units for distribution throughout southeast Asia.

Chinese officials defended the book piracy by claiming that people are too poor to pay for Western books, "yet we must obtain this knowledge so that we can develop our economy. Furthermore, our printers give Chinese people jobs. Your companies are rich and your country is rich, yet always you want more." American diplomats countered that although the argument offered surface appeal, the reality was that American publishers priced

---

27. International Intellectual Property Alliance (1989, pp. 57–66).

books much lower in developing country markets than in industrialized countries. In addition, they observed that because books are heavy, they are better printed in the developing country and transported locally for distribution. Thus American publishers would also give Chinese people jobs. Finally, the publishers maintained that the official defense on behalf of Chinese consumers and workers masked a corrupt support of pirate printers by government officials. (The same defense was used by the South Korean government before that country's printers and music CD and video cassette makers became licensee partners of American companies in the 1990s.) China was named a priority foreign country again in 1990, but on-and-off negotiations produced little change in policy.

After the April 1991 announcement that China would again be priority, the USTR was ready to become aggressive about using trade sanctions. In May the Chinese government agreed to provide copyright protection for computer software, and in June a new copyright law took effect. USTR negotiators pressured Beijing to agree by the end of November to accede to the Berne Convention and the Geneva Phonogram Convention or face sanctions. In January 1992 China agreed to sign both treaties and make the legislative reforms necessary to implement treaty conditions.

The commitments did not come until the USTR threatened to raise tariffs on $1.5 billion of Chinese goods, including beer, footwear, clothing, leather goods, televisions, watches, and nuts and bolts. Later in 1992 American and Chinese negotiators reached agreement, the so-called Memo of Understanding, on adopting international standards of patent protection for pharmaceuticals and chemicals. Although the Chinese took some important initiatives, such as creating a special court in Beijing to hear copyright and trademark disputes, USTR negotiators nevertheless knew only too well that treaty accessions and legal reforms did not mean that the intellectual property dispute was settled.

By 1994, losses to Chinese patent infringement, copyright piracy, and trademark counterfeiting were estimated at $1 billion and mounting rapidly. For the Clinton administration, as they had for the Bush administration, the losses became a high-priority problem. The trade deficit with China was $30 billion in 1994, and the president recognized that only aggressive trade diplomacy could assuage business criticism and keep the initiative on trade policy away from a Congress that was easily tipped toward protectionism. Executive branch officials at the Office of the U.S. Trade Representative and the Commerce Department recognized that forecasts of the Chinese economy predicted 10 percent annual GDP growth for at least the medium term and that infringement of pharmaceutical, chemical, and semiconductor patents would grow extensively. *Lion King* videos today, pentium chips tomorrow. The administration was also motivated by a desire to be perceived as tough with China on trade policy in the wake of human rights violations that were controversial in U.S. domestic politics.

American negotiators could count on significant bargaining leverage with the Chinese. China was especially dependent on exports of textiles and apparel, toys, and simple manufactured goods of plastic, metal, and leather to the U.S. market. These goods were produced by factories in Guangdong Province along the southern Chinese coast, which were run by China's newly rich and increasingly powerful young entrepreneurs, many with Hong Kong and Taiwan connections, and by the Defense Ministry, a paragon of traditional power. Negotiators could find additional leverage in Beijing's professed goal of rejoining the GATT regime as a founding member of the World Trade Organization.[28]

The Americans, however, needed to balance aggressiveness with respect for Beijing's bargaining leverage. China's nuclear and conventional warwaging capabilities make its neighbors wary during even the best of times, and U.S. policymakers wanted Chinese cooperation in restraining North Korea's nuclear policy and Middle East arms sales. And despite diminishing political capacity, the Beijing government remained able to link military security with trade policy. Its one billion consumers, even if most are poor, and its centralized economy give the government great power over direct investment and import contracts, particularly in telecommunications, energy, agriculture, natural resources, construction, and transportation. Chinese trade negotiators regularly threatened AT&T, Boeing, Chrysler, and midwestern farmers with lost investment and sales if U.S.demands to protect intellectual property rights were too stringent.

The Clinton administration raised the protection of intellectual property rights in China to the top of the USTR's agenda in late 1994 by renewing a section 301 investigation. The administration emphasized that it was willing to impose sanctions to achieve greater protection of intellectual property rights in China, even if multilateral obligations did not then demand it. The USTR set the end of December as the deadline for a

---

28. The Chinese government claims that it is "rejoining" the GATT regime because China was an original member, although it was then represented by the Nationalist government. This is a controversial point of international law made effectively moot by the establishment of the World Trade Organization.

settlement. When negotiations broke down, it announced in January 1995 that it was readying a list of Chinese imports worth $2.8 billion to be sanctioned with higher tariffs. The agency remained firm, even in the face of severe criticism. The Hong Kong Trade Department protested that it would be an innocent victim of the sanctions—$470 million worth of goods were reshipped through its port. In the United States, the National Retail Federation, which represents the big American retailers, and other groups cautioned that American consumers would pay more for many goods if the tariffs were imposed.

The Chinese responded by threatening to freeze the Big Three automakers out of any new deals. But they also made highly publicized raids on street vendors of counterfeit CDs and software. In late February the government closed the largest of the more than two dozen software knock-off factories in Guangdong Province and brought charges in the Beijing intellectual properties court against some prominent software retailers. When negotiators for the two countries settled the dispute, the United States announced that it would drop the threat of sanctions. The agreement committed the Chinese to close all two dozen software knock-off factories within three months. Chinese customs authorities were to create by December 31, 1995, a centralized records system that would include the names of infringers, types of products, quantities, and disposition of the cases and products. The U.S. government would provide experts from the Customs Service and FBI to help Chinese officials design effective customs enforcement procedures and training for customs workers. The agreement provided that customs officials would seize and destroy counterfeit goods and fine the purveyors of them.

The agreement provided that beginning March 1, 1995, all CDs and CD-ROMs were to be protected through an identification system that would authenticate the products. The agreement required continued improvement of court procedures and police enforcement of intellectual property rights through interagency task forces that would be established at all levels of Chinese government—central, provincial, and local—and would include personnel from the National Copyright Administration, the State Administration for Industry and Commerce, the Patent Office, and the police. The task forces would be empowered to investigate, enter premises, seize property, and impose fines. Telephone numbers for local task forces were to be made available to foreign firms to encourage participation and action. These were extraordinary terms: never before had a bilateral trade agreement done so much to build national institutions.

The agreement also linked intellectual property enforcement with market access. China was to remove quotas on imports of American audio-visual products and, subject to censorship, the entire catalogs of music companies. Joint ventures for software production were to be permitted in Guangzhou and Shanghai immediately and phased in over five years in eleven other cities. A week after the agreement was signed, Time Warner announced that it had reached a deal to distribute television programming through the formation of China Television Enterprises, Inc.

Dissatisfied with the Chinese government's enforcement efforts, especially against the pirating of computer software, movies, and music recordings, the USTR announced in May 1996 that it would increase tariffs on textiles and apparel goods, consumer electronics, bicycles, and sporting goods by $3 billion. The expectation was that China, which sent $45 billion in exports to the United States (one-third of its total exports), would be compelled to step up enforcement efforts. But Beijing declared that it would retaliate against imports and investments involving automobiles and parts, cotton, audio-visual products, and vegetable oils. And for good measure it was offering a thirty-airliner deal to Airbus instead of Boeing.

Chinese bilateral diplomacy with the United States has been consistently combative since the dispute over textile subsidies and quota noncompliance in the 1980s. This pattern is a stark contrast with U.S. bilateral trade diplomacy with the Japanese, Korean, and Taiwanese governments, which have often been clever but in the end have usually capitulated. A country with a billion consumers and a relatively open investment regime need not capitulate to every U.S. trade policy demand.

Targeting sanctions at exporters in Guangdong Province has worked at least for the moment: in June 1996 Chinese authorities closed a dozen government-authorized factories and several underground, unauthorized factories that illegally produced CDs, CD-ROMs, and music and video tapes, seizing the manufacturing equipment and destroying their output, and closed 5,000 theaters that were showing pirated movies.[29] These actions, along with customs officials' seizures of pirated goods, were augmented by greatly improved verification and monitoring procedures. All legitimate products now bear signature codes, and all factories will have inspectors who monitor production around the clock to ensure that only coded, legitimate goods are produced and that no illegal production takes place.

---

29. U.S. Trade Representative,"Report on Chinese Enforcement Actions under the 1995 IPR Agreement," June 17, 1996.

As impressive as the details of the 1996 understanding are, businesses and local governments in Guangdong Province and elsewhere continue to condone piracy and support weak enforcement of intellectual property laws. Thus the U.S. willingness to threaten sanctions appears to be a necessary diplomatic tool. The threat against exporters in Guangdong Province worked because local export interests were more powerful than local pirates. But once Beijing and Washington reached agreement during the 1995 negotiations and the threat of sanctions was lifted, local economic and political life in Guangdong returned to normal—until the cycle was repeated in 1996. American copyright-intensive firms boiled again with frustration; Washington alleged perfidy on the part of Beijing; Beijing threatened a trade war; and nationalists in China accused the United States of pursuing a deliberate, insidious strategy of economic containment.

U.S. Bilateral Intellectual Property Diplomacy, 1989–96

The USTR implemented regular section 301 to defend the interests of globally competitive U.S. industry sectors, thus blunting the domestic politics of trade deficits and the calls for protectionism and contributing to the agency's multilateral diplomatic goals within the GATT.[30] Special 301 intellectual property policy has similarly been used for the benefit of some of the most globally competitive American industry sectors—pharmaceuticals and fine chemicals, films and music recordings, computer software— and these industry groups have shaped the USTR's diplomacy agenda for protecting intellectual property.

Since 1989 the USTR has put dozens of countries, mostly but not always emerging markets, on its watch list (table 4-1). In 1989 and 1992 the Pharmaceutical Research and Manufacturers of America explained to the USTR that the primary problem in each country on its list was that pharmaceuticals could not receive product patents. By 1994 the association noted that countries such as Brazil, China, Korea, and Thailand had legally extended product patents to pharmaceuticals (or at least drafted legislation) so that the issues were in the main regulatory agency interpretations of these laws. In 1989 the International Intellectual Property Alliance stated that Korea, Taiwan, Thailand, China, India, Indonesia, Malaysia, Brazil, Egypt,

---

30. Ryan (1995b).

Table 4-1. *Countries on Agency and Organization Agendas for Violations of Intellectual Property Rights, 1989, 1992, 1994*

Year	Country
USTR bilateral diplomacy agenda	
1989	Brazil, China, India, Korea, Mexico, Saudi Arabia, Taiwan, Thailand
1992	Australia, Brazil, European Community, Egypt, Hungary, India, Korea, Philippines, Poland, Taiwan, Thailand, Turkey
1994	Argentina, China, European Union, India, Japan, Korea, Saudi Arabia, Thailand, Turkey
PhRMA patent agenda	
1989	Argentina, Chile, India, Korea, Mexico, Thailand
1992	Brazil, Hungary, India, Thailand, Turkey, Venezuela
1994	Argentina, Brazil, China, Egypt, India, Indonesia, Korea, Thailand, Turkey
IIPA copyright agenda	
1989	Brazil, China, Egypt, India, Indonesia, Korea, Malaysia, Nigeria, Philippines, Saudi Arabia, Taiwan
1992	Australia, Egypt, Germany, Greece, Korea, India, Italy, Philippines, Poland, Taiwan, Thailand, Paraguay, Turkey, United Arab Emirates
1994	Brazil, China, El Salvador, Indonesia, Japan, United Arab Emirates

Sources: U.S. Trade Representative, "Special 301," press releases (various dates); Pharmaceutical Research and Manufacturers of America, "Special 301 Submissions," public file, Office of the U.S. Trade Representative (various years); and International Intellectual Property Alliance, "Special 301 Submissions," public file, Office of the U.S. Trade Representative (various years).

and Nigeria had adopted acceptable copyright laws, so that the problems were the lack of enforcement, lack of criminal penalties, and poorly functioning judiciaries for dispute settlement. The complaints have remained the same since then.

For the Business Software Alliance, the complaints have been not only pirated software (which is emphasized in the IIPA's submission) but also the lack of explicit extension of copyright protection to computer software and databases in many countries—including China, Mexico, Korea, and Thailand, but also Italy and Germany—which BSA described as "rampant organizational piracy."[31] For video game maker Nintendo, the biggest problem was in Taiwan, where producers loaded stolen games onto EPROMs, assembled them into game players, and exported them.[32]

American bilateral intellectual property diplomacy was conducted with multilateral trade negotiation objectives in mind, as is discussed later. From its beginning with the Korea negotiations, including the Special 301 policy initiated in 1989, and through the signing of the Agreement on Trade-

31. Business Software Alliance (1989).
32. Arter and Hadden (1996).

Related Aspects of Intellectual Property Rights (TRIPS) in 1994, USTR intellectual property diplomacy was in the main a rule-writing effort. Negotiators used bilateral and multilateral diplomacy to encourage governments, especially in developing countries, to draft legislation, sign international treaties, and reach agreement on TRIPS. The USTR has regularly used the threat of revoking GSP tariff benefits to convince countries to protect intellectual property rights. Since 1995 the agency's emphasis in copyright matters has shifted from rule writing to enforcement. But rule writing continues concomitant to developing country's implementation of TRIPS agreement requirements, and USTR-initiated WTO dispute settlement regarding TRIPS implementation will be common well into the next century. The strategy toward China represents the kind of institution building that is increasingly the focus of the agency's efforts in copyright protection.

In 1996 the USTR presented the following priorities for bilateral intellectual property negotiations.[33]

—Argentina: strengthen patent protection, especially regarding pharmaceuticals.

—European Union: lower excessive patent fees and patent maintenance fees.

—Greece: reduce copyright piracy.

—India: strengthen patent protection, especially for pharmaceuticals and agricultural chemicals.

—Indonesia: reduce copyright piracy.

—Japan: broaden definition of patent claim, strengthen trade secret protection.

—Korea: reduce computer software piracy, strengthen trade secret protection.

—Turkey: reduce copyright piracy.

The USTR's 1996 watch list spotlighted countries with weak copyright enforcement practices: Brazil, Chile, Colombia, El Salvador, Italy, Kuwait, Oman, Paraguay, Peru, Russian Federation, Saudi Arabia, Singapore, Thailand, United Arab Emirates, and Venezuela.

Because the USTR's Special 301 list is generally congruent with those of the copyright and patent interest groups, the industry petitions suggest what its likely priorities for intellectual property diplomacy will be in the late 1990s. The International Intellectual Property Alliance has urged the

33. U.S. Trade Representative (1996, pp. 9–19).

agency to take up the issue of film rental rights with countries such as Argentina, Indonesia, Pakistan, Paraguay, and the Philippines. It has complained of the lack of criminal remedies in Greece, India, Indonesia, Italy, Mexico, Paraguay, Philippines, Poland, Thailand, Turkey, and Venezuela. Finally, the alliance has protested the lack of civil remedies and the sievelike borders in many developing countries, especially NAFTA partner Mexico.[34] The Software Publishers Association has also urged USTR action on rental rights, criminal and civil remedies, and border tightening but in addition has emphasized that software piracy by governments in developing countries is rampant and sets the interests of the software industry apart from the entertainment copyright industries.[35] Nintendo confronts Taiwanese producers that have moved their pirate game player and game tape production to other parts of southeast Asia for export throughout Asia and Latin America.[36]

In 1996 the USTR spotlighted countries with inadequate patent laws: Australia, Chile, Costa Rica, Egypt, Guatemala, Pakistan, Peru, and Venezuela. The list generally follows the recommendations made by the pharmaceutical makers.[37] These manufacturers continue to urge protection for their products—so-called pipeline protection for drugs under patent but pending safety and efficacy approval, a twenty-year patent term, and severely limited compulsory licensing. They add that judicial and legal institutionalization is crucial during the TRIPS implementation so that remedies provided by legislation are remedies in practice.

The interest groups, formed with the declaration of a mission, have been made effective through leaders who have designed strategies, encouraged membership, financed operations, and recruited capable staffs.[38] Both of the key special interest groups, the Intellectual Property Committee and the International Intellectual Property Alliance, survived the globalization of intellectual property in the late 1980s by being effective advocates for their members and being able to adapt their agendas and strategies to changing circumstances. In 1997 the Intellectual Property Committee includes General Electric, Hewlett-Packard, IBM, Johnson & Johnson, Merck, Microsoft, Pfizer, Procter & Gamble, Rockwell, Texas Instruments, and

---

34. International Intellectual Property Alliance, *Special 301 Recommendations* (1996).
35. Software Publishers Association (1996).
36. Arter and Hadden (1996).
37. Pharmaceutical Research and Manufacturers of America (1996).
38. Walker (1991).

Time Warner. The challenge for these special-interest groups is to encourage the full legal implementation of TRIPS obligations in all the developing countries.[39] And they must help ensure that these laws are enforced with vigor, a tall task.

---

39. Jacques Gorlin, director, Intellectual Property Committee, Testimony before the Subcommittee on Trade of the House Committee on Ways and Means, September 11, 1996.

FIVE

TRIPS Diplomacy and International Legal Change

THE INTERNATIONAL LAW of patents, trade secrets, copyrights, industrial designs, and trademarks is based on a series of treaties promulgated late in the nineteenth century and amended throughout the twentieth to adapt to changing technologies and patterns of business competition. During most of its history, the international law of intellectual property existed in a world apart from the international law of trade in real property: while the law of intellectual property institutionalized government intervention into markets, the law of trade institutionalized government withdrawal from them. The diplomacy of intellectual property rights was conducted by obscure administrators at the World Intellectual Property Organization forum or its predecessors. The diplomacy of trade in real property was conducted by high-profile ministers at the GATT forum. Although they existed on different planes, the two worlds finally met in the Uruguay Round of GATT multilateral trade negotiations to establish minimum national standards of protection of intellectual property rights under the authority of revised treaties.

When U.S. business people and government representatives called for the creation of new international laws because the institutions to protect intellectual property in many developing countries were weak or nonexistent, the developing countries made clear at WIPO forum that they wanted no part of reformed institutions. One-nation, one-vote decisionmaking at WIPO gave developing countries control over the WIPO agenda. For the U.S. business interests and policymakers, breaking the refusal to negotiate seriously depended on understanding how states interacted in multilateral bargaining settings. The diplomacy of making international law is a two-level exercise in which states bargain with their domestic groups even as they bargain with each other.[1] The domestic level may require including new groups and issues, making concessions, and even redefining issues from low priority to high national interest in the minds of opinion-leading policymakers, legislators, and domestic groups.[2]

According to some students of trade negotiations, the key to getting agreement is getting the right mix of issues on the table, even if they are previously unrelated, so that they can be linked for bargaining purposes.[3] A negotiator offers to the opposing negotiator something important in order to receive in return a concession that otherwise would not have been offered. Linkage-bargain diplomacy can be exploited to achieve treaties in diplomatically and politically difficult areas in which agreement would otherwise be elusive. WIPO, with its authority limited to intellectual property issues, could not offer linkage-bargaining opportunities. GATT multilateral trade negotiations, however, could offer opportunities for creative bargaining, because the proposed agenda for the 1980s round of negotiations included textiles and apparel, agriculture, services, foreign direct investment, and government procurement. Many developing countries had much to gain from liberalized trade in textiles and apparel and agricultural products; the United States and other industrialized countries had much to gain from liberalization of services and an easing of controls on foreign direct investment. U.S. trade diplomats hypothesized that linkage bargaining in the GATT forum could achieve unprecedented multilateral agreement.[4] When the Agreement on Trade-Related Aspects of Intellectual Property Rights (TRIPS) was finally achieved as part of the Uruguay Round, it appeared that linkage-bargain diplomacy explained the outcome. And it seemed that international intellectual property lawmaking would from that time forward be linkage-bargain, trade-related diplomacy.

Linkage bargaining within the GATT regime worked because U.S. negotiators held fast to their position that the Uruguay Round agreements had to be accepted in their totality. There would be no à la carte picking and choosing among agreements, as had happened at the Tokyo Round, and the

1. Putnam (1988).
2. Friman, 1993; and Schoppa, 1993.
3. Hoekman (1989); Tollison and Willett (1989); and Sebenius (1983).
4. Rubin and Graham (1984); and Hufbauer and Schott (1985, pp. 73–75).

U.S. position was strong because the final Uruguay Round package included the agreements establishing the World Trade Organization and the Dispute Settlement Understanding. The Dispute Settlement Understanding offered less developed countries, especially, some respite from the threat of Special 301 and trade sanctions carried out by the U.S. Trade Representative. The Special 301 threat loomed larged in the minds of policymakers from developing countries. They had little to fear from a European Community lukewarm on TRIPS from the beginning but much to fear from a USTR that had initiated 301 actions over intellectual property rights violations by Korea and Brazil in 1985 to get the two countries to the table and that pursued an aggressive Special 301 diplomacy throughout the eight years of the Uruguay Round to keep them there.

Closer examination of TRIPS diplomacy, however, reveals that linkage bargaining during the Uruguay Round only worked because there was a draft TRIPS agreement on the table as the final bargains were being struck. Expert specialists crucially helped cooperation in the international regime by deploying their technical knowledge, conducting what can be called function-specific diplomacy.[5] Under the leadership of the TRIPS negotiation chair, the GATT Secretariat culled ideas from the negotiators and offered a compromise text to the combatants, providing a draft composite text that was incorporated into the "Dunkel Draft" offered by the director general as a compromise final agreement.[6] When the endgame concluded, the Draft Composite Text became the final TRIPS agreement. Function-specific diplomacy contributed as much as linkage-bargain diplomacy to achieving the agreement. The TRIPS agreement may have, in an immediate sense, rested on the economic power and diplomatic agressiveness of the United States. But American power and aggressiveness would have come to little if a detailed agreement drafted by intellectual property specialists had not been on the table.

U.S. power within North American trade relations, comparatively much greater than within the GATT, allowed U.S. negotiators to write terms of agreement considered model by many observers. NAFTA demands some positive obligations not imposed by TRIPS and confers no lengthy phase-in for implementation of its terms. Nevertheless, the TRIPS agreement fundamentally changes international intellectual property institutions, and its

---

5. Jacobson (1984, pp. 62–67).
6. The official name of the Dunkel Draft is Draft Final Act Embodying the Results of the Uruguay Round of the Multilateral Trade Negotiations.

implementation profoundly reforms national intellectual property policies and practices in many countries.

The TRIPS agreement establishes important minimum standards for intellectual property protection, but it does not completely harmonize national intellectual property policies, which at the outset had been the goal of the U.S. negotiators. During the eight-year-long negotiations, U.S. power and linkage bargaining produced agreements on intellectual property rights within the North American Free Trade Agreement that are more demanding and detailed than TRIPS. Nevertheless, given the differences in scale and scope between NAFTA and the Uruguay Round, TRIPS must be seen as an impressive achievement with such far-reaching implications for developing countries as to justify calling it the single most important agreement concluded in the Uruguay Round. TRIPS establishes obligations for developing countries with potentially profound implications for their economies and polities.

International Treaties on Intellectual Property

The international law of intellectual property as established by pre-TRIPS international treaties is described below. The TRIPS agreement greatly changes the international law of intellectual property, introducing minimum standards of protection in some areas of intellectual property and obligating enforcement. It includes detailed provisions regarding judicial proceedings with respect to intellectual property disputes whereas WIPO conventions had little to say on enforcement provisions. The TRIPS reforms, however, do not discard the provisions of traditional treaties negotiated in WIPO forums. Thus these treaties remain in force and important sources of international law.

The Paris Convention

The Paris Convention for the Protection of Industrial Property was signed in 1883 and periodically amended in the twentieth century, most recently in 1979. The convention does not obligate minimum standards of patent protection among its signatory states. Each Paris Union member is free to offer any standard of patent protection it wishes. However, the convention does demand that members not discriminate against foreign property owners, an obligation known as national treatment. National patent laws must be administered even-handedly whether the property is owned by citizens or by foreigners. An important provision of the convention establishes a right of priority throughout the membership once an application for a patent, utility model, industrial design, or trademark is filed in any one member state. However, the provision ought not be misinterpreted to mean that a patent application filed in one member state is filed in all member states, for it does not mean this, and article 4 of the convention explicitly says so. The right of priority simply means that a date has been established throughout the membership should any disputes arise over who was first to file.

Article 5 of the treaty provides that states have the right to legislate compulsory licenses so as "to prevent the abuses which might result from the exercise of the exclusive rights conferred by the patent, for example, [the invention's] failure to work." In theory a compulsory license law permits the government to assign a foreign-owned invention to a local company for production and distribution to ensure that the invention is available to its citizens. In practice, a compulsory license law may be used by a government to ensure that a favored domestic company is granted exclusive distribution rights within the country and the actual foreign owner is denied both the right to make and distribute the product itself and the right to select a local maker and distributor licensee. This provision is thus among the most controversial of the Paris Convention.

Article 10 binds members to ensure effective protection against unfair competition, particularly attempts to create confusion in the marketplace by trying to sell goods through unauthorized use of trademarks or trade names. (Article 9 provides that "all goods unlawfully bearing a trademark or trade name shall be seized on importation into those countries of the Union where such mark or trade name is entitled to legal protection.") Article 12 obligates each member to establish an industrial property service office to administer policy regarding patents, utility models, industrial designs, and trademarks. The office is to publish a record of intellectual property grants and registrations. The Paris Convention created a forum for the members to consult with each other, an executive committee of member representatives to meet more often, and a secretariat known as the International Bureau.

The Paris Convention bears the marks of a modest agreement among generally like-minded industrialized countries. Even if they disagreed on particulars, the Paris Union agreed that the patent institution was important for industrial innovation, acknowledging that Europeans decide patentability based on the concept of the "inventive step" and maintain a "first-to-file" priority system, while Americans decide patentability based on the concepts of "nonobviousness" and "novelty" and maintain a "first-to-invent" priority system. Although a few developing countries joined early in the convention's history—Brazil in 1884, the Dominican Republic in 1890, Mexico in 1903, and Cuba in 1904—62 developing countries joined the Paris Union after 1962 and many former socialist republics and states have joined in the 1990s, bringing the total membership to 134.[7]

The Patent Cooperation Treaty

The Patent Cooperation Treaty, signed in Washington in 1970 and later amended, makes it possible to seek patent protection simultaneously in each of a large number of countries by filing an international patent application. The treaty details the application process within the International Patent Cooperation Union. The application contains the name of the applicant, the title of the invention, a description, including an abstract, that "shall disclose the invention in a manner sufficiently clear and complete for the invention to be carried out by a person skilled in the art" (article 5), the claim or claims for patent, and the member states or region in which patent is sought. The applicant indicates in which of the contracting states of the union the application should have effect, which is the same as if application had been independently filed in the state's patent office. The international application is then subjected to an international search of the prior art, which is carried out by one of the major patent offices (Australia, Austria, China, Japan, the Russian Federation, Spain, Sweden, United States, and European Patent Office). The search report is communicated to the inventor, who may withdraw the application if the result of the search indicates that patentability is modest. If the applicant decides to continue with the international application, the application and search report are sent to all the designated national and regional patent offices in proper form and, if necessary, translated. The WIPO International Bureau publishes the international application (after eighteen months) and the international search report.

The Patent Cooperation Treaty provides innovators an efficient way of applying to multiple national authorities but does not provide a mechanism for an international patent. Indeed, as article 27 makes clear, "Nothing in

---

7. World Intellectual Property Organization (1995d, pp. 5–6).

this Treaty and the Regulations is intended to be construed as prescribing anything that would limit the freedom of each Contracting State to prescribe such substantive conditions of patentability as it desires." Definitions of "prior art" and standards for patentability are reserved to the member states. The treaty does, however, establish an "international preliminary examination." For an additional fee, treaty administrators will request that one of the national or regional patent offices do a preliminary examination and offer a nonbinding opinion on "whether the claimed invention appears to be novel, to involve an inventive step (to be non-obvious), and to be industrially applicable." It offers the applicant better information regarding patentability than does the international search.

The treaty's establishment of the International Patent Cooperation Union includes an assembly composed of the contracting parties, an executive committee of representatives drawn from the membership, and administering authority vested in the WIPO's International Bureau. Financed by the fees paid for its services, the bureau also provides technical services to national patent office authorities: training, counseling on administrative reform, and advice on record keeping and processing. Eighty states have acceded to the treaty, including twenty-four developing countries—Brazil and India (1975), Vietnam (1993), and China (1994) among them.[8]

The UPOV Convention

The International Convention for the Protection of New Varieties of Plants (the UPOV Convention, signed in 1971 and amended in 1991) establishes a union of contracting parties who agree to confer "breeder's rights" on those who discover or develop new varieties of plants. *Variety* is defined in article 1 as "a plant grouping within a single botanical taxon of the lowest known rank." The Union for the Protection of New Varieties of Plants is headquartered at WIPO and administered under authority of its director general, who also serves as secretary general of the union.

Article 4 of the convention provides that contracting parties confer national treatment on each other. Articles 5 through 9 establish the conditions under which breeder's rights are granted. The right "shall be granted where the variety is new, distinct, uniform, and stable." The treaty goes on to provide that the breeder's rights "shall not be subject to any further or

---

8. World Intellectual Property Organization (1995d, p. 17).

different conditions," as long as the applicant is in compliance with application procedures and pays the fee. That a variety is new means that it has never been sold or otherwise exploited earlier than one year before the application date in the territory of application and earlier than four years before in territories outside that of application (six years in the cases of trees and vines). Thus the plant breeder's novelty standard is lower than the patent novelty standard, yet more demanding than the originality standard of copyright law. The variety must be "distinct," that is, "distinguishable from any other variety whose existence is a matter of common knowledge at the time of the application." It must be sufficiently "uniform" in its "relevant characteristics." Finally, it must be stable in that its "relevant characteristics remain unchanged after repeated propagation."

Article 10 provides that the breeder has the right to select the country of priority application but need not wait until the process is complete before applying for secondary rights in other contracting national jurisdictions. Article 11 provides that the applicant has a twelve-month right of priority beginning with the application date, and article 13 provides that the applicant has "provisional protection" against infringement during the pendency period. The breeder, according to article 14, maintains exclusive rights regarding "production or reproduction (multiplication), conditioning for the purposes of propagation, offering for sale, selling or other marketing, exporting, importing, stocking for any of the purposes mentioned" in the earlier articles.

Exceptions to these rights, provided in article 15, include "acts done privately and for noncommercial purposes, acts done for experimental purposes, and acts done for the purpose of breeding other varieties." Article 15 also provides that "Each Contracting Party may, within reasonable limits and subject to the safeguarding of the legitimate interests of the breeder, restrict the breeder's right in relation to any variety in order to permit farmers to use for propagating purposes, on their own holdings, the product of the harvest which they have obained by planting, on their own holdings, the protected variety." Article 16 further provides for the exhaustion of breeder's rights by stating that they "shall not extend to acts concerning any material of the protected variety," when "material" means "propagating," "harvesting," and "any product made directly from the harvested material." Article 19 provides that the breeder's right "shall be granted for a fixed period" and "shall not be shorter than 20 years from the date of the grant of the breeder's right" (twenty-five years for trees and vines). Article 20 provides terms by which the new variety is "designated by a denomination which will be its generic designation" and that may be trademarked. Twenty-seven states belong to the UPOV, but only a few are developing countries: Argentina, South Africa, and Uruguay.[9]

The Budapest Treaty

The Budapest Treaty on the International Recognition of the Deposit of Microorganisms for the Purposes of Patent Procedure, signed in 1977 and amended in 1980, establishes a union of contracting parties who either allow or require the deposit of microorganisms for the purposes of patent procedure and who agree to recognize the legitimacy of deposit with any international depository authority. Article 6 provides that for a state to become an international depository authority, it must become signatory to the treaty and comply with certain specified procedures. Article 7 provides that WIPO's International Bureau, as administrator of the treaty, determines whether a national depository is in compliance and designates international depository status. Thirty-five states, including China, Korea, Singapore, and the Philippines, have joined the Budapest Treaty.[10] The operation of the treaty is further discussed in chapter 6.

The Hague Agreement

The Hague Agreement Concerning the International Deposit of Industrial Designs, signed in 1925 and amended through the years, allows nationals of any of the contracting parties to secure protection for the industrial designs in all the contracting parties by depositing their design with WIPO's International Bureau. To register, the designer submits an application along with a graphic of the design. Article 7 provides for a fifteen-year duration of protection for international industrial designs, divided into a five-year phase when the design may be accepted under sealed cover and a ten-year phase when the design must be accepted only under open cover. The International Bureau publishes notice of industrial design registrations monthly in the *Industrial Design Bulletin*. Only twenty-five states have acceded to the Hague Agreement, including, surprisingly, North Korea in 1992.[11]

---

9. World Intellectual Property Organization (1995d, p. 24).
10. World Intellectual Property Organization (1995d, p. 41).
11. World Intellectual Property Organization (1992, p. 12)

The Berne Convention

The Berne Convention for the Protection of Literary and Artistic Works was signed in 1886 and has been amended many times. It is administered by WIPO's International Bureau, which receives financial assessments from the member states of the Berne Union and charges fees for the services it provides.

Article 2 of the convention defines "literary and artistic works" to include

> every production in the literary, scientific and artistic domain, whatever may be the mode or form of its expression, such as books, pamphlets and other writings; lectures, addresses, sermons and other works of the same nature; dramatic or dramatico-musical works; choreographic works and entertainments in dumb show; musical compositions with or without words; cinematographic works to which are assimilated works by a process analogous to cinematography; works of drawing, painting, architecture, sculpture, engraving and lithography; photographic works to which are assimilated works expressed by a process analogous to photography; works of applied art; illustrations, maps, plans, sketches and three-dimensional works relative to geography, topography, architecture or science.

The Berne Convention also covers translations, adaptations, musical arrangements, encyclopedias, anthologies, and other collections and arrangements of expression. All these "enjoy protection in all countries of the Union."

However, article 3 qualifies this by stating, "'published works' means works ... whatever may be the means of manufacture of the copies, provided that the availability of such copies has been such as to satisfy the reasonable requirements of the public, having regard to the nature of the work." Thus "published works" does not include "the performance of a dramatic, dramatico-musical, cinematographic or musical work, the public recitation of a literary work, the communication by wire or the broadcasting of literary or artistic works, the exhibition of a work of art and the construction of a work of architecture." A songwriter may copyright printed lyrics; a singer may not copyright a performance of a song. An architect may copyright a drawing of a building; neither architect nor constructor may copyright the building.

National treatment is offered in article 5: "when the author is not a national of the country of origin of the work for which he is protected under this Convention, he shall enjoy in that country the same rights as national authors." Article 5 clearly states, however, that "the extent of protection, as well as the means of redress afforded to the author to protect his rights, shall be governed exclusively by the laws of the country where protection is claimed." Article 6 confers moral rights: "the author shall have the right to claim authorship of the work and to object to any distortion, mutilation or other modification of, or other derogatory action in relation to, the said work, which would be prejudicial to his honor or reputation." These rights pass to the author's heirs. Article 7 provides a term of protection of the life of the author plus fifty years. For cinematographic works the period is fifty years after the work has been made available to the public. Photographic works enjoy protection for a minimum of twenty-five years from their making.

Article 9 states that authors maintain the exclusive right to authorize reproduction of their works "in any manner or form." Article 14 grants authors of literary and artistic works the exclusive right to authorize broadcasting, publishing, or other public communication, performance, and distribution of their works. They enjoy exclusive right to authorize adaptations, arrangements, and other alterations, including adaptation into a cinematographic work and "the distribution of the works thus adapted or reproduced." This right includes importantly "the inalienable right to an interest" in resales of the work.

These exclusive rights are constrained by the provision in article 13 that national governments may "determine the conditions" under which the rights are exercised, although governments may not "be prejudicial to the rights of these authors to obtain equitable remuneration." The author's exclusive rights do not take away from the public the right to "make quotations from a work which has already been lawfully made available to the public, provided that their making is compatible with fair practice, and their extent does not exceed that justified by the purpose." This provision of article 10 is qualified by the statement that press or broadcast transmissions of current events are matters of national legislation to determine, with respect to "the extent justified by the informatory purpose," whether they may "be reproduced and made available to the public."

The exclusive rights of authors are further limited by the sweeping language of article 17: "The provisions of this Convention cannot in any way affect the right of the Government of each country of the Union to permit, to control, or to prohibit, by legislation or regulation, the circulation, presentation, or exhibition of any work or production in regard to which the competent authority may find it necessary to exercise that right." Article 16 states that infringing copies of a protected work are subject to seizure, which "shall take place in accordance with the legislation of each country."

In stark contrast with the Paris Convention on patents, the Berne Convention demands that minimum standards be maintained with respect to literary and artistic works. The Berne Union membership totals 114 governments, including countries such as Brazil, China, Egypt, India, Malaysia, and South Africa.[12] The utility of the copyright for promoting the creation of expression products has long been recognized in developing countries, which have rich traditions in literature and the arts.

The Rome Convention

The Rome Convention of 1961, formally the International Convention for the Protection of Performers, Producers of Phonograms and Broadcasting Organizations, grants national treatment to performers, phonogram producers, and broadcasters. The protection provided for performers by article 7 includes preventing the broadcast or public communication, fixation, and reproduction of their works without their consent. Article 10 provides that producers of phonograms enjoy the right to authorize or prohibit the direct or indirect reproduction of their phonograms. Article 13 provides that broadcasters of phonograms enjoy the right to authorize or prohibit the rebroadcast, fixation, and reproduction of their broadcasts. The term of these rights is twenty years from the end of the year in which fixation of the phonogram, performance, or broadcast takes place. The member states, however, may limit these rights through domestic laws and regulations regarding private use, the use of short excerpts in connection with the reporting of current events, broadcast by the states' own facilities, and use in education and scientific research. As discussed later, TRIPS did not modify these rules, but the Internet-inspired 1996 Diplomatic Conference would address these rights. Forty-eight states have joined the Rome Convention, including Brazil, Chile, Mexico, and some other Latin American and African countries.[13]

---

12. World Intellectual Property Organization (1995d, pp. 7–9).
13. World Intellectual Property Organization (1995d, p. 15).

The Geneva Convention

The Geneva Convention for the Protection of Producers of Phonograms against Unauthorized Duplication of Their Phonograms, signed in 1971, states in the preamble that the contracting states are "concerned at the widespread and increasing unauthorized duplication of phonograms and the damage this is occasioning to the interests of authors, performers and producers of phonograms." Article 2 provides that member states "shall protect producers of phonograms who are nationals of other Contracting States against the making of duplicates without the consent of the producer and against the importation of such duplicates . . . and against the distribution of such duplicates to the public." Article 4 establishes a minimum twenty-year period for the protection of phonogram rights against infringement, while article 3 provides that the member states will implement their obligations through "one or more of the following: protection by means of the grant of copyright or other specific right; protection by means of the law relating to unfair competition; protection by means of penal sanctions." Article 6 provides that compulsory licenses must fulfill all the following conditions: duplication is for use solely for the purpose of teaching or scientific research; the license is valid only within the territory of the state that granted the license; and "equitable remuneration" is provided. The membership, amounting to fifty-three states, includes developing countries such as Brazil (1975), China (1993), Egypt (1978), India (1975), Mexico (1973), and Korea (1987).[14]

The Madrid Agreement

The Madrid Agreement Concerning the International Registration of Marks, dating to 1891 but amended a number of times, establishes the Madrid Union and provides that nationals of any of the contracting countries may secure trademark protections applicable to the nationals' goods and services, registered in their country of origin, in all member countries by filing their marks with WIPO's International Bureau. When filing the application for registration, the trademark holder must comply with rules in the Madrid Convention and additional regulations of WIPO and must specify the goods and services for which protection is requested. These

14. World Intellectual Property Organization (1995d, p. 19)

goods and services are classified according to terms specified by the Nice Agreement Concerning the International Classification of Goods and Services for the Purposes of the Registration of Marks, which was signed in 1957 and has been amended. The Trademark Law Treaty, signed in Geneva in 1994, provides further rules for the international registration of marks for goods and services. Forty-four states have acceded to the Madrid Agreement, forty-two have acceded to the Nice Agreement, and forty-four have acceded to the Trademark Law Treaty.[15]

TRIPS Diplomacy in the Uruguay Round

By the last quarter of the twentieth century it had become clear to many business people and policymakers in the industrialized countries that the standards of the Paris Convention were too weak to provide adequate international patent protection. The treaties obligated members to do little more than provide national treatment of foreign products. American patent interests determined that minimum standards needed to be added because the era in which treaty members were mostly like-minded industrialized countries was over. Developing countries had become important sources of the production of intellectual property products, and much of the production was pirated. Even in countries that belonged to the patent treaty, local laws offered little chance of remedy for infringement.

Beginning in the late 1970s, some of the more visionary pharmaceutical companies and representatives from the U.S. Patent and Trademark Office took their case for minimum standards of patent protection to WIPO with a request for new negotiations. Their goal was to hold a diplomatic conference of the Paris Union that would fundamentally reform the Paris Convention. The WIPO director general declined to support the request, explaining that the developing countries vehemently opposed changes to the treaty. To press forward despite this opposition would yield nothing for the United States or its patent-based industries, and WIPO itself might well be fatally damaged because developing countries would reject any reformed treaty and to reinforce their displeasure might even leave the organization.

---

15. World Intellectual Property Organization (1995d, pp. 11, 13, 23).

The Advisory Committee on Trade Policy and Negotiation, established by the 1979 Trade Act to institutionalize business advice to the president, provided the forum to create the trade-related strategy to reform the international intellectual property institutions. The ACTPN, led by the CEOs of Pfizer and IBM, persuaded the U.S. Trade Representative that the next round of multilateral trade negotiations should be used to adapt the institutions to a world economy in which developing countries were major producers of intellectual property goods. Patent protection regulations, the CEOs said, should be harmonized at a high standard, and computer software, increasingly important to the U.S. economy, should be explicitly protected by the Berne Convention. U.S. business interests and the USTR constructed a "GATT strategy" to overcome the developing-country opposition within the WIPO. GATT negotiations had a record of success in creating new laws in politically thorny trade policy matters, and the organization's flexible institutional design offered the prospect of successfully reforming international intellectual property laws by linking intellectual property issues with conventional issues of trade negotiations.

The GATT rounds of negotiations in the 1950s had focused on tariff reduction. An "offer-concession" negotiation scheme was developed whereby the major trading states bargained in essentially bilateral fashion, requesting and offering concessions, trading off agreements in one product area for those in another. The GATT's most-favored-nation rule institutionalized tariff cuts throughout the membership.[16] For the 1960s Kennedy Round of tariff negotiations, representatives established a "linear-cut" negotiation scheme whereby an across-the-board cut was the starting point for exceptions-oriented bargaining.[17] Linear tariff cutting produced a one-third reduction in world tariff levels in the Kennedy Round and another in the 1973–79 Tokyo Round, but of greater import to world trade was that the multilateral trade negotiations (MTN) forum had proved capable of winning international agreements to reduce nontariff trade barriers. Nontariff barriers such as unreasonable customs procedures, import-licensing schemes, and export subsidies posed special challenges to trade negotiators because they were difficult to quantify and thus tricky to value and weight when offers and concessions were being made. But Tokyo Round negotiators had been able to create linkage opportunities provided by the round's

---

16. Dam (1970, p. 61).
17. Preeg (1970, pp. 58–81); and Curzon (1965, pp. 76–78).

broad agenda to get important new agreements on matters such as anti-dumping, government procurement, and safeguards (clauses allowing escape from free trade obligations).[18] In addition, the GATT Secretariat had earned a reputation for providing objective technical support, either through the leadership of a more active director general during the Kennedy Round, who hosted in his office the final, late-night linkage bargaining, or of a more modest director general during the Tokyo Round, who kept to the background.[19]

The GATT multilateral trade negotiations had been hailed at the conclusion of the Tokyo Round as the most important institutional innovation in world trade since the creation of the GATT itself.[20] The new GATT round was to begin in the early 1980s with a proposed agenda of reducing agricultural and textile trade barriers, matters known to be important to many developing countries.[21] The U.S. Trade Representative (USTR) and American business leaders agreed that GATT negotiations could achieve what could not be achieved in the WIPO forum. They could provide the forum for negotiators to link concessions on intellectual property protection on the part of the less-developed South to concessions lowering agriculture and textiles tariffs on the part of the northern industrialized countries. But for the strategy to work, it would need a crucial change from the one used in the Tokyo Round: there could be no à la carte shopping among agreements, no selective acceptance of agreements. All agreements would have to be accepted by all contracting parties or developing countries would be able simply to refuse an intellectual property rights agreement.

Before their GATT strategy could be set in motion, U.S. policymakers faced a problem in their own camp. The countable indicators provided by the International Intellectual Property Alliance demonstrated to the USTR that American businesses had extensive film, music, and book piracy problems in developing countries. Thus copyright protection as well as patent protection should be on the agenda. But a few copyright-based businesses adamantly opposed the idea of including copyright reform on the agenda of

18. Winham (1986, pp. 256–305); and Finlayson and Zacher (1983).
19. Eric Wyndham White had been executive head of the GATT Secretariat since its inception in 1948 and played a key brokering role in the Kennedy Round. See Preeg (1970, pp. 184–90). White's successor, Olivier Long, receives only one mention in the history of the Tokyo Round by Winham (1983, p. 96). Analytically, however, I note that Winham makes almost no reference to the GATT Secretariat in the entire book.
20. Jackson (1980).
21. Cline (1983).

the trade negotiations. True, the international standards did not expressly protect computer software, but they were in general acceptable to copyright-dependent U.S. companies. The problem was lack of enforcement in developing countries. The film, music, and book producers preferred to bet that the bilateral section 301 strategy would get enforcement levels up. Besides, the GATT rounds were wild affairs and the results were unpredictable. The copyright interests feared that they might lose bilateral policy options or even lose multilateral rights by the time the negotiations were concluded. The USTR hosted several meetings, described by participants as "testy" and "acrimonious," to get the copyright interests to support the multilateral GATT strategy. USTR policymakers explained that the long-term interests of copyright owners were best served through a TRIPS process of reforms. Copyright advocates, concluding that USTR was committed to including copyright issues, reluctantly supported copyright negotiations in the Uruguay Round.

Getting intellectual property onto the new negotiations agenda was no easy task. Believing that European support in particular would be necessary and Japanese support helpful to making it happen, the USTR recommended to the CEOs of Pfizer and IBM that they encourage their European and Japanese counterparts to pressure their governments and the European Community Secretariat to support the idea.[22] Although the large companies were competitors in global markets, they shared an interest in improved intellectual property protection, especially in emerging markets. Various European and Japanese trade associations, however, had to be talked into supporting the initiative. Neither they nor their governments were as committed to protecting intellectual property rights as were some groups in the United States because the multilateral negotiations would consider many issues they perceived to be of greater importance, and the opposition of developing countries was well known.

The developing countries maintained that WIPO, not the GATT, was the appropriate forum for discussions of intellectual property rights and that patent policies especially ought vary by the level of a country's development and not be harmonized. Extensive piracy of patented pharmaceutical and chemical products and copyrighted films, music, books, and software meant that local interests in these countries opposed policy change. Inside and outside the governments, health care interests claimed that pharmaceu-

22. Santoro and Paine (1995, p. 10).

tical piracy benefited the people, agricultural interests claimed that piracy of fertilizers and weed-control chemicals promoted local food production, and book and software interests claimed that piracy contributed to local learning and technology transfer. The so-called Group of Ten developing countries within the GATT—India, Brazil, Argentina, Cuba, Egypt, Nicaragua, Nigeria, Peru, Tanzania, and Yugoslavia—opposed placing intellectual property on the agenda just as they opposed placing services and more lenient policies for foreign direct investment on the agenda.[23] During several years of preround negotiation, they did not budge from their opposition, so the USTR decided to take the unprecedented step of initiating 301 action against South Korea and Brazil to bully the developing countries to the GATT negotiating table. The action was intended to signal that negotiations could go on one-by-one under threat of bilateral trade sanctions or they could take place within the GATT round, but negotiations would take place.

The gambit worked: aided by some draftsmanship maneuvering, forty countries, which included the United States, European Community members, Japan, and twenty developing countries, agreed to the inclusion of intellectual property in the Uruguay Round. In July 1986 a final draft text for the Punta del Este Ministerial Declaration, written by the Swiss and Colombian ambassadors, was submitted to all the trade ministers and adopted as an agenda item.[24] The declaration gave the following mandate to the negotiators:

In order to reduce the distortions and impediments to international trade, and taking into account the need to promote effective and adequate protection of intellectual property rights, and to ensure that measures and procedures to enforce intellectual property rights do not themselves become barriers to legitimate trade, the negotiations shall aim to clarify GATT provisions and elaborate, as appropriate, new rules and disciplines. Negotiations shall aim to develop a multilateral

---

23. Telecommunications services in developing countries are typically government monopolies that provide poor service but are major employers and substantial revenue sources for government. Financial services similarly are considered central to economic policy and providers of development capital and tend to be tightly linked with government finance ministries. Liberalization of services upsets all these patterns and relationships. Foreign direct investment was in the 1980s strictly controlled by many developing countries, and the industrialized country agenda of getting public international law commitments to offer rights of establishment contradicted predominating policies.

24. G. Evans (1994, pp. 160–61).

framework of principles, rules and disciplines dealing with international trade in counterfeit goods, taking into account work already undertaken in the GATT.

The Uruguay Round would in the late 1980s and early 1990s become the forum for international intellectual property rights negotiations, but because the text of the talks declaration was deliberately loosely worded, the first task for the Trade-Related Intellectual Property Rights Negotiating Committee was to establish an agenda. The United States insisted that the TRIPS negotiations ought comprehensively to cover patents, trade secrets, industrial designs, integrated circuit designs, copyrights, and trademarks. The negotiations also ought to set as goals agreements that achieved most-favored-nation status, national treatment, transparency, and minimum standards. The coverage of any agreement ought be geographically universal. In general, the OECD and newly industrialized countries had converged toward a consensus that the TRIPS agreement ought to incorporate the Paris Convention and the Berne Convention, apply Berne rules to computer programs by defining them as literary works, and go beyond the two conventions to establish minimum standards. India, on behalf of the G-10, contended that an anticounterfeiting code limited to fashion goods and trademark infringement ought be the only issue under discussion and bitterly opposed any negotiation regarding patents and trade secrets.[25]

Negotiations proceeded, but months would pass between formal meetings among negotiators, and a chasm separated American negotiators from G-10 negotiators. American trade negotiators in Geneva were in frequent contact with the primary Washington-based advocacy groups, including the Intellectual Property Committee, International Intellectual Property Alliance, Pharmaceutical Research and Manufacturers of America, and various company and trade association representatives. European business was represented by the Union of Industrial and Employers' Confederation of Europe, which comprised thirty-three member federations from twenty-two European countries. Japanese business was represented by the Keidanren, the Japanese Federation of Economic Organizations. In June 1988 these groups jointly proposed a draft "Basic Framework of GATT Provisions on Intellectual Property, Statement of Views of the European, Japanese and United States Business Communities."[26] To get a deal, European business

25. G. Evans (1994, p. 162).
26. G. Evans (1994, p. 165).

groups recommended that developing countries be offered most-favored-nation treatment, pledges of increased technical assistance, and transition periods for implementation of an agreement. (This last was at the time it was suggested and remained until the end of the negotiations opposed by U.S. pharmaceutical manufacturers.)

For their part, India and Brazil denounced the "Basic Framework," especially the patent rules. India argued that developing countries should be free to exclude pharmaceuticals, food, and chemicals from patent protection, shorten patent protection periods for other sectors, and license foreign patents under preferential terms. A patent conferred in a host country, the Indian negotiators contended, was an obligation on the multinational company, and compulsory licensing should be recognized as a legitimate government policy tool to prevent these corporations from misusing their rights in the host country.[27]

Seeking to bridge the North-South gap on TRIPS, an international conference was held in 1989 at Vanderbilt Law School at which an industrial design scholar proposed that the TRIPS negotiators moderate their demands and adapt the fair use doctrine of copyright law to patent law.[28] The proposal was rejected by patent and copyright specialists alike as a perversion of policy purposes in both their houses and the copyright interests in particular recalled why they had opposed at the outset the inclusion of copyright in TRIPS, but that it was even offered emphasized that the negotiation gap remained so wide that deviant thinking could be aired. At the same conference, two senior congressional staff members insisted that the minimum the U.S. delegation should obtain in a TRIPS agreement was

(1) substantive standards for intellectual property protection; (2) effective enforcement measures at the border and internally; (3) a multilateral consultation and dispute settlement mechanism; and (4) traditional GATT provisions, including transparency and national treatment applied to intellectual property.[29]

A GATT Secretariat official pointed out to the developing countries that they were acting as though the choice of forum was the GATT or WIPO when the reality was that the choice was GATT or the USTR. The developing countries were failing to recognize that their bargaining leverage was

---

27. G. Evans (1994, p. 167).
28. Reichman (1989, p. 809).
29. Kastenmeier and Beier (1989, p. 291).

greater in the Uruguay Round negotiations than with U.S. bilateral section 301 procedures.[30]

The turning point in the the negotiations came in April 1989 when a compromise between the industrialized and developing countries was achieved to draft a framework agreement that would outline mimimum standards for intellectual property rights and enforcement but leave off the table the question of whether WIPO or GATT was the appropriate forum for discussion.[31] In September India accepted the principle of international enforcement of intellectual property within the context of the Uruguay Round, which allowed the negotiations to focus on substantive provisions of an agreement. Negotiators from the United States, other industrialized countries, and the G-10 developing countries put proposals on the table. But, countries such as Mexico and even Canada stated that they shared India's concerns that patents could lead to anticompetitive monopolies, so there was no wholesale shift in thinking within the TRIPS negotiation committee toward consensus for agreement. This phase of the negotiations resulted in January 1990 in the creation of a document, the "Checklist of Issues," which listed some 500 points of disagreement.[32]

Led by the U.S., EC, Japanese, Swiss, and Indian negotiating teams, the committee circulated draft texts to bridge the checklisted differences. The chairman of the TRIPS negotiating group brokered the process, and the GATT Secretariat staff culled ideas and proposals from the texts. The negotiation chairman presented a "Draft Composite Text" at the Brussels Ministerial Meeting in December 1990.[33] The TRIPS draft text indicated that significant disagreement persisted on first-to-file versus first-to-invent policies for patents, compulsory licensing, patents for plant and animal varieties, copyright versus neighboring rights for performers, moral rights under copyright, and rental rights under copyright. The chairman of the TRIPS committee established a "ten-on-ten" structure—ten industrialized countries, ten developing countries—to move the negotiations toward consensus.

The whole Uruguay Round multilateral trade negotiation was in danger of foundering because the U.S.-EC conflict was over agricultural subsidies, and quotas were hardening into a round-buster. So GATT Director General

30. Subramanian (1990).
31. G. Evans (1994, p. 169).
32. G. Evans (1994, p. 170).
33. Lars Anell, the ambassador to GATT from Sweden, chaired the intellectual property negotiation committee.

Arthur Dunkel and the secretariat compiled the results achieved to that point by all the negotiation committees, draft TRIPS composite text included, and presented the "Dunkel Draft" to the states in December 1991 for final negotiation.[34] Negotiations continued in 1992 and 1993 based on the draft and, when the agriculture conflict was settled, the member states agreed to a whole package of agreements: the creation of the World Trade Organization, amended dispute-settlement procedures, trade in goods, agriculture, application of sanitary and phytosanitary measures, textiles and clothing, technical barriers to trade, trade-related investment measures, subsidies and countervailing duties, antidumping measures, preshipment inspection, rules of origin, customs procedures, safeguards, services, among, among several other matters, trade-related intellectual property rights.[35] The draft TRIPS composite text was codified as an Uruguay Round agreement essentially without change.[36]

Policymakers from developing countries did not like the TRIPS agreement, but the Uruguay Round package offered much that they did like. In particular, the amended dispute-settlement procedures, they believed, would offer them some respite from U.S. section 301 policy unilateralism and trade sanctions. Liberalization of international trade in textiles and apparel through the phasing-out of the Multifiber Arrangement and trade in agricultural products would confer export benefits. The creation of the World Trade Organization conferred a new international legitimacy to the international organization of trade, and signing the Uruguay Round agreement made a country a founding member of the new organization. As discussed later, the TRIPS agreement also left some loopholes and loose language that developing-country policymakers believed they would be able to exploit.

Looking back on the negotiations, participants acknowledged that without the secretariat-drafted Draft Composite Text there would have been no TRIPS agreement: "we would have gotten little or nothing just as happened in investment and services." They were effusive in their praise for the chair of the negotiation committee, whom several called the hero of the story, and of the secretariat. Indeed, the TRIPS agreement was a great achievement of the round and contrasted with the agreement on liberalizing policies toward direct foreign investment that contained only modest provisions and negotiations on services and yielded only a framework agreement, while sector-specific commitments were put off for further negotiation after the round.

The TRIPS Agreement and Legal Change

In the end the TRIPS negotiations produced agreement regarding protection for patents, copyrights, trademarks, integrated circuit layout designs, industrial designs, and trade secrets. The agreement builds on the legal base provided by the Paris Convention on industrial property (amended in 1967), the Rome Convention on performers, producers, and broadcasters (1961), the Berne Convention on literary and artistic works (amended in 1971), and the Washington Treaty on integrated circuits (1989).

Article 27 of the agreement offers product and process patents to nearly all types of inventions "in all fields of technology, provided that they are new, involve an inventive step and are capable of industrial application" with the understanding that *inventive step* is synonymous with *nonobvious* and *useful*. The article, which explains that patent rights are "enjoyable without discrimination as to the place of invention, the field of technology and whether products are imported or locally produced," is the most important achievement for U.S. negotiators, for it legitimizes the patentability of pharmaceuticals, transgenic plants and animals, and computer software. However, it also allows states to exclude inventions from patentability for reasons of "public order" or "morality." This clause is pregnant, for it confers on states the right to prohibit patents to protect "human, animal or plant life or health or to avoid serious prejudice to the environment," including but not limited to "diagnostic, therapeutic and surgical methods for the treatment of humans or animals" and "plants and animals other than microorganisms, and essentially biological processes for the production of plants or animals other than non-biological and microbiological processes." The passage explicitly permits patents on plant varieties and provides that the language should be revisited "four years after the entry into force of the Agreement establishing the WTO." The precise meaning of the passage can only become known through interpretation over time and when the issues are readdressed in 1999.

TRIPS provides patent holders with exclusive rights to make, use, sell, import, assign, or transfer a patent through license. However, these rights may be limited in certain ways. Compulsory licensing, though not prohibited, is constrained by article 31 so that it must be a nonexclusive license, "predominantly for the supply of the domestic market of the Member authorizing such use," with "adequate remuneration," and "subject to judicial review." Article 32 requires an opportunity for judicial review of any decision to revoke or forfeit a patent, while article 33 provides for a minimum twenty-year patent term from the date the application is filed. For process patents, when the "product obtained by the patented process is new" or when "there is a substantial likelihood that the identical product was made by the process and the owner of the patent has been unable through reasonable efforts to determine the process actually used," article 34 places the burden on the alleged infringer to prove that the identical product was produced by a different process.

Article 3 of the agreement requires that signatories offer national treatment: "Each Member shall accord to the nationals of other Members treatment no less favorable than that it accords to its own nationals with regard to the protection of intellectual property." Article 4 requires that signatories offer most-favored-nation terms to each other; that is, "any advantage, favor, privilege or immunity granted by a Member to the nationals of any other country shall be accorded immediately and unconditionally to the nationals of all other Members." The twin requirements of national treatment and MFN, which have been hallmarks of the GATT/WTO regime since its founding, aim to generalize the rights and responsibilities among weak states and powerful states alike.

Despite these terms of agreement, which go a long way toward establishing minimum international standards of patent protection, the TRIPS agreement in article 8 appears to offer some wiggle room for members regarding their commitments in TRIPS:

Members may, in formulating or amending their national laws and regulations, adopt measures necessary to protect public health and nutrition, and to promote the public interest in sectors of vital importance to their socio-economic and technological development, provided that such measures are consistent with the provisions of this Agreement. Appropriate measures, provided that they are consistent with the provisions of this Agreement, may be needed to prevent the abuse of intellectual property rights by right holders or the resort to practices which unreasonably restrain trade or adversely affect the international transfer of technology.

The precise meaning of article 8 will only become known through the inevitable litigation of international dispute settlement.

TRIPS aims to prevent disputes by demanding in article 63 the transparency of laws, regulations, administrative practices, and court decisions (although it permits witholding information out of concern for public interest or proprietary interest). Transparency would be achieved through publication and reporting to the TRIPS Council certain aspects of policy and practices. When disputes between signatories do arise, article 64 provides that the disputants use the GATT/WTO settlement procedures. These call for bilateral negotiation with or without the good offices of the WTO Secretariat first, then formal dispute settlement if needed. The settlement mechanism is a three-member panel that assesses the arguments of the disputants and issues a decision that typically offers an interpretation of relevant international law and an opinion regarding a state's policy compliance with that law.[37] The agreement in article 68 establishes a council for TRIPS, a body composed of representatives from member states who monitor the operation of the agreement. The council offers a continuing forum for consultation about intellectual property policy issues, a mechanism that may resolve disputes without the need for formal settlement.

For copyright, article 9 establishes that signatories comply with the 1971 terms of the Berne Convention. Article 10 explicitly provides that computer programs and databases are to be protected as literary works under the convention. Article 12 establishes a general fifty-year minimum term dating from the year of publication or creation but does not diminish the longer terms many states offer to their copyright holders. Article 11 grants owners of computer software and cinema copyrights the right "at least" to authorize or prohibit rental of their products. For rights related to sound recordings, performers control fixation, reproduction, and broadcasting of their performances. Producers of sound recordings have the right to authorize or prohibit the reproduction of their phonograms. Broadcasters have the right to authorize or prohibit the fixation, reproduction of fixations, and rebroadcasting of their broadcasts. These rights and obligations are further specified in the Rome Convention, which is embodied in TRIPS article 14. TRIPS does not specify moral rights.

Owners of trademarks are granted by article 16 and through application of the Madrid Agreement exclusive right of use when two firms are engaged in the same or closely related trade and "such use would result in a likelihood of confusion." That is, Apple Computer, for example, may

---

37. Pescatore, Davey, and Lowenfeld (1996); and Hudec (1993).

protect its trademark against others in computer and related businesses with the expectation of fairly wide rights, but the company receives considerably less protection under trademark law in unrelated businesses. The courts look for "confusion" in the minds of consumers when adjudicating trademark disputes. Article 16 further strengthens protection for internationally well known trademarks, although not with absolute clarity: "In determining whether a trademark is well-known, account shall be taken of the knowledge of the trademark in the relevant sector of the public, including knowledge in that Member obtained as a result of the promotion of the trademark." Sustained use of the trademark combined with its registration with trademark authorities appears to be the best means to maintain and extend trademark rights globally, for article 19 requires that registration may be cancelled "only after an uninterrupted period of at least three years of non-use" by the holder. Article 18 provides that a trademark registration term mimimum is seven years, but that it may be renewed indefinitely. Article 21 prohibits compulsory licensing of trademarks, conferring to the owner the exclusive right to assign a trademark.

Articles 25 and 26 of TRIPS require that member states protect industrial designs "that are new or original" and that the owner of a protected industrial design has the right to prevent third parties from making, selling, or importing articles "bearing or embodying a design which is a copy, or substantially a copy." The agreement provides that the term of protection be at least ten years.

In the 1984 Washington treaty on semiconductors, TRIPS negotiators agreed to include layout design (topography) protection for integrated circuits. Article 36 states that members should consider it unlawful to import, sell, or distribute a product that is or contains an unauthorized copy of a protected integrated circuit layout design (sometimes called a semiconductor mask). Article 38 states that this protection ought to last for at least ten years, beginning with registration filing or first commercial exploitation "wherever in the world it occurs."

Trade secret protection, although the term *trade secret* is not used, is provided in article 39. "This was an area of heated North-South debate, with developing countries opposing the treatment of trade secrets as an intellectual property right."[38] In accordance with the article 10 unfair competition section of the Paris Convention, members are to protect "undisclosed infor-

---

38. Primo Braga (1995, p. 393).

mation." Persons should be able to protect their information as long as it is secret, has commercial value because it is secret, and has "been subject to reasonable steps under the circumstances . . . to keep it secret." However, neither TRIPS nor the Paris Convention establishes rules regarding judicial remedies for theft of trade secrets.

Article 40 of TRIPS similarly concerns competition, in this case the licensing of intellectual property rights. The article assumes that certain types of licensing agreements can restrain trade or impede the transfer and dissemination of technology; thus it explicitly reserves to the members the right to enact legislation that controls these types of licensing agreements.

Considerable text is devoted to enforcement, a matter especially important to U.S. copyright interests. The general obligation is presented in article 41: members "shall ensure that enforcement procedures . . . are available under their national laws so as to permit effective action against any act of infringement of intellectual property rights . . . including expeditious remedies to prevent infringements and remedies which constitute a deterrent to further infringements." The general obligations include enforcement procedures that are "fair and equitable" but are not "unnecessarily complicated or costly, or entail unreasonable time limits or unwarranted delays." Procedures are to be transparent; decisions are to be delivered "without undue delay" and "based only on evidence in respect of which parties were offered the opportunity to be heard." Article 41 further obligates states to offer the opportunity for judicial review of administrative decisions, but it makes no demand that they create a special separate judicial review procedure regarding intellectual property law.

Civil judicial procedures are outlined in article 42, including the right to timely written notice, the right to independent legal counsel, and the right to present relevant evidence. Article 43 gives the judicial authorities the power to order that evidence be produced by the opposing party when the complainant has "presented reasonably available evidence sufficient to support its claims and has specified evidence relevant to substantiation of its claims which lies in the control of the opposing party." Judicial authorities, article 44 states, shall have injunction authority, which is "the authority to order a party to desist from an infringement, inter alia to prevent the entry into the channels of commerce in their jurisdiction of imported goods that involve the infringement of an intellectual property right, immediately after customs clearance of such goods."

Article 45 empowers judicial authorities to order infringers to pay damages "adequate to compensate for the injury the right holder has suffered because of an infringement of his intellectual property right by an infringer who knew, or had reasonable grounds to know, that he was engaged in infringing activity." Article 50 enables judicial authorities to "order prompt and effective provisional measures" to prevent infringement from occurring by preventing the distribution for sale or importation of infringing goods and by preserving evidence." The article further lays out guidelines regarding procedures for exercising provisional measures.

Members are obligated by article 51 to adopt administrative or judicial procedures that afford rights holders the opportunity to stop the importation of infringing goods at the border through customs action. The rights holder must provide "adequate evidence" of infringement, however, before customs action need be taken, and the goods may only be held up at the border for ten days without the initiation of full judicial procedures or revocation of the suspension order.

In addition to civil actions, members are required to provide criminal procedures in cases of "willful trademark counterfeiting or copyright piracy on a commercial scale." The remedies prescribed by article 61 "shall include imprisonment and/or monetary fines sufficient to provide a deterrent, consistent with the level of penalties applied for crimes of a corresponding gravity." The article also provides that seizure, forfeiture, and destruction of the infringing goods be made an available remedy.

Because the agreement establishing the World Trade Organization, the GATT's successor, requires member states to accept all WTO agreements, most developing countries will be party to the TRIPS agreement. However, TRIPS included the important reservation that no member was bound to comply until one year after the January 1, 1995, date the WTO came into force. Middle-level developing countries are given an additional five-year implementation grace period, while the least developed countries receive ten-year phase-in periods. Perhaps as important, de jure implementation of TRIPS obligations in some less developed countries may not indicate de facto implementation by local governmental and judicial authorities. Thus in the final assessment, implementation of intellectual property laws in the national legal systems of industrializing countries will occur gradually during the decade to come, but at a pace and vigor that may vary considerably among them.

The transition periods were strenuously opposed by the pharmaceutical interests, yet they, the copyright interests, U.S. government negotiators, and many other business and government participants were generally pleased with the agreement because developing countries were finally obligated under public international law to meet basic standards of intellectual property protection, thereby achieving deep integration in an important policy area. The points of continued disagreement that had been specified in the Draft Composit Text could, in the minds of the participants, be addressed another day.

Intellectual Property and NAFTA

The interest-group mobilization that led the USTR to put intellectual property rights on the Uruguay Round agenda also led it to put the issue on the NAFTA negotiations agenda. Chapter 17, article 1701, of the North American Free Trade Agreement among the United States, Canada, and Mexico establishes mutual obligations regarding intellectual property rights: "Each Party shall provide in its territory to the nationals of another Party adequate and effective protection and enforcement of intellectual property rights, while ensuring that measures to enforce intellectual property rights do not themselves become barriers to legitimate trade." Thus NAFTA was the first multilateral treaty to impose positive obligations on its contracting parties. The obligation exceeds national treatment: it is to provide "adequate and effective protection and enforcement of intellectual property rights." Article 1701 provides that the member states must "at minimum" implement all the obligations defined in chapter 17 and the substantive provisions in the Geneva Convention on phonograms, Berne Convention on literary and artistic works, Paris Convention on industrial property, and UPOV Convention on plant varieties. Article 1703 imposes a national treatment obligation on the member states, and article 1704 reserves to the states the right to adopt laws that control anticompetitive practices.

The member states are bound by article 1705 to protect the copyrights of the kinds of works specified in the Berne Convention and "any other works that embody original expression," including "all types of computer programs" and "compilations of data or other material, whether in machine readable or other form, which by reason of the selection or arrangement of their contents constitute intellectual creations." Authors retain the right to allow or prohibit the importation of unauthorized goods, the first public distribution of the original and each copy of the work to the public, the communication of a work to the public, and the commericial rental of the original or a copy of a computer program. They retain these rights for at least fifty years. Article 1705 defines copyrights as "economic rights" in deliberate contrast with moral rights:

> Any person acquiring or holding economic rights may freely and separately transfer such rights by contract for purposes of their exploitation and enjoyment by the transferee; [and] any person acquiring or holding such economic rights by virtue of a contract, including contracts of employment underlying the creation of works and sound recordings, shall be able to exercise those rights in its own name and enjoy fully the benefits derived from those rights.

Article 1706 provides to the producer of a sound recording the right to authorize or prohibit reproduction of the recording and public distribution of the original and each copy of the recording by "sale, rental or otherwise" and prohibit importation of unauthorized recordings. As in the Rome Convention, the copyright term is a minimum of fifty years, but deliberately unlike the Rome Convention (which is prominent by its absence from the list of treaties given application in article 1701), the member states are given considerably less leeway to restrict copyrights: "Each party shall confine limitations or exceptions to the rights provided for in this Article to certain special cases that do not conflict with a normal exploitation of the sound recording and do not unreasonably prejudice the legitimate interests of the right holder."

Article 1707 declares that it is a "criminal offense to manufacture, import, sell, lease or otherwise make available a device or system that is primarily of assitance in decoding an encrypted program-carrying satellite signal without the authorization of the lawful distributor of such signal." It is a "civil offense to receive, in connection with commercial activities, or further distribute, an encrypted program-carrying satellite signal."

Trademarks, covered in article 1708, are to be protected indefinitely for successive terms of ten years. Each state must provide a system for registering trademarks. In determining whether a trademark is well known, the Paris Convention is augmented so that "account shall be taken of the knowledge of the trademark in the relevant sector of the public, including knowledge in the Party's territory obtained as a result of the promotion of the trademark." Policymakers of the member states may legislate in the area of copyright, but their policy freedom is limited: "No Party may encumber the use of a trademark in commerce by special requirements." Article 1708 goes on to say, "A Party may determine conditions on the licensing and assignment of trademarks, it being understood that the compulsory licensing of trademarks shall not be permitted and that the owner of a registered trademark shall have the right to assign its trademark with or without the transfer of the business to which the trademark belongs." In addition, "A Party may provide limited exceptions to the rights conferred by a trademark, such as a fair use of descriptive terms, provided that such exceptions take into account the legitimate interests of the trademark owner and of other persons."

Article 1709 provides that "each Party shall make patents available for any inventions, whether products or processes, in all fields of technology, provided that such inventions are new, result from an inventive step and are capable of industrial application." The terms *inventive step* and *capable of industrial application* are defined to be synonomous with *nonobvious* and *useful*, respectively. Language from the Paris Convention is taken to exclude from patentability "diagnostic, therapeutic and surgical methods for the treatment of humans or animals"; "plants and animals other than microrganisms"; and "essentially biological processes for the production of plants or animals, other than nonbiological and microbiological processes of such production." Nevertheless, member states are to provide protection for plant varieties through patents, "an effective scheme of *sui generis* protection," or both. Member states must provide both process and product patents for pharmaceutical and agricultural chemicals, including patents "for subject matter that relates to naturally occurring substances prepared or produced by, or significantly derived from, microbiological processes and intended for food or medicine."

Policymakers are constrained by the provision that "a party may provide limited exceptions to the exclusive rights conferred by a patent, provided that such exceptions do not unreasonably conflict with a normal exploitation of the patent and do not unreasonably prejudice the legitimate interests of the patent owner, taking into account the legitimate interests of other persons." The rationales for revocation of patents are limited to grounds that "would have justified a refusal to grant the patent" or that "the grant of a compulsory license has not remedied the lack of exploitation of the patent." NAFTA provides that "each party shall permit patent owners to assign and transfer by succession their patents, and to conclude licensing contracts."

Compulsory licenses, or "use of the subject matter of a patent . . . without the authorization of the right holder," are restricted by a number of provisions, beginning with their characterization as exceptional: "authorization of such use shall be considered on its individual merits." Other provisions are that "the proposed user has made efforts to obtain authorization from the right holder on reasonable commercial terms and conditions and such efforts have not been successful within a reasonable period of time." Furthermore, the scope and duration shall be limited; such use shall be nonexclusive, nonassignable, and predominantly for the supply of the domestic market. Review and termination of the use shall be provided, adequate remuneration offered to the patent holder, and the legal validity of the use subject to judicial review.

Process patents explicitly assign responsibility to defendants to establish that their process does not infringe whenever the "patented process is new" or "a substantial likelihood exists that the allegedly infringing product was made by the process and the patent owner has been unable through reasonable efforts to determine the process actually used." The term of protection is at least twenty years from the date of filing an application or seventeen years from the date of a patent's grant.

Regarding layout designs for integrated circuits, article 1710 makes it

unlawful for any person without the right holder's authorization to import, sell or otherwise distribute for commercial purposes any of the following: a protected layout design; an integrated circuit in which a protected layout design is incorporated; or an article incorporating such an integrated circuit, only insofar as it continues to contain an unlawfully reproduced layout design.

In cases of inadvertent infringement, compensation to the rightholder is required for any stock sold after notification has been given to the infringer. Article 1710 provides for a minimum ten years of protection and leaves no room for interpretation on the matter of compulsory licenses: "No Party may permit the compulsory licensing of layout designs of integrated circuits."

Article 1711 declares that trade secrets are to be protected, provided that the information is secret, has commercial value, and reasonable steps have been taken to keep the information secret. In addition, "No party may limit the duration of protection for trade secrets," and "no party may discourage or impede the voluntary licensing of trade secrets by imposing excessive or discriminatory conditions on such licenses or conditions that dilute the value of the trade secrets." Data, such as test results that are submitted to the government during approval processes for pharmaceuticals and chemicals, must be held confidential for five years.

New or original industrial designs are protected under article 1713, although "designs are not new or original if they do not significantly differ from known designs," and "such protection shall not extend to designs dictated essentially by technical or functional considerations." For textile designs in particular, the member states must prevent procedural costs from impairing the seeking and obtaining of industrial design protection.

The NAFTA chapter 17 text extensively discusses enforcement provisions for intellectual property rights, including administrative and judicial procedures. Article 1714 declares that "each Party shall ensure that enforcement procedures . . . are available under its domestic law so as to permit effective action to be taken against any act of infringement of intellectual property rights . . . including expeditious remedies to prevent infringements and remedies to deter further infringements." In general, each member state is to "ensure that its procedures for the enforcement of intellectual property rights are fair and equitable, are not unnecessarily complicated or costly, and do not entail unreasonable time-limits or unwarranted delays." The states are also to

> provide that decisions on the merits of a case in judicial and administrative enforcement proceedings shall preferably be in writing and preferably state the reasons on which the decisions are based; be made available at least to the parties in a proceeding without undue delay; and be based only on evidence in respect of which such parties were offered the opportunity to be heard.

Final administrative decisions must be reviewable by the judiciary.

Civil procedures are covered by article 1715: defendants have a right to written notice; parties to proceedings have a right to legal counsel; procedures cannot include "overly burdensome requirements"; parties are entitled to present relevant evidence; and confidential proprietary information should be protected. Article 1715 goes into considerable detail regarding the power the judicial authorities ought to possess. When a party has specified that evidence possessed by the opposing party is necessary to a proceeding, the courts should have the authority to order production of the evidence. When a party fails to provide requested information, the courts should have the authority to make preliminary or final determinations based on the evidence at hand. The courts should possess the authority to stop infringement by preventing entry into channels of distribution, dispose of counterfeit goods, and order infringers to pay legal fees and compensation to the rights holders. As a principle, when making these decisions, "judicial authorities shall take into account the need for proportionality between the seriousness of the infringement and the remedies ordered as well as the interests of other persons."

Article 1717 provides for criminal procedures and penalties "at least in cases of willful trademark countefeiting or copyright piracy on a commercial scale." The penalties include imprisonment and monetary fines imposed "sufficient to provide a deterrent, consistent with the level of penalties applied for crimes of a corresponding gravity." Article 1718 describes how rights holders may go about stopping infringing goods at a border through action by customs authorities.

SIX

WIPO and the International Organization of Intellectual Property

THE World Intellectual Property Organization is the international government organization most central to the international intellectual property regime, and it has been changing and adapting to a turbulent environment. As industrialized country creators of intellectual property have confronted developing country governments about weak intellectual property institutions, WIPO has helped these developing countries comply with international intellectual property conventions. WIPO has faced encroachment from the World Trade Organization, which sponsored Uruguay Round multilateral negotiations that resulted in the 1994 Agreement on Trade-Related Aspects of Intellectual Property Rights (TRIPS), thus challenging its own position as the forum for making international intellectual property law. WIPO is being asked to expand greatly the scope of its teaching regarding the purpose, implementation, and enforcement of intellectual property policy in order to help developing countries meet their TRIPS agreement obligations. Many of its developing country members are altering their development strategies from import substitution to more liberal policy mixes, thereby rethinking policies toward patents and copyrights. Technological revolutions in bioengineering, digitizing, microprocessing, and electronic networking have challenged conventional concepts of intellectual property, the organization's core concern.

In the past WIPO has, however, successfully adapted to change imposed upon it by its member states. The 1974 agreement to join the UN system turned the organization from a rich man's club of industrialized countries into a potentially universal membership, international governmental organization of developing countries that needed considerable educational services. The Patent Cooperation Treaty of 1978 required WIPO to administer international patent applications, a task that would ultimately result in its recruitment of scores of new employees skilled in patent application review and the creation of an administrative structure to manage processes quite unlike those traditional at the organization. The director general led the adaptation through the roles of idea generator, organizer, and diplomat; and professional staff acquired new competencies related to their roles as teachers about intellectual property policy and administration and as intermediaries in negotions for making international intellectual property law. Nevertheless, in the late 1990s WIPO is challenged as an organization to learn and adapt to changes more profound than ever in its history and must do so with new leadership because of the retirement in 1997 of its long-time director general.

Organizational Mission and Tasks

WIPO is among the most venerable of international governmental organizations, dating its origins to the secretariats established to administer the Paris Convention for the Protection of Industrial Property in 1883 and the Berne Convention for the Protection of Literary and Artistic Works in 1886, which were united by the Swiss Federation into a single secretariat in 1893.[1] In 1962 the U.S. representative to the Paris Union and Berne Union (as the memberships are formally known to this day), Arpad Bogsch, took the lead in drafting a proposal for a reformed organization, becoming its deputy director general the next year in order to turn the proposals into treaty text. He organized the 1967 diplomatic conference that resulted in fifty-one mostly industrialized country governments promulgating the Convention Establishing the World Intellectual Property Organization and ascended to the position of director general in 1973. The WIPO story of institution-building leadership by one person is matched in the history of international

1. Bogsch (1992, pp. 7–21).

governmental organizations only at GATT and at the International Labor Organization.[2]

Largely through the diplomacy of the director general, WIPO joined the UN system in 1974. The postcolonial enlargement of the United Nations in the 1960s and 1970s, in the judgment of the director general, offered the best institutional setting to become a universal organization with the goal of promoting "the protection of intellectual property throughout the world." It was a judgment, however, that was not shared at the time by all in the international intellectual property policy community. That same year the developing country Group of 77 was forged in the United Nations, inspired by the success of the OPEC oil cartel to become the economic strategy mirror of the security strategy of the nonaligned movement. Using their superior numbers in the United Nations (where one-nation, one-vote decisionmaking afforded them power they did not have in the weighted-voting International Monetary Fund and World Bank and the rarely voting GATT), they passed a Declaration on the Establishment of the New International Economic Order (NIEO), which asserted state rights to nationalize foreign enterprises, create commodity cartels, and regulate multinational corporations.[3] It was an agenda very much at odds with the U.S.- and European-dominated economic international governmental organization agenda for developing countries: currency convertibility and macroeconomic stability at the International Monetary Fund; dam and irrigation project construction at the World Bank; and import policy liberalization at the GATT.[4] The developing countries' economic development strategy emphasized greater independence by substituting domestically produced goods and services for imports by restricting imports and foreign direct investment—the so-called import substitution industrialization strategy.[5] The implication of the strategy for intellectual property policy was that industrial property ought not to receive patent protections and compulsory licensing ought to be demanded of foreign owners of technology.

From the very first as a UN agency, the organization was shaped and directed by its director general's articulation of a compelling mission that was durable in its long-term usefulness and could be explained simply and

2. Eric Wyndham White at the GATT and David Morse at the International Labor Organization each served as director general for some twenty years beginning in 1948 and were instrumental in institution building.
3. Bhattacharya (1976).
4. Garritsen de Vries (1987); Ayres (1983); and Hudec (1987).
5. Gilpin (1987, pp. 273–88).

repeatedly to internal and external audiences. The mission is composed of three primary tasks: help member states create multilateral norms, help developing countries write and administer national laws, and serve the member states through administration of the treaties. Over the years the director general ensured that the mission was adhered to unwaveringly.

WIPO's services not only carry out its mission but support the agency financially. Its relationship with the United Nations carries with it limitations on numbers of staff, job classifications and descriptions, and compensation—a substantial concern in recent years as the U.S. government in particular has urged institutional reforms regarding UN agencies' secretariat activities and budgets. However, whatever the procedural constraints of UN status, the agency has become increasingly financially independent from member contributions, and it has done so through the service it provides to patent applicants under the Patent Cooperation Treaty (PCT). Some 40 percent of this service is provided to U.S. multinational enterprises.

The PCT was the international policy solution to the growing problem created by companies that were filing multiple applications for patent protection. By the 1960s this practice was straining the capacity of national patent offices to make fair and timely administrative decisions regarding patentability and straining the legal resources of patent-intensive firms.[6] According to the director general at the time,

> One of the most important [diplomatic factors that led to the negotiation of the PCT between 1966 and 1970] was the interest of the United States of America, then by far the leading country in the field of technology and patenting. The Patent Office of the United States supported the scheme, and I like to believe that the decisive step towards the solution was found in a conversation between the then Commissioner of Patents, Edward J. Brenner, and myself in the former's office. . . . The two of us stood before a blackboard on which we chalked the diagram of the proposed system [for the PCT] on June 8, 1966.[7]

Extensive preparatory work of meetings, document creation, and diplomacy to encourage national patent offices and their political leaders and legislatures to become signatories put the treaty in force in 1978.

6. Bogsch (1995, p. 10).
7. Bogsch (1995, p. 11).

The PCT does not confer an international patent. Rather, the system establishes an international clearinghouse to which an applicant may submit one patent application that may take effect in several, many, or all (eighty-nine in 1997) PCT member states. The effect in each designated state is the same as if an application had been filed with the national patent office of the state. The PCT administrative staff submits the application to one of the major national patent offices (or the European Patent Office) for international search of the prior art and patentability examination. The treaty administrators then publish an international application notification.[8] There is only one fee, which establishes priority without multiple national submissions. The applicant may put off until the patentablility decision is final the list of countries in which the patent is to have effect and need not pay national fees until the patent decision is reached and a final list of countries for effect is drawn.[9]

During its first five years, the PCT lost money, and the member states made up the deficits with special contributions; but in 1982 it started turning a surplus. By 1988 surpluses exceeded 25 percent, and by 1993 refunds were given to the states that had helped the organization in the early years. The surpluses contributed by PCT administration lowered membership contributions from about 35 percent of the budget in the early years to 25 percent in the early 1990s and are projected to be about 10 percent by the end of the 1990s. The surpluses have also permitted WIPO to offer special discounted membership fees to poor countries, especially since 1989, when a new formula meant that the difference between the countries paying the highest and lowest contributions in the Unions has been changed from 25:1 to 800:1. The result is that many of the developing countries have a burden that is one-tenth of what it was before.[10] Unlike in the General Assembly where the United States is supposed to contribute 25 percent of the budget, the U.S. government contributes a tiny share (perhaps 1.5 percent in the early 1990s), and that share continues to shrink as the PCT incomes climb.

8. "The Patent Cooperation Treaty (PCT) and Its Importance to Developing Countries," PCT/Gen/7 (1996).
9. Putting off the decision of where the patent is to have effect is meaningful for inventors: the exploitation of a patentable invention is ultimately a decision of business strategy, which must take account of many competition, marketing, and regulatory factors. And, of course, circumstances may change during the period of patent pendency.
10. WIPO staff member source, February 1997.

Perhaps no other international governmental organization has executed such an ambitious, sustained program of teaching seminars and expert conferences than has WIPO. The organization estimates that 23,000 people, most from developing countries, had participated in their training seminars by 1992.[11] In 1980 the director general wrote,

> Our goal is that intellectual property should accelerate the development of developing countries. Naturally, each developing country's government sets its own economic goals. It is in the service of those goals that intellectual property should play a significant and realistic role. Such service requires trained persons, well-equipped and well-functioning industrial property offices and adequate legislation. My objective is that in every case where a developing country asks for advice and training, WIPO should be in a position to furnish it.[12]

The training programs typically last five days and involve WIPO professional staff as well as outside experts. The main annual industrial property course offered since 1978 and the main annual copyright course offered since 1988 are held in Geneva, the Hague, or Munich, but most of the courses are held in developing countries. Curricula emphasize the role and functioning of a patent office, copyright law and so-called neighboring rights (of broadcasting, performance, and so forth), and enforcement, judicial practices, and mock trials. Occasional courses involve tours for participants such as university law professors who are taken to the top intellectual property law programs in the United States and Europe. In 1981 the WIPO Secretariat leadership helped establish the International Association for the Advancement of Teaching and Research in Intellectual Property. The decision regarding where national and regional training courses are to be offered is made within WIPO at the highest level, for these are among the organization's highest-profile activities, and diplomacy toward the organization's members calls for sensitive judgments.

When offered in the industrialized countries, seminars are mostly marketing efforts aimed at introducing potential users to the PCT program. In 1996 PCT staff put on 21 seminars in cities as disparate as Istanbul and Singapore, Nagoya and Newark. The training curricula have gradually changed to reflect the demands of global trade. Once they focused almost

---

11. Bogsch (1992, p. 55).
12. *WIPO 1980 Activities* (1981, p. 133).

exclusively on patent and industrial property, but in recent years, copyright has become equally important. In 1970 WIPO conducted 10 programs, including patent (8), trademark (1), and copyright (1). Through the 1980s it conducted about 30 programs a year, including patent (20), trademark (2), and copyright (8). In 1995 it conducted more than 140 programs, including patent (55), trademark (8), copyright (49), enforcement (12), and general courses (19).[13] Until the PCT surpluses became substantial, the programs were about half funded by member contributions and about half by the UN Development Program. The UNDP contribution was $30 million by the early 1990s, but has been declining because of the agency's changing agenda, diminishing resources, and WIPO's growing financial independence.

The agency's activities have been varied. For some years the staff have offered several hundred one-on-one consulting missions annually, giving advice on subjects such as the use of information technology to improve patent office operations. In 1979 the organization established an annual award for inventors, which it calls the WIPO gold medal. There were 264 winners, 155 from developing countries, by the early 1990s. The organization was also instrumental in creating the International Federation of Inventors' Associations and sponsors periodic conferences focusing on innovation and invention and the role of intellectual property policy.

Business enterprises from the industrialized countries praise the teaching function of WIPO—when they know about it. But in general the intellectual property–intensive firms were dissatisfied with the level of protection offered by the international regime administered by the organization. Like other institutions associated with the United Nations (with its dominance by developing countries), the international intellectual property regime developed with loose rules, weak dispute settlement mechanisms, and no ability to enforce the provisions of international treaties. The Paris and Berne Conventions and other significant treaties obligated national treatment of their signatories but did not demand minimum standards of protection. Industrializing countries tended not to have patent and trademark laws, although some such as Brazil and India many years ago institutionalized copyright laws to protect the works of their own artists. Still, even these laws have been poorly enforced in recent years.[14] Policymakers in develop-

---

13. *WIPO Activities* (various years).
14. Gadbaw and Richards (1988).

ing countries contended that weak patent protection made sense because they wanted to diffuse technology from the industrialized countries at prices as low as possible.

It is no surprise then that beginning in the early 1980s, globally ambitious, U.S.-based intellectual property–intensive industries and associations, along with government representatives, turned away from WIPO with its domination by less developed countries and toward the GATT multilateral trade negotiations as the main way to establish American standards of international intellectual property protection. It may well be that the patent issue (especially the pirating of pharmaceuticals), debated furiously between the United States and many developing country governments, could not have been settled anywhere but in the GATT negotiations. The final TRIPS agreement, however, refers to and amends WIPO-administered treaties on patents, copyrights, trademarks, semiconductor masks, industrial designs, and trade secrets.

The agreement establishing the World Trade Organization, the GATT's successor, requires member states to accept all WTO agreements, which means most developing countries will be party to the TRIPS agreement. This brings a new urgency to WIPO development cooperation. Because the countries must be in compliance with the provisions of the treaty within no more than a decade, the organization must offer more training programs and more one-on-one consulting missions, greatly straining its human resources. It must do so with all deliberate speed, for about one hundred developing countries are WTO members. And because TRIPS imposes demands on copyright as well as patent policies, WIPO has greatly expanded its development cooperation in this policy area. In 1987 it organized six training courses on copyright; in 1997 it will conduct eighty-seven. Since copyright administration is primarily about enforcement, the organization began in 1995 to teach programs on police and customs methods of applying the laws. The organization has pledged to the WTO by formal agreement to provide technical assistance to WTO members so that they will come into compliance with TRIPS.[15]

15. Article 4, "Agreement between the World Intellectual Property Organization and the World Trade Organization," concluded in Geneva on December 22, 1995, and entered into force on January 1, 1996.

Organizational Design and Behavior

WIPO is led by a director general, 2 deputy directors general (for development cooperation and industrial property norms), 3 assistant directors general (for copyright norms, copyright development cooperation, and general administrative services), and 22 directors. It has a permanent staff of 500, including 180 professionals and 100 temporary staff members. About half the general service staff members are employed in the PCT Administrative Division; most of the professionals are involved with development cooperation and the creation of norms. It is a structure that has evolved to meet changing needs and appears likely to evolve further in the direction of recommendations from the new director general and the member countries.

WIPO is a wealthy IGO: the surpluses brought by the administration of the PCT ensure that staff get the information they need and travel frequently to provide technical assistance for development cooperation. The organization does, however, work under some important budgetary constraints. As a UN agency its budgets must be prepared a year in advance and approved by governing bodies of state members. Thus when circumstances call for reallocation of resources, the director general cannot simply order a change. For example, when the significance of digital technologies and the World Wide Web became clear in 1995–96, the organization could reallocate only limited professional staff and resources because the budget had not anticipated the rapid rise in the importance of the Internet. (Not even Microsoft has emphasized Web strategies for much longer than that, but, unlike WIPO, its leadership could shift resources quickly.) Furthermore, as a UN agency, WIPO must comply with New York–established rules regarding staff size and compensation. Thus, some complaint is heard at the organization that too much of the professional staff's time is spent doing clerical and administrative tasks because UN rules say that the organization has all the general services staff it needs.

When it became a UN agency WIPO had to be reconfigured to serve at once the needs of countries rich in industrial property, which represented the core of the institution's history, and the demands of LDCs poor in industrial property, which could be crucial to the institution's future. Furthermore, the entire UN system was challenged by cold war tensions, so organizational structure and procedures, activities, and staffing would all need either to resolve the North-South, East-West contradictions or evade them. To effect the necessary changes, in 1975 two positions of deputy director general were created, one to encourage and oversee development cooperation (first headed by a national from a developing country) and the other to supervise industrial property matters (first headed by a national from a socialist country). This structure was fitted for the primary tasks of WIPO service: technical training programs to improve the functioning of offices for industrial property (patent, industrial design, and trademark) in developing countries, administer international applications under the Patent Cooperation Treaty, and provide a forum for the creation of international norms.

Over the years the organization was restructured to fulfill its primary tasks flexibly and responsively. The position of deputy director general for industrial property norm creation was established, as were divisions headed by directors to deal with multilateral treaties, member laws, and PCT administration. Until recently WIPO has been focused on industrial property, but in response to growing infringements of copyright the organization created the position of assistant director general for copyright who reported to the director general, not to one of the deputies. And only a few years ago a second assistant director general for copyright development cooperation (again, reporting to the director general) was created so that the first position can concentrate on creating copyright norms. Thus an organizational structure was created that is flat: each principal reports to the director general without intervening layers. The result has been a flexible organization that, despite occasional budget-driven lapses, has proved capable of quickly responding to challenges.

If an organization is to learn and adapt to changing conditions, it requires stability, a motivated staff, and rewards, which include financial compensation, opportunities for career advancement, and recognition. Most of the senior staff have been with WIPO for a long time, a few nearly as long as the director general, and have been promoted to their positions from within the organization. Turnover in the rest of the staff seems modest. (I did not conduct interviews with people who have left the organization nor with junior professional staff, so the evidence may not be balanced.) Some of the staff probably could make more money in the private sector, especially since UN-imposed salary limits have created disparities with pay at the European Commission and some national governments. Nevertheless, the positions confer status when staff members travel internationally, and daily meetings offer opportunities for public recognition of good work. There are no women at the level of assistant director general or higher. And because WIPO is a small organization, it has a promotion bottleneck somewhat reminiscent of a small, family-owned business.

Most of the professional staff regularly attend conferences in their areas of expertise and communicate with their counterparts in other organizations. These activities are institutionalized in the organization by virtue of two of its primary tasks: conducting training programs and doing preparatory work for creating norms. The training programs always involve outside academic experts and practicing lawyers (whether private counsel or counsel within big companies) in addition to internal specialists, thus ensuring that new ideas and the latest thinking are introduced to the staff. For example, to begin taking account of the implications of artificial intelligence for intellectual property law, WIPO organized a symposium at Stanford in 1991 that brought together leading technologists and legal specialists.[16] To move along the copyright preparatory work for a 1996 diplomatic conference to amend the Berne Convention, the agency sponsored major conferences with international experts in 1991 in Cambridge, Massachusetts, 1994 in Paris, and 1995 in Mexico City and Naples.[17] To bring the best thinking to bear on private settlement of intellectual property disputes (as well as to announce publicly its movement in that direction), the organization hosted a major international conference on the issue in Geneva in 1994.[18] WIPO's Arbitration Center began in 1996.

Bringing valuable information into the organization, however, is only the beginning of organizational learning: the information must be acted on and must become part of the life of the organization. As former Director General Bogsch commented,

It is a basic working principle [at WIPO], which has been applied during the whole [1967 to 1992] period, that the work of each staff member will be far more efficient if he or she is well informed of what is happening in the house of WIPO and in the outside world of intellectual property. Such information or knowledge allows the staff member to see his or her duties in context, to see the relative importance and urgency of the duties. Such a view enhances the execution of the tasks with intelligence and an increased sense of responsibility. It makes cooperation among the various services natural and easy. It makes work more interesting.[19]

---

16. WIPO (1991).
17. WIPO (1993b); WIPO (1994b); WIPO (1995a); and WIPO (1995b).
18. WIPO (1994a).
19. Bogsch (1992, p. 67).

The director general institutionalized several methods to encourage internal communication. In WIPO jargon, they are "days," "weeks," "couriers," and "management meetings." Each day and at the end of each week, all professional staff submit a short report about their external contacts and communications. The courier is the daily 8:30 a.m. meeting chaired by the director general and attended by some one hundred of the professional staff. The director general "reads out or summarizes the most important pieces of mail (hence the word courier) received since the last courier and sorted out immediately beforehand. Then come oral reports by any staff member who has just returned from a mission." After the formal meeting concludes, informal meetings and consultations among small groups of staff members take place. The management meeting takes place more or less quarterly and involves about thirty of the senior staff. "It is to be noted," the former director general wrote, "that each participant hears about, without necessarily speaking on, all matters, not only those for which he or she is directly responsible. This, again, creates awareness of the tasks, achievements, and difficulties of [WIPO] as a whole, and thereby allows each participant to see his role in context." This system appears to be important to organizational learning at the agency. Staff members are indeed well informed about not only the activities of the organization but also about the technical and diplomatic milieu in which it is operating.

WIPO has not had formal staff training programs because the organization has been designed for a relatively small group of professionals. However, formal training programs have been institutionalized during the past few years for general service staff of the PCT who have come to number several hundred. Training is offered in procedures and technical matters and also in human resource management. The PCT operation, which was organizationally reformed in 1996, is very different from that of the rest of WIPO.

Students of international business competition note that skills, knowledge, and competences tend to cluster in certain regions: automobile technology in Bavaria, financial services knowledge in London, electronics manufacturing know-how near Tokyo, information technology in Silicon Valley.[20] Skills, knowledge, and competences related to social and political life also tend to cluster in certain regions: government competencies in Washington and nonprofit arts knowledge in New York, for example. So it

20. Porter (1990, pp. 148–73).

could be hypothesized that skills, knowledge, and competences related to international government diplomacy cluster in Geneva to the benefit of WIPO, given that the World Trade Organization, World Health Organization, International Telecommunications Union, World Meteorological Organization, United Nations Conference on Trade and Development (UNCTAD), and the European Headquarters of the United Nations, and major intergovernmental organizations are located there. However, review of the annual reports at WIPO (a good source of evidence, given the systematic way the organization gathers internal information regarding contacts) shows that in the 1970s and early 1980s there were occasional contacts with organizations such as UNCTAD, the International Labor Organization, and Paris-based UNESCO, but nothing resembling active dialogue, and actual cooperation was minimal.

The GATT-WTO has had a big impact on WIPO as an organization and on its regime during the past decade, but it appears that each organization has delineated its role, and the two cooperate where their roles intersect— TRIPS implementation, creation of new norms, intellectual property dispute settlement—but it does not appear that staff at the organizations have much to discuss in general. There appears to be no Geneva clustering effect as it relates to learning at WIPO. As to how WIPO employees stay informed about important issues, no one mentioned any other IGO. Rather, they talked about nongovernmental organizations, transnational epistemic communities to which they belonged, the media (especially the American media, which people pointed out was where a lot of the action was regarding new technologies, cultural products, and aggressive diplomacy), and their own international conferences.

WIPO staff appear to be achievement oriented: the organization claims that employees work longer hours on average than do those at other UN agencies. I observed that many of the professional staff work on Saturday or Sunday. All were actively taking on new challenges, whether preparing for new treaties, expanding development cooperation, getting the new Arbitration Center off the ground, or managing the growth of PCT administration. For example, the PCT system, which has become so important to patent administration worldwide and to the operation of WIPO, was only modestly popular during its first several years in force. A PCT administrator studied the system and recommended reforms to improve its functioning. The reforms took effect in 1984, and by the following year submissions by U.S. and European companies rose rapidly—and have been rising significantly every year since.

Recruitment of professional staff at WIPO has been consistent: although they are nationals from various countries, developing and industrialized, almost all are intellectual property administrators or attorneys, and most have been specialists in industrial property until recently, when copyright specialists have been recruited. Most possess technical or expressive (for example, literature) backgrounds in addition to legal study. Very few have backgrounds in economics, political economy, or general public administation. Many were recruited through having been national participants in a WIPO training program who had caught the eye of a WIPO staff member. (This is a practice that brings relationship building with member governments' intellectual property administrators, who may brag to their bosses that their people are so good that WIPO wants to recruit them.) Staff members are highly committed to the organization's mission and tasks: they value the utility of intellectual property law and administration but do not get caught up in economic development debates about intellectual property and foreign direct investment, trade, or economic growth. WIPO staff members are a relatively cohesive group who generally share the same worldview.

Organizational learning appears to proceed both top down and bottom up. It is explained by characteristics of organizational climate and culture that enable leadership, flat organizational structures, staff members who belong to professional communities, shared worldviews, and internal communication mechanisms and that encourage motivation—rewards and achieving attitudes. These characteristics exist at WIPO largely because of the leadership of the director general, who designed an organization that is flexible, externally oriented, and achieving. A study of decisionmaking at IGOs nearly twenty-five years ago concluded that "the key task for any executive head is to use his strategic location in his organization's communications network and the platform his position affords him to mobilize a consensus in support of organizational goals. How influential an executive head will be be depends in large measure on his success in performing this task."[21] The director general of WIPO has used every available means of communication to mobilize the organization to achieve his vision. As he departs in 1997, it remains to be seen whether he has planned for his own succession with as much foresight.

---

21. Cox and others (1973, p. 398).

For a World Intellectual Property Organization born during the era of the Group of 77 and the New International Economic Order, the past decade has been turbulent. TRIPS brought big changes, but WIPO's climate and culture seem to have facilitated organizational learning, adaptation, and renewal in the face of that turbulence. The challenges ahead concern technology. Digitization, networking, the World Wide Web, and biotechnology are the present and future challenges for WIPO norm creation for the patent and copyright institutions and for development cooperation with emerging-market countries.

SEVEN

TRIPS Implementation and Development

THE IMPLEMENTATION of the Agreement on Trade-Related Aspects of Intellectual Property Rights offers the potential for increased innovation and expression activity in developing countries. TRIPS is also a program of "deep integration"—harmonizing the policies and laws of developing countries with those of the global community—initiated by American multinational corporations and foreign policymakers.[1] But the support of domestic interest groups in developing countries even for shallow integration, nondiscriminatory trade policies, and measures to reduce tariffs and other trade barriers remains unconsolidated.[2] Because of the extensive intellectual property enforcement obligations, TRIPS is also an unprecedented initiative of the industrialized world to strengthen the judicial systems of developing countries. Implementation of the agreement by third world governments in the late 1990s and beyond will challenge accepted strategies of economic development, the governments' capacity to enforce policy, and the effectiveness of the judiciary.

Putting TRIPS policies into practice in developing countries will occur in a context of international trade and development that is far different from the context in which TRIPS negotiations were begun in 1986. Industrializing countries are increasingly engaging in the world economy through deliberately open, liberal-tending strategies. The old economic develop-

1. Lawrence (1996); and Kahler (1995).
2. Haggard (1995).

141

ment policy of substituting domestically produced goods and services for imported ones has clearly failed, and the debt crisis of the 1980s and the export-oriented success of Singapore, South Korea, and other East Asian countries motivated policymakers in developing countries to rethink their ideas about which development strategies worked, and how and why. As the TRIPS negotiations were going on, researchers discovered evidence that weak policies for protecting intellectual property rights discouraged investment, trade, and technology transfer. Indigenous innovation and expression activity could be better encouraged by protection of intellectual property rights than by piracy and other violations of them. The uniformity and consistency of development policy's opposition to intellectual property rights, which had been overstated anyway, cracked.

Nevertheless, the implementation of TRIPS provisions still faces considerable opposition from domestic interest groups and national governments. The reform of the patent institution is staunchly resisted by pirates, who have been making fat profits, and health care and agriculture interests, who are certain that health care and food will become more expensive. National governments must implement policy within state structures that often confer significant independence on regional and local governments. This federalism means that deals struck by the capital with other capitals must be rebargained with these local governments if national policies are to achieve full compliance throughout the country, a problem of particular significance in matters of protecting intellectual property.

Trade and commercial competition based on intellectual property cause law and policy enforcement problems that are qualitatively different from those created by financial capital flows and trade in real property. The enforcement of policies concerned with financial assets and trade is essentially a matter of a central government's power and its capacity to control its borders. But enforcing intellectual property rights depends on a state's capacity to reach deeply into its country to enforce policies at local levels. It can be argued that the TRIPS agreement aims to help developing-country signatories better institutionalize the capacity to enforce policy through their obligation to reform their judiciaries to improve enforcement of intellectual property rights. The extensive demands the TRIPS agreement makes on governments to reform courts, judicial procedures, and public administration of enforcement are extraordinary.

For public international law, TRIPS is a multilateral agreement of historic significance. Sovereignty, that is, state control over lawmaking and enforcement over a defined territory, is eroding before the global interdependence of the late twentieth century. Under traditional notions of international law, there has always been a reserved domain of exclusive domestic jurisdiction over a nation's legislative, administrative, and judicial affairs, although its boundaries have long been recognized to be unclear.[3] Developing countries have ceded sovereignty to the community of states in important aspects of economic policy. The International Monetary Fund has circumscribed state sovereignty by demanding extensive macroeconomic policy adjustments as a condition for loans that would solve balance of payments problems.[4] The GATT eroded sovereignty by demanding extensive trade policy reforms in exchange for trade benefits from industrialized countries.[5] States have also given up significant elements of sovereignty through interdependence with other states. The interdependence of financial markets reduces states' policy independence.[6] Dependence on trade with the United States makes its trade partners vulnerable under authority of the U.S. section 301 policy to American demands for changes in trade policy.[7] And under authority of the extraterritorial reach of U.S. antitrust "effects doctrine" laws, trading partners are subject to demands to change the structure and concentration of their industries when they have anti-competitive effects in the United States.[8] By becoming signatories to TRIPS, however, states have for the first time through their membership in the World Trade Organization ceded to a global organization significant elements of their sovereignty over their administrative and judicial structures and procedures—essential features of polity, not policy.

TRIPS Implementation and Economic Development Ideas

The TRIPS obligations contradict the policies of many developing countries. The agreement is premised on economic theories favoring innovation and expression, and it takes full cognizance the nature of competition of patent-dependent and copyright-dependent businesses. These premises are considerably at odds with the guiding rationale for intellectual property policies in many countries. TRIPS implementation engages the government

3. Brownlie (1990, pp. 389–407).
4. Frenkel and Goldstein (1991); Garritsen de Vries (1987); and Williamson (1983).
5. Hudec (1987).
6. Goodman and Pauly (1993).
7. Ryan (1995a).
8. Scherer (1994).

and business elite in a fundamental debate about economic development strategy. Implementation through national legislative and administrative acts in developing countries also threatens established relationships of business and government. Thus, TRIPS poses challenges that are at once intellectual and political.

Changes in Economic Development Strategies

In response to U.S. pressure under authority of its Special 301 trade law, many developing countries reformed their intellectual property rights laws even before TRIPS was signed. In the late 1980s five governments reformed their patent laws, two their trademark laws, and nine their copyright laws. In the early 1990s, intellectual property reforms proliferated widely as twenty-nine countries reformed patent laws, three reformed trade secret laws, twelve reformed trademark laws, and thirty-three reformed copyright laws (table 7-1).

Some observers, however, question the sincerity of the reforms. One contends that intellectual property laws in developing countries have been changed in response to U.S. pressure, but minds have not been changed.

In nearly every instance the targeted countries have engaged in foot dragging and chosen not to implement and enforce the new policies. The continued monitoring and repeated threats of renewed Section 301 action in the absence of satisfactory enforcement of the new policies suggest that the trend toward greater protection of intellectual property is not being as ardently embraced as the United States would wish. The targeted states acquiesce on paper and do just enough to free themselves of U.S. pressure—but no more. While these countries have changed their policies, they have not changed their minds about the merits of intellectual property protection. Even when the United States carried out its threats by imposing sanctions on Brazil, India, Mexico, and Thailand, the targeted countries did not comply. Free riding on others' intellectual property and the profits of piracy still outweigh the liberal norm of respect for property rights.[9]

The description of developing countries' behavior is accurate. Indeed, when TRIPS was concluded, twenty-five developing countries offered no

9. Sell (1995, p. 332).

Table 7-1. *Countries Making Changes in Intellectual Property Policies,*
1985–88, 1989–94

Period	Policy subject			
	Patent	Trade secret	Trademark	Copyright
1985–88	Taiwan		Taiwan	Taiwan
	Malaysia		Mexico	Japan
	Mexico			Singapore
	Korea			Turkey
	Japan			Malaysia
				Indonesia
				Korea
				Canada
				Brazil
1989–94	Indonesia	Mexico	Mexico	China
	Chile	China	Chile	Taiwan
	Saudi Arabia	Taiwan	India	Indonesia
	Yugoslavia		UAE	Malaysia
	Spain		Thailand	France
	Mongolia		Philippines	Saudi Arabia
	Poland		Switzerland	Colombia
	Czechoslovakia		Ukraine	Portugal
	Venezuela		Jamaica	Italy
	Bugaria		Ecuador	Mongolia
	Mexico		South Africa	Poland
	Germany		Honduras	Czechoslovakia
	Brazil			Japan
	Argentina			Bulgaria
	New Zealand			Egypt
	Romania			Romania
	Andean Pact			Greece
	Thailand			Germany
	UAE			European Union
	Peru			South Africa
	European Union			UAE
	Korea			Turkmenistan
	Turkmenistan			Pakistan
	Russia			Chile
	Philippines			Bolivia
	Ukraine			Philippines
	Jamaica			Ukraine
	Equador			Jamaica
	Honduras			Ecaudor
				Venezuela
				El Salvador
				Honduras

Source: U.S. Trade Representative, "Special 301," press releases (various dates).

patent protection to pharmaceuticals (thirteen did not even confer patent protection to chemicals), and fifty-seven did not offer copyrights for computer software.[10] However, it is less clear whether opposition to intellectual property laws as a matter of economic development strategy is universal. Some minds in developing countries may be changing as new strategies are being adopted to encourage investment, licensing, and indigenous innovation and expression. The positive role of intellectual property in national economic development is not yet well appreciated, notwithstanding that many individuals in most countries are frustrated by inadequate protection. This pent-up demand for better protection has not yet found a political voice, the voice of the past, as always, being louder than the voice of the future.[11]

Policymakers in developing countries have long tended to think differently about copyrights than they have about patents. The utility of the copyright has been acknowledged by many developing countries, while the utility of the patent has been controversial. Brazil has had copyright law for a generation and India for two generations, although neither has enforced the laws effectively, but both are only now moving toward the adoption of world-standard patent laws. The institutional histories of patent and copyright in the third world are characterized by a philosophical tension between natural property rights and incentives for risky investment in innovation and expression. This tension results in a tendency to confer legitimacy on the copyright because it appears to protect the "moral rights" of (local) authors and to deny the "economic rights" of (foreign) firms. Yet, despite the opposition to intellectual property law reforms, especially of patent policies, the context in which development strategy is formulated in the era of TRIPS implementation is very different from the context in any previous era.

The GATT initiatives in the 1960s to help solve the economic problems of the developing countries were feeble except for the tariff cutting offered by the Generalized System of Preferences, which were trade preferences valuable to exporters in developing countries even if critics charged that importers manipulated the system for their own benefit.[12] Neither the Kennedy Round negotiations nor the subsequent Tokyo Round contributed much to development. If anything, they propounded the antidumping and

10. Primo Braga (1995b, p. 396).
11. Sherwood and Primo Braga (1996).
12. Wilson (1992, p. 44).

subsidy–countervailing duty agreements and the Multifiber Agreement that worked against the interests of developing countries.[13]

As a result, most developing-country political and academic leaders, especially the so-called *dependencia* school in Latin America, rejected the GATT-based international trade regime. The world economy, they charged, was structured to ensure that developing countries were burdened with overdependence on exports of raw material exports, which tended toward price volatility; maldistribution of national income that created elite preferences for imported foreign luxury goods; and investments in manufacturing by multinational corporations that destroyed local production. These observers also contended that the agreements facilitated foreign domination of local capital markets, introduced technology inappropriate to local skills, created an international division of labor, prevented indigenous, self-sustaining technological development, distorted the local labor market because multinational corporations pay higher wages than local firms can afford, and promoted reliance on foreign capital, which encourages authoritarian government.[14] The critics argued that greater independence would be achieved if domestically produced goods and services were substituted for imported goods and services and if governments in the third world imposed restrictions on imports and foreign direct investment restrictions—so-called import substitution industrialization. In the 1960s and 1970s many of these governments demanded joint equity with multinational corporations and local managerial control. In some cases the governments expropriated the companies' assets.

Developing countries presented proposals for restructuring the world political economy at the first UN Conference on Trade and Development (UNCTAD) in 1964. They requested trade preferences for their manufactured goods, commodity price stabilization, resource and technology transfers, reductions in freight and service charges, debt rescheduling and reductions, and a new forum to replace the GATT.[15] Creating an economic strategy to mirror the security strategy of the nonaligned movement and inspired by the success of the OPEC oil cartel, in 1974 the Group of 77 developing countries used their numbers in the United Nations (in which one-nation, one-vote decisionmaking afforded them power they did not have in the weighted-voting International Monetary Fund and World Bank

13. Hudec (1987).
14. Gilpin (1987, pp. 263–305).
15. Cutahar (1984).

and the rarely voting GATT) to pass a Declaration on the Establishment of the New International Economic Order (NIEO). The NIEO reiterated the UNCTAD demands and asserted the right to nationalize foreign enterprises, create commodity cartels, and regulate multinational corporations.[16] Thus the G-77 used the UNCTAD forum to establish raw materials and agricultural cartels—the Commodity Common Fund—intended to monitor and manage supply, demand, and therefore prices. The Commodity Common Fund managed supply by amassing stocks of the commodities, much as the OPEC cartel managed the supply of oil.[17] It was an era in which third world governments weakened intellectual property policies, as India did with its changes in patent policy in 1972.[18]

Whether the measure is economic growth rates, current account balances, or income distribution, the strategy of import substitution performed poorly. The Commodity Common Fund achieved some success in stabilizing then raising prices but turned out to be fool's gold; oil is the only exception to the rule that commodities are substitutable with alternatives.[19] Furthermore, the oil shocks of the 1970s increased the dollar needs of the developing countries that were not oil producers and falsely raised the hopes of the oil-producing developing countries. The commercial banks of the industrialized countries recycled petrodollars through the developing countries, creating levels of national debt that became a debt crisis in 1982 before subsiding into a debt problem by the end of the decade.

The Group of 77 lacked the power in the world political economy to achieve the New International Economic Order. By the end of the 1980s the proposal was dead, UNCTAD mattered little in the world economy, and import substitution had come to be seen as a failed strategy. It failed, however, not because of greedy foreign banks or the structure of world power but because the strategy itself was flawed. Import substitution may have been the best available response of countries such as Mexico and Brazil to the external economic and political shocks of the Great Depression and World War II.[20] But in the 1970s and 1980s it depended on markets that were too small to provide economies of scale and on demand conditions that were too isolated to produce globally competitive industries; typically the strategy resulted in inefficient production and bad products. These

16. Bhattacharya (1976).
17. Finlayson and Zacher (1990).
18. Gadbaw and Richards (1988, p. 200).
19. Krasner (1974).
20. Haggard (1992, pp. 161–90).

underlying economic realities came into high relief when the oil shocks produced the third world debt crisis.

The International Monetary Fund used its power as source of capital and guarantor to other public and private lenders to lend to developing countries on the condition that they adjust their economic policies to follow liberal-tending, market-oriented prescriptions.[21] Perhaps as important, by the 1990s developing countries had a new economic development model in the strategies of South Korea and Taiwan. Both countries had adopted import substitution policies after the end of Japanese colonialism, had experienced their own balance-of-payments problems, and had depended heavily on U.S. aid. In the late 1950s they were met with American demands that they wean themselves from that aid and, confronted with serious external security threats, the governments in Seoul and Taipei adopted export-led strategies to achieve balance-of-payments equilibrium and earn foreign exchange for domestic development and industrialization.[22]

Korea and Taiwan were "late industrializers," and late industrializers are good learners.[23] They visit international expositions, attend international conferences, visit foreign plants, consult foreign suppliers, hire foreign experts, and beg, borrow, and buy foreign designs. In South Korea and Taiwan the strategy involved a great deal of planning and intervention by government; very high levels of investment in key industries, more investment than would have occurred without government intervention; and the exposure of industries to international competition in foreign, though typically not in domestic, markets.[24] The governments intervened in the markets through land redistribution, financial system controls to put industrial production ahead of consumer spending, price controls, undervalued foreign exchange rates, wage controls (and union repression), export performance rewards, foreign direct investment controls, foreign technology acquisition, and sector-specific subsidies and export promotion assistance. By the late 1980s the Korean Foreign Ministry was planning for admission to the OECD (which took place in 1996). Taiwan was by then even richer than Korea, although diplomatically isolated in world politics.

Thus inspired, the political leaders of developing countries have been dropping import substitution strategies and adopting strategies that seek

21. Kahler (1986); and Williamson (1983).
22. Haggard (1992); and Cheng (1990).
23. Amsden (1989).
24. Wade (1990).

fuller engagement in the world economy, including export promotion and (qualified) liberalization of import and direct investment policies. Until 1978 China's economic policy had been classic import substitution: import barriers, foreign exchange controls, and foreign direct investment restrictions.[25] This resulted in chronic poverty, poor infrastructure, a widening technological gap between world standards and Chinese capabilities, and a much lower standard of living than that enjoyed by its rapidly industrializing East Asian neighbors. About 1960 a famine killed millions of people, and economic, political, and social chaos ruled the late 1960s and the 1970s.[26] Advocates for change argued that "socialism" in China must not mean "egalitarianism on the basis of universal poverty."[27] After a consolidation of power by Deng Xiaoping, the Chinese government announced in December 1978 a new open door policy to stimulate the country's modernization in science and technology. The logic of the policy was not liberalization but the adoption of Western technology and the export of manufactured goods.[28] Thus import barriers would be removed and trade and investment decisionmaking would be decentralized only when necessary. China initially adopted a capitalist development strategy similar to Japan's and South Korea's, although China's reform policies toward multinational companies evolved very differently from the Japanese archetype.[29]

Motivated by forces similar to those that confronted Mao's political successors, by the end of the 1980s the socialist command strategies of the Soviet Union and its eastern European satellites underwent their own upheavals. Under the command strategy the Soviet state had seized nearly complete control of the means of production and resource allocation. Through its republics and satellites it imposed a largely dyadic and asymmetrical regional economy, thereby maintaining independence in the world political economy.[30] Resource deployment in socialist states favored agriculture, heavy manufactures, and energy production to build military capabilities, but at the cost of underinvested light, consumer-oriented industries.[31] Nevertheless, the system might have survived had not the pace of

---

25. Lardy (1992).
26. Friedman, Pickowicz, and Selden (1991, p. xxiii).
27. Pearson (1991, p. 62).
28. Ho and Huenemann (1984).
29. Johnson (1986, p. 559); and Shirk (1993).
30. Marrese (1986).
31. Commisso (1986).

technological progress in the West and the Chernobyl disaster delegitimized the Soviet state—and had not information technologies such as fax machines and satellite television not been there to be the instruments of death.

Challenged by debt crisis, Mexico acceded to the GATT and negotiated a free trade agreement with the United States and Canada, liberalizing its trade and investment policies in the process. Many developing countries acceded to the GATT and its WTO successor during the 1990s, taking the total membership toward universality. Latin American governments have been liberalizing trade and investment policies and negotiating free trade agreements to create bigger, more efficient markets, thus attracting more foreign direct investment. India is liberalizing its economy, if more slowly and erratically than China; Vietnam is pursuing *doi moi* reforms; and the ASEAN countries have agreed to phase in a free trade agreement. The countries of Latin America are joined by China, India, northeast and southeast Asia, eastern Europe, central Asia, and southern Africa as emerging markets.

Emerging Markets and Foreign Direct Investment

Emerging market countries in the 1990s want to encourage more investment by multinational corporations. During the 1970s and concomitant with their import substitution policies and the New International Economic Order proposals, third world governments attempted to stop new foreign direct investment and renegotiated the terms that governed existing investments owned by multinational corporations. But changes in economic strategy since the debt crisis have brought renewed interest in foreign direct investment. Governments in developing countries and those making transitions from nonmarket economies recognize that investment, while not scarce, is limited and they are competing for it. Thus some have been exploring the usefulness of investment incentives, including tax abatements, investment credits, subsidized loans, and performance requirements. These inducements affect the potential investor's revenues, cost of inputs, factors of production, and profitability.[32] Some of these policies may encourage inward foreign direct investment, but they must be considered in

32. Guisinger (1986)

the light of restrictions placed on export subsidies under the GATT. The direction of policy in the world economy seems to be toward multilateral agreement to restrict investment incentives because they could lead states into costly bidding wars.[33] When offering incentives, states that make certain their policies are stable and that their commitments are credible do better.[34]

Incentives matter less to multinational corporation managers than do political stability, asset control, earnings remittance, monetary and fiscal policies, transportation and communication infrastructures, business behavior standards, import barriers, export quotas, and regulatory factors.[35] Clever incentives tend to matter less than fundamentals: market opportunities, foreign exchange, infrastructure, political and legal predictability. Developing countries with small populations, however, do face special challenges to gain the attention of decisionmakers in multinational corporations.[36]

In the late 1980s and the early 1990s, research sponsored by international governmental organizations started to demonstrate with systematically gathered evidence what anecdotal evidence had been saying for some years: weak intellectual property protection discourages foreign direct investment in certain industry sectors, especially pharmaceuticals, chemicals, and information technologies. An UNCTAD study in 1986 found that investment in new technology areas such as computer software, semiconductors, and biotechnology was influenced by intellectual property policies.[37] A 1987 OECD study found weak intellectual property policies to be significant barriers to international technology licensing.[38] A study by the UN Commission on Transnational Corporations in 1989 found that weak intellectual property protection reduced computer software investment. Another study by the UNCTC announced in 1990 that weak patent policies reduced pharmaceutical investment.[39] Survey research sponsored by the International Finance Corporation of the World Bank found that, with variations by sector, country, and technology, at least 25 percent of American, German, and Japanese high-technology firms refused direct invest-

33. Hufbauer (1984).
34. Murtha (1991).
35. Wallace (1992).
36. Goodman (1987).
37. United Nations Conference on Trade and Development (1986).
38. Organization for Economic Cooperation and Development (1987).
39. United Nations Commission on Transnational Corporations (1989, 1990).

ment or joint ventures in industrializing countries with weak intellectual property policies.[40] Given scarce resources, they invested in countries where the intellectual property risks were lower.

During the TRIPS negotiations, this emphasis on international technology and capital flows became an important new variable to the political economy of intellectual property policy. Previously, some American economists argued that intellectual property policies ought to depend on levels of development and that the least developed countries should not adopt international standards but that middle-income countries possibly should.[41] These studies may not have taken sufficient account of trade, investment, capital, and technology flows. More recent World Bank research supports the conclusions of the survey research by tracing actual patterns of U.S. foreign direct investment and finding that countries with weak intellectual property policies do indeed have less foreign direct investment than would otherwise be expected.[42]

It is often said that developing countries have no stake in technological innovation because they lack the capacity for market-leading discovery and invention. However, this viewpoint is likely wrong; developing countries such as Korea have demonstrated a capacity to absorb new technologies and know-how faster than other developing countries and have grown faster as a consequence.[43]

Technological innovation, economists explain, is the engine for long-run economic growth; and innovative ideas, methods, and products depend on knowledge and human capital, on information-rich workers with know-how and learning capacity.[44] Knowledge is not "out there" someplace; it is often embedded in organizations, and commercially valuable knowledge is often embedded in business enterprises, their very existence declaring when they organize information better than markets do.[45] When they are multinational, these enterprises are diffusers of knowledge, but their knowledge is much more than discrete facts. Business enterprises possess organizing principles that are deeply embedded not only within their organization but

---

40. Mansfield (1995, p. 5). Mansfield's research was first circulated in 1992 as "Unauthorized Use of Intellectual Property: Effects on Investment, Technology Transfer and Innovation," University of Pennsylvania, Philadelphia.

41. Deardorff (1992); and Maskus (1990).

42. Primo Braga (1995b).

43. Kim (1997).

44. Grossman and Helpman (1991); and Rosenberg, Landau, and Mowery (1992).

45. Kogut and Zander (1992).

within their particular industry sector. Organizational and managerial capabilities diffuse across national boundaries at different rates depending on the absorptive capacity of countries.[46] Incremental product and process innovations can often be quickly imitated by producers in developing countries, but organizational innovations are substantially more difficult to learn and incorporate into routine activities. Thus, foreign direct investment, whether by joint venture or wholly owned subsidiary, contributes essential new knowledge that cannot be obtained by reading books and journal articles.

Competition in intellectual property–intensive industries demands extremely high commitments of financial capital (10 to 30 percent of sales rather than the 3 to 5 percent typical in manufacturing), extremely high commitments of human capital (scientists, engineers, and creative talent do not come cheaply), and highly developed and specialized organizational and managerial capablities. Not only must the innovative or expressive product be created, but it must be produced and distributed: neither technological innovation in the laboratory nor creative expression on the sound stage is enough to win in these high-risk businesses. Intellectual property–intensive winners organize to produce and market, and they do so globally to capture economies of scale, cross-subsidize within their firms, and face the most demanding, sophisticated customers.

Many of these firms have reacted to emerging markets by locating product development and production in these countries as well as by acquiring local distribution capabilities. Effective marketing often means collaboration with local partners who bring specific competencies in local distribution, advertising, management of workers, and business-government relations. Collaboration with local partners is a means toward reducing or at least diversifying the risks associated with international business activities.[47] In many developing countries, collaboration with local partners also is one of the means employed to combat the piracy of intellectual property. For example, pharmaceutical production is an exacting process such that would-be imitators find the capital barriers to market entry high, higher than, for example, the barriers to piracy of music CDs. Nevertheless, except in the poorest of developing countries, the barriers to entry are not insurmountable, and piracy of pharmaceutical products in developing countries is widespread.

46. Kogut (1991).
47. Moran (1985).

Yet in the minds of pharmaceutical company managers, completely staying out of markets such as China is the wrong solution to the piracy problem. The pharmaceutical market in China is large and its potential is vast. In 1992, total pharmaceutical imports were $319 million and prescription medicines about $128 million.[48] The Chinese government allocated $4.5 billion for 1991–2000 for investment in capital construction and the renovation of existing manufacturing plants. The Chinese population is aging; the primary causes of death in China's urban areas are similar to those in the West: cancer, heart disease, stroke. Furthermore, Chinese physicians are no longer the "barefoot doctors" of the Cultural Revolution. They not only prefer Western-style medicines to traditional Chinese remedies, but also Western brand medicines to local imitations, which they find substandard. Thus, antipiracy action in the pharmaceutical industry includes a standard tactic of marketing: demonstrate that your product is better than your competitor's. Western pharmaceutical makers make their product packaging distinctive and teach users how to tell the difference between the genuine product and the (even skillfully executed) pirated product.

International business strategies of the copyright industries in the emerging market countries differ from those of the manufacturing-oriented pharmaceutical, fine chemical, and information technology hardware businesses because manufacturing adds little value to the product and the barrier to market entry at the point of production is low. Computer application software, books, and CD-ROMs and entertainment products such as film videocassettes, video games, and compact music disks often require tens of millions of dollars in development costs but are inexpensively copied and sold either as "good as the real thing" or "good enough" for less discriminating customers. Thus these firms aggressively enforce their intellectual property rights through worldwide antipiracy teams, cooperation with local police, telephone hotlines, and Special 301 trade diplomacy. To turn pirates into partners, they also sign licensing deals with local manufacturers to produce legitimate products; create joint ventures with local software writers, publishers, music houses, and film studios to expand production of works by local talent for local consumption; and sign contracts with local agents to advertise and distribute legitimate products to create brand awareness.

48. Sullivan (1993).

Marginal participation in intellectual property–intensive competition is possible through piracy, but real engagement, exploitation, and contribution of indigenous innovation and expression depends on effective implementation of TRIPS policies and their enforcement in the national political economies, for the important holders of commercially valuable intellectual property are neither governments nor universities but business enterprises such as McGraw-Hill and Dun & Bradstreet, Time Warner and Disney, Microsoft and Oracle, DuPont and Monsanto that possess the organizational capabilities to design and distribute innovation and expression products. Just as these companies compete with each other, however, they are cooperating with each other, and partners do not steal from each other if they expect to maintain good business relationships. In the emerging markets as in the industrialized countries, the real rewards go to the partners, firms that gain skills and know-how and long-term relationships in addition to sales and profits, not to the pirates, who learn little more than how to evade antipiracy enforcement.

Intellectual Property Enforcement and the Judiciary

Economic strategy alone is not enough to sustain growth and development. Implementing economic reforms and the TRIPS commitments takes much better governance than most developing countries are accustomed to. Trade in intellectual property and commercial competition places on states an enforcement problem qualitatively different from that of financial capital flows and real property trade. Enforcing policies toward financial assets and trade are essentially problems of central government power and capacity to control a country's borders. Policies in developing countries regarding financial assets such as capital controls and more general macroeconomic policies have frequently been subject to change at the behest of IMF bankers, and the implementation challenges they impose on states is of the power of the central government to act contrary to the demands of domestic interest groups. Trade policy obligations, as illustrated by the Uruguay Round agreements, tend to fall into three categories: customs and border measures, subsidies and "unfair" trade practices, and product regulations and standards testing. As with the IMF's conditionality-imposed policy changes, implementing the GATT-imposed trade policy changes challenges the power of the central government to resist the demands of domestic interest groups. The additional burden of imposing GATT laws is the capacity to control border flows of traded goods.

By contrast, the enforcement of intellectual property rights depends on a government's capacity to to enforce policies at local levels when localized corruption and cronyism are ways of life in many developing countries. The essence of the state is its capacity to enforce policy as well as make it, and the TRIPS agreement poses an enforcement challenge that, it may be argued, helps developing countries better institutionalize the capacity to enforce policy through the multilaterally committed obligation to reform their judiciaries.

The copyright industries of the United States and Europe, through their initiative to improve the enforcement of copyright laws, have been urging enforcement by means of the U.S. Special 301 process and the TRIPS agreement for judiciary building. Courts, customs, and police are the agents of enforcement, and in many developing countries they have performed poorly and often been corrupt. The annual Special 301 recommendations of the International Intellectual Property Alliance, the Software Publishers Association, and Nintendo detail the inadequacies of enforcement country by country. "Mexican criminal procedures," said IIPA in its 1997 report, "are often unfathomable, intricate, ad hoc, and seemingly random." The report also said, "Criminal elements dominate much of urban Brazil." Bulgaria is the biggest source of CD piracy in Europe because of government-owned pirate factories and exports controlled by organized crime. The courts in Pakistan are "hopelessly backlogged." Nintendo offers the assessment that "Venezuela's legal system has not evolved at the same pace as its modern economy. . . . Until Venezuela addresses some of these serious deficiencies that have given their judicial system the reputation of being 'among the most corrupt in the world,' Nintendo and other U.S. intellectual property owners will continue to suffer irreparable harm and loss."[49] An effort has been made to survey systematically and rate numerically the intellectual property laws, administrative procedures, and enforcement capabilities of developing countries, and it confirms the bleak experience of the copyright industry antipiracy teams.[50]

Courts, if they are to provide effective dispute settlement, must be independent, competent, and effective. The World Bank has undertaken a study of judicial institutionalization in developing countries. Independence

---

49. Arter and Hadden (1996); and International Intellectual Property Alliance (various years).
50. Sherwood (1997a).

means detachment from interest groups, the executive and legislature, and fellow judges and attorneys.[51] It means rendering adjudicatory decisions according to law rather than the interests of politics or commerce. Judicial independence is achieved by ensuring that judges are insulated from political and commercial pressures through secure judicial terms and salaries and control over case assignment and court scheduling. Judicial competence is achieved through procedures that ensure merit-based appointments of highly qualified and respected judges and evaluation procedures that ensure ethical conduct and professional training. Judicial effectiveness is achieved through adequate staffing and competent administration to aid the timely disposition of cases. The World Bank has found that corruption may be as much the product of overburdened courts and delays that cause frustrated litigants to pay bribes as of conventional payola to swing adjudicatory outcomes in one direction or the other.

The World Bank has provided capital to build infrastructure to relieve poverty and has recommended strategies for developing open economies, but has had no sustained commitment to state building, even if its 1997 *World Development Report* announces that intention by emphasizing the state and institutional sources of development.[52] Concomitant to the pursuit of profits and of anticommunist containment of the Soviet bloc and its supposed revolutionary ideology, American multinational corporations and foreign policymakers have long been accused of propping up authoritarian regimes in developing countries with little regard for local rule of law.[53] Thus TRIPS is a seminal initiative of international law and organization. However, neither the laws of intellectual property protection nor the judicial reforms necessary for their effective enforcement will be easily implemented in developing countries.

51. Dakolias (1995).
52. Ayres (1983); Dornbusch and Helmers (1988); and Shihata (1991).
53. Kwitny (1984); Gaddis (1982); and Krasner (1978).

EIGHT

The Communication Revolution and Intellectual Property

EVEN AS the TRIPS negotiations were grinding along, a communication revolution was under way, born of telephony deregulation, which increased providers and need for high-capacity fiber-optic cable, an important breakthrough in digital compression technologies that is increasing channel capacity and may foment a digital convergence of communication media, and the spectacular increase in the use of the Internet. The revolution challenges conventional instititions of intellectual property such as copyright to adapt to new technological capabilities and new commercial behaviors. It also challenges recent practices such as the assignment of domain names (electronic addresses) to adapt to the global reach of the Internet.

At the World Intellectual Property Organization in December 1996 the future of global electronic communication and commerce was at issue as representatives of communications and information companies, nongovernmental organizations, and national governments convened to amend for the era of digital communication the copyright and performer's rights explicated in the Berne and Rome Conventions.

Digital convergence and networked, interactive communication offer the prospect of new services and conveniences, including a powerful new medium by which to distribute copyrighted materials. They also, however, offer the prospect of unauthorized piracy of digitized music, films, and software, downloaded again and again with no loss of quality. Internet-based electronic commerce poses challenges to information technology (encryption, e-cash, and so forth) and the copyright institution even as it offers a paradigm shift in product distribution. Does going digital require a complete rethinking of international copyright law? U.S. policymakers confront the same questions with respect to U.S. domestic law and policy preferences toward international institutional change.

Interests and policy preferences in the United States and internationally have arranged themselves into four groups: producers of copyrighted entertainment, information, and software content; users of copyrighted content, including libraries, governments, and universities; on-line and communication service providers, the deliverers of content; and makers of hardware, including computers and peripheral equipment, video and audio equipment and other consumer electronics, and broadcast equipment. Content producers have aimed to ensure their ownership rights, content users to ensure access, communication service deliverers to ensure delivery free of liability for piracy, and hardware makers to ensure equipment production free of liability for piracy. Ownership, access, and piracy have looked different depending on the point of view.

Two treaties were negotiated and signed at the 1996 Geneva Diplomatic Conference under the auspices of WIPO, and the outcome was just as predicted by the WIPO Secretariat assistant director general more than a year before at the Naples conference. The agreements aim to preserve the intent of the intellectual property policy of expression: to confer exclusive rights of authorship and distribution to provide incentives for risky investment in expression products while maintaining the public's access to the information and expression. Although new communication technologies make it a tricky balance to achieve, the copyright agreements were achieved through function-specific diplomacy built on five years of WIPO educational initiative and despite the absence of the linkage-bargaining opportunities that led to the TRIPS agreement. *Wired* magazine described through its on-the-spot journalism the interest group advocacy and diplomacy at the diplomatic conference but, by ignoring the institutional history of the international copyright law reform process undertaken through the leadership of the WIPO Secretariat over the previous five years, mischaracterized how the new international copyright law was achieved there.[1] However, the final text omitted crucial issues, so the 1996 diplomatic conference only begins the process of creating new rules regarding communication technology change and copyright.

1. Browning (1997); Samuelson (1997).

Intellectual Property and National Information Infrastructure

Digital compression is a breakthrough technology that has driven the communications revolution. Although it was long recognized that digitizing video—storing video information as bits of ones and zeroes in the same way as text is digitized in computing systems and audio in compact discs—was possible, the practical problem was that video requires much more storage space than audio. For example, 75 minutes of music takes up 600 megabytes of storage on a CD, while a typical 120-minute feature film takes up 216,000 megabytes, the equivalent of 360 CDs.[2] But video encoded through high-speed computer hardware can be digitized, an operation analogous to a photograph's being projected through a fine screen so that each tiny square in the bitmap is assigned a binary value of one or zero for on or off pulses. Through a process called multiplexing, the audio and video signals are compressed and synchronized, then decoded to reconstruct the picture. The result: 360 discs reduces to 1 disc, so that the digital video disc becomes possible. Another result: television can be broadcast digitally just as computers proof information digitally, at least in theory. A sea change will occur in broadcasting and home television with implications much greater than higher-quality pictures wedded to CD-quality sound.

The unexpected success of digital compression technologies in 1990, integrated with huge-capacity fiber-optic cables and broadcast and wireless technologies, fomented turbulence in markets, causing convergence of communications media, challenging conventional ways of doing business in many industries, and establishing a new era of citizen interactivity. "By 1995, the Internet could be accessed over TV cables; TV signals could travel over power and phone lines; phonelike service could be provided over the Internet; the Internet and networking could be transmitted wirelessly."[3] Businesses and policymakers have been strongly challenged by the interactivity:

It is coming by telephone wires, optical fiber, coaxial cable, and microwave. It is coming from local phone companies, cable operators, and Internet service providers, both large and small. It is coming

2. "The Big Squeeze: Digital Data Compression," *Popular Science* (November 1995), p. 100. This section is based on the research of Vanessa Fuhrmans, School of Foreign Service, Georgetown University, 1996.
3. "Technology 1996: Analysis and Forecast," *IEEE Spectrum* (January 1996), p. 30.

into your personal computer and into your television set. "It" is entertainment, shopping, and information services, and all of it is interactive.[4]

Market participants in computer, telephony, wireless, Internet, television, information services, retailing, and entertainment are potentially all competitors and all collaborators: "No company anywhere in the world knows how to do all those things."[5]

To devise policy to regulate this national information infrastructure (NII), in February 1993 the Clinton administration formed the Information Infrastructure Task Force under the direction of the secretary of commerce. The task force established four committees: the Telecommunications Policy Committee, Committee on Applications and Technology, Security Issues Forum, and Information Policy Committee. Within the Information Policy Committee, the Intellectual Property Rights Working Group was created with Commissioner of Patents and Trademarks and Assistant Secretary of Commerce Bruce Lehman as chair.

At a public hearing in November 1993 business associations, companies, and nongovernmental organizations, primarily from the copyright industry associations (film, music, publishing, software) and library associations, presented some seventy written statements.[6] The Information Industry Association (representing information product and service companies such as Dow Jones, McGraw-Hill, and Dun & Bradstreet) emphasized that "after all the high-speed networks are built, all the leading-edge switches and routers are installed, all the hardware and software are put in place, the advanced information infrastructure will need one more element to realize its potential: information."

The information companies were emphasizing that the new communication technologies offered potential new business risks to loss and piracy of their hard-earned investments even as they offered potential new business opportunities. They argued that copyright law be amended to ensure that incentives to invest in the creation of information products be preserved and incentives hinged on the electronic age meaning of key phrases in copyright law. What is the precise meaning of "reproduction in copies"? The meaning under copyright law had been clear when printed in books or catalogs by

4. "Wired for Interactivity," *IEEE Spectrum* (April 1996), p. 21.
5. Maney (1995, p. 10).
6. National Information Infrastructure Task Force, Working Group on Intellectal Property, Public Hearing, November 18, 1993, USPTO public file.

publishers, and ownership rights of producers were balanced against fair use rights of the public. The meaning evolved under copyright law when the copy machine empowered people to reproduce the copies themselves. But the new technologies empowered individuals to manipulate with ease the information then disseminate it at will nearly limitlessly. What is the precise meaning of "temporary storage of data" in the era of computer-based, Internet communication? Downloading, uploading, sending, diskette storing: when were rights of the producer violated? They were asking the questions, even if they were not certain themselves how the law ought to be amended.

Libraries, the traditional advocacy antagonists of the information companies, similarly were not certain of the precise language needed to reform copyright law, but a representative emphasized that the principle of public access mattered most: "The NII should preserve fair use and the library exemptions and allow for a variety of pricing structures." There were no submissions during the initial call for public comment on intellectual property and national information infrastructure on behalf of on-line service providers or network computing firms, which did not then realize that their interests were at stake. The wakeup call would soon arrive, however.

In July 1994 the working group released a draft green paper on copyright and the national information infrastructure for discussion and comment, and by August comments poured into the Patent and Trademark Office from the American Library Association, the Business Software Alliance, Dow Jones, IBM, the Recording Industry Association, Time Warner, and West Publishing, among other interests whose policy positions were well known to the working group. The green paper also got the attention of heretofore disengaged interests, including America Online, Bell Atlantic, the Computer and Communications Industry Association, CompuServe, and US West. US West stated that although the company was a creator of information and thus depended on copyright, it was also a distributor of content and thus criticized that "despite the balance indicated [by the premise of the green paper], the bulk of the analysis in the green paper is on the protection of content, rather than on users' expectations regarding access to and use of the content." The Computer and Communication Industry Association commented, "The Green Paper consistently takes the view that copyright law's primary task is to increase the ability of copyright owners to sue users and distributors of works on the NII and to increase the ability of owners to control the use of their works. . . . The impact of the proposed expansion of owners' rights, without a corresponding expansion of limitations on these rights, is far-reaching." The association specified some problems:

> Adoption of a new *digital transmission* right suggests a repeal of the public performance and display rights of copyright, to be replaced by an exclusive right to control *all* performances and displays of copyrighted works distributed in digital forms. . . . Any person that began to make multiple copies of a work for further distribution could be prevented under the exclusive reproduction right of the copyright holder. . . . Many NII service providers plan in the coming months to sell products, via digital transmission, that are just as tangible as any product at a store. If this change in the first sale doctrine is enacted, it will jeopardize a consumer's legitimate rights to further distribute a lawfully acquired and paid for copy of a downloaded movie, CD-ROM title, or software program. This change could eliminate an important new method of distribution that will almost certainly emerge on the NII.

The on-line service providers emphasized that liability was their concern, criticizing the court decision in *Playboy* (discussed later in this chapter) and praising the outcome in *Universal v. Sony* (see chapter 3): "The Working Group should examine whether or when service providers—as distinct from their subscribers and other information providers—should be held liable for copyright infringement." The liability standard, he said, should be "actual knowledge" plus "failure to stop." Bell Atlantic explained that

> telephone companies, as the deep pockets, will face continuous threats of litigation because they are simply the conduit for copyrighted material over which they may not, as a matter of law, exercise any control. . . . Contributory or vicarious liability should not apply to information conduits in the absence of willful conduct or knowledge of infringing activities. . . . Users will be able to interact freely with information by uploading, downloading, modifying and distributing information from one platform to another.

America Online criticized the implicit comparison that had guided the making of new policy:

> This strict liability standard has been imposed on print publishers of copyrighted materials, whether or not the publisher intended to in-

fringe or had knowledge of the infringement. However, print publishers have the opportunity to review what they publish in advance of publication. This is not the case for on-line service providers. . . . We are simply not publishers. We are interactive service providers and we need new ideas and new rules in our new medium.

Although the working group hosted public hearings in Chicago and Los Angeles in September 1994, the issues had all been spotlighted and the positions of the parties involved staked out in the responses to the green paper.

In September 1995 the working group released its final report, which came to be known as the Lehman report. It stated that the primary challenge for copyright law was digitalization combined with fiber optic cables, two technologies that would permit the creation of a "high-speed, interactive, broadband, digital communications system."[7] The system would be a national information infrastructure that would link computers, telephones, televisions, radios, and fax machines as never before, thereby possessing "tremendous potential to improve and enhance our lives." The report offered sweeping language regarding the nascent new era: "The NII can provide access to rich cultural resources around the world, transforming and expanding the scope and reach of the arts and the humanities. It will provide opportunities for the development of new markets for cultural products. It can broaden our cultural experiences through diversity of content, and increase our understanding of other societies." The NII would improve education and promote creativity in America. "Individuals and entities that heretofore have been predominantly consumers of works can now become authors and providers through the NII. It can put easier, more sophisticated communication and publishing tools in the hands of the public, increasing the ability to communicate with, and disseminate works of authorship to, others." Because the U.S economy was already the world's premier producer of information products, the NII would contribute to job creation and higher economic growth rates.

However, the report emphasized that the copyright institution would be needed to help make all this happen:

The full potential of the NII will not be realized if the education, information, and entertainment products protected by intellectual

7. Information Infrastructure Task Force (1995, pp. 8–9).

property laws are not protected effectively when disseminated via the NII. Creators and other owners of intellectual property rights will not be willing to put their interests at risk if appropriate systems—both in the U.S. and internationally—are not in place to permit them to set and enforce the terms and conditions under which their works are made available in the NII environment. Likewise, the public will not use the services available on the NII and generate the market necessary for its success unless a wide variety of works are available under equitable and reasonable terms and conditions, and the integrity of those works is assured. All the computers, telephones, fax machines, scanners, cameras, keyboards, televisions, monitors, printers, switches, routers, wires, cables, networks and satellites in the world will not create a successful NII, if there is not *content.* What will drive the NII is the content moving through it.[8]

The report cautioned that the fact that new technologies made unauthorized reproduction easy did not legitimize such behavior: "such a legal free-for-all would transform the NII into a veritable copyright Dodge City." The report noted that although some of the computer software companies did occasionally give their software away, it was not a dismissal of the importance of copyright but a marketing strategy to win such general acceptance in the marketplace that they could establish a standard that affords profit making in related, often copyrighted, products and services. The conventional copyright industries—films, music, and publishing—would continue their strategy of copyright vigilance.

Regarding copyright, the report stated that it was the means toward the goal of expression that added to public welfare: "The Constitution outlines both the goal that Congress may try to achieve (to promote the progress of science and useful arts) and the means by which [it] may accomplish it (by securing for limited times to authors and inventors the exclusive right to their respective writings and discoveries)."[9] It explained that copyright law requires "fixation" and that the courts had determined in the *Atari* case that protectable fixation took place in an interactive software setting such as a video game.[10] "The sufficiency of the fixation of works transmitted via the NII, however, where no copy or phonorecord has been made prior to the transmission, may not be so clear."

8. Information Infrastructure Task Force (1995, pp. 10–11).
9. Information Infrastructure Task Force (1995, p. 20).
10. Information Infrastructure Task Force (1995, p. 26).

A transmission, in and of itself, is not a fixation. While a transmission may result in a fixation, a work is not fixed by virtue of the transmission alone. Therefore, "live" transmissions via the NII will not meet the fixation requirement, and will be unprotected by the Copyright Act, unless the work is being fixed at the same time as it is being transmitted. The Copyright Act provides that a work "consisting of sounds, images, or both, that are being transmitted" meets the fixation requirement "if a fixation of the work is being made simultaneously with its transmission." To obtain protection under this "simultaneous fixation" provision, the simultaneous fixation of the transmitted work must itself qualify as a sufficient fixation. A simultaneous fixation (or any other fixation) meets the requirements if its embodiment in a copy or phonorecord is "sufficiently permanent or stable to permit it to be perceived, reproduced, or otherwise communicated for a period of more than transitory duration." Works are not sufficiently fixed if they are "purely evanescent or transient" in nature, "such as those projected briefly on a screen, shown electronically on a television or cathode ray tube, or captured momentarily on a television or cathode ray tube, or captured momentarily in the 'memory' of a computer."

The crucial sentence was the next one: "Electronic network transmissions from one computer to another, such as e-mail, may only reside on each computer in RAM (random access memory), but that has been found to be sufficient fixation." The report cited two cases in which the federal courts had determined that electronic transmission is fixation, meaning that a film or music or book being electronically transmitted is already fixed and hence subject to copyright protections.[11]

The report explained the doctrine of first sale, that the copyright holder has only the right to authorize or prohibit the initial distribution of lawful copy. It reviewed recent case law on the exclusive right to display in the context of the Internet.[12] A critical precedent is *Playboy Enterprises, Inc.* v. *Frena*, in which the question was whether the on-line bulletin board service provider was liable for copyright infringement when a subscriber put copyrighted pictures on the electronic bulletin board and they were downloaded

---

11. *Advanced Computer Services of Michigan Inc.* v. *MAI Systems Corp.*, 845 F.Supp. 356, 363 (F.D. Va. 1994); and *Triad Systems Corp.* v. *Souheastern Express Co.*, U.S. Dist. LEXIS 5390 at 15–19 (N.D. Cal. March 18, 1994), cited in Working Group on Intellectual Property Rights (1995, p. 28).

12. Information Infrastructure Task Force (1995, p. 68).

by another subscriber. The court determined that the bulletin board provider was indeed liable. Supporters of this conclusion often draw analogy to bookstores, which are liable for infringing works. But opponents raise doubts about the capability of the on-line service provider to monitor and police its marketplace the way a bookstore does.[13] They contend that the on-line bulletin board is more like a telephony service provider and ought to be treated the same way: telephone companies are neither expected to monitor communication traffic nor as a matter of privacy does society wish that they do so. The bookstore analogy, they argue, is better drawn to the World Wide Web than to interactive communication. The electronic commerce provider ought be expected to be able to monitor what is offered for sale through its medium and as a matter of business strategy has powerful incentives to ensure that it does.

The report also elucidated the fair use doctrine as stated in the 1976 Copyright Act, laying out its four key concepts for analysis: purpose and character of use, nature of the copyrighted use, amount and substantiality of portion used, and effect of the use on the potential market.[14] Citing Supreme Court case language (as in the cases involving the Ford memoirs and Sony Betamax), the report concluded that the courts have put the least emphasis on the portion used and the greatest emphasis on the economic harm of the use. Citing the *Playboy* and *Sega games* cases, it explained that the courts have determined that downloading of copyrighted materials is infringement not protected by the fair use doctrine.[15]

The report reviewed the information-technology aspects of the global information infrastructure, including encryption, digital authentication, e-cash systems, and the Electronic Copyright Management System administered by the Copyright Office, noting that the technological means were available to establish a market environment that would encourage continued development of the Internet in a way that preserved essential copyrights. The report concluded, with optimism encouraged by the evidence of the introduction of digital audio tape recorders and the passage of the Audio Home Recording Act in 1992, that "ensuring consumer access to and enjoyment of both copyrighted works and new technologies is an attainable goal."[16] With the passage of the audio CD act in 1992 Congress "incorpo-

13. Information Infrastructure Task Force (1995, p. 114).
14. Information Infrastructure Task Force (1995, pp. 74–75).
15. Information Infrastructure Task Force (1995, p. 81).
16. Information Infrastructure Task Force (1995, p. 11).

rated both technological and legal measures to protect the interests of both consumers and copyright holders."

Unlike some government reports that describe, summarize, and present an agenda of problems without stating a policy prescription, the Lehman report recommended actions to preserve copyrights in a digitally converged, interactive environment. Most significant, it recommended that "the Copyright Act be amended to expressly recognize that copies or phonorecords of works can be distributed to the public by transmission, and that such transmissions fall within the exclusive distribution right of the copyright owner." There is, it stated, "no reason to treat works that are distributed in copies to the public by means of transmission differently than works distributed in copies to the public by other, more conventional means. Copies distributed via transmission are as tangible as any distributed over the counter or through the mail."[17] It went on to recommend that the exclusive right to publication include distribution by digital transmission. The doctrine of first sale would change to reflect the digital reality that the first purchaser could upload the digitized document and share it with millions of people. Devices with a primary purpose of infringing on copyrights would be banned.

Digital interests—on-line and communication service providers, network software producers, information technology service providers, consumer electronics manufacturers—and librarians criticized the recommendations.[18] Precisely when is a copyrighted work "fixed" in a tangible medium? Is browsing on the World Wide Web an act of copyright infringement? What is the liability of the on-line provider? Is the on-line provider liable as a contributor to infringement if a person illegally downloads a copyrighted work? What is the liability of the consumer electronics manufacturer of personal computers? Were they contributors to infringement in the way that VCR manufacturers were once accused of being? Precisely how would infringing devices be defined? Were PCs to be banned? Would librarians be unable to disseminate information without becoming in effect bookstores?

An influential commentary in *Wired* magazine asserted that the answers to these questions were already known. "Browsing through a borrowed book, lending a magazine to a friend, copying a news article for your files—all seem innocuous enough. But the Clinton administration plans to

---

17. Information Infrastructure Task Force (1995, pp. 213, 216).
18. Information Technology Association of America (1995).

make such activities illegal for works distributed via digital networks."[19] The administration's motivation to turn the NII into a "publisher-dominated toll road" was, the author explained, campaign contributions: "The administration wants to please the copyright industry, especially members of the Hollywood community, who are vital to the president's reelection bid." Recalling Hollywood's setback in the VCR case, she commented, "Ever since they began to realize that digital technologies could 'free' information dissemination, the established copyright industry has been shaking in its boots."

Participants, observers, and prophets, although not engaged in producing the Lehman report, raised the question: Is intellectual property, and especially copyright, fundamentally challenged in the new electronic, interactive communication era? "Legislators," explained one analyst offering a widely held view, "have not understood what distinguishes this medium from newspapers and television networks. It's more interactive. It's more participatory." These observers contend that "content on line is something that is continuous, changing, and evolving."[20] They point out that papers, magazines, and books can be transported free: "information wants to be free." Esther Dyson, perhaps the best-known and most influential commentator, wrote, "The future world of electronic content and commerce . . . is . . . not the world most intellectual property owners have been planning for, contracting for, securing rights for."[21] She has presented a distinctly different future for content in an interactive era:

> The idea of copyright will still be important because it is the law and it is moral. Second, a content producer will still want to control the integrity of the work. Even if I get royalties, I want to make sure that my work isn't dumbed down and sold under someone else's name. . . . All I'm saying is that you need to figure out how to be paid for producing content because the business models are going to change. They'll get money for performances, readings, for going on-line and interacting with their audiences. The free copies of content are going to be what you use to establish your fame. Then you go out and milk it. . . . Content will be sponsored somewhat in the way network television programming is today. . . . Like everyone else, I get lots of free information on the Net. . . . Why should I pay to get

19. Samuelson (1996, p. 135).
20. Denise Caruso and David Bunnell quoted in Brockman (1996, pp. 66, 32).
21. Esther Dyson quoted in Brockman (1996, p. xxviii).

more when I have too much already? . . . Future scenarios on this are obvious. A consultant will write a book, hand it out for free and then charge higher fees for his services.[22]

Another information technologist put it bluntly: "Intellectual Property is an oxymoron."[23] *Wired* magazine, the unofficial journal of the interactive community and the institution perhaps most responsible for establishing a distinctive "cyber culture," consistently argues that the "copyright cartel" aims to grab all it can get and will do all it can to prevent the revolution of the interactive, universally wired world. "The one thing about intellectual property that will not change is the complete chaos of intellectual property laws."[24]

Producers of movies, music, books, databases, and computer software, who are all too well aware that their expression products can be transported for free in the interactive era, have replied to the dismissals of cyber culture's defenders that expression of the information is not created free; indeed, creation is an expensive process. And Esther Dyson's vision indicates no understanding of the idea-expression dichotomy institutionalized in the copyright. The Internet's historic development in government and university-subsidized communication among researchers has provided false premises for a future in which interactivity converges with the mainstream, commercial world where it takes profits to pay for the investments in new expression. But, like the information technologists, the media interests see interactivity as the biggest communication revolution since telephony and radio and believe that it introduces great promise for product and service distribution, even if they are not sure exactly how it should be used or what all the technological capabilities are.

Digital Distribution and Copyright Diplomacy

Over a five-year period leading up to the December 1996 diplomatic conference WIPO sponsored international conferences, attended by experts in communication technology and intellectual property law, in Palo Alto, California, in March 1991; Cambridge, Massachusetts, in April 1993; Paris in June 1994; Mexico City in May 1995; and Naples in October 1995. The

22. Esther Dyson quoted in Dreifus (1996, p. 18).
23. John Perry Barlow quoted in Brockman (1996, p. 12).
24. Paul Saffo quoted in Brockman (1996, p. 262).

1993 Harvard conference began by providing context. An editor at *Digital Media* outlined for the 300 participants the special characteristics of digital information and expression:

—intangible until processed and projected through a microprocessor-controlled device;

—copied indefinitely with no loss in quality;

—information malleable; can be combined, altered, mixed, manipulated with relative ease;

—infinite life, unlike old movie film and 78 rpm recordings, which decay.[25]

Two American copyright attorneys reminded the participants that governments have a long, embarrassing history of tardy response to technological innovations in expression media.[26] They recalled that the U.S. Supreme Court in 1908 denied copyright protection to the paper music rolls of player pianos because they were not tangible copies in the minds of the justices, since *tangible* had always meant intelligible to a human mind and music rolls could not be deciphered by the eye. Congress did not officially make the paradigm shift regarding tangibleness and extend copyright protection to sound recordings for another sixty years, after three generations of opposition by broadcasters and owners of traditional copyrighted works.[27]

Conference presentations indicated widespread recognition that the new technologies would fundamentally change businesses and that policy reform would shape that change in some important ways. Transnational interest groups disagreed with one another about basic policy preferences: producers were concerned about ownership rights and the prevention of piracy; users were concerned about access. Nevertheless, "producers" often include both actual creators, such as authors, musical artists, and film directors, and distributors, such as publishers, music producers, and movie studios, and their interests and rights are not the same.

Representatives of the music industry pointed out that the music business was truly global in part because it had already successfully embraced digital technology: "Without question, compact disc wins the award for best audio technology not invented by Thomas Edison."[28] But the industry

25. David Baron in World Intellectual Property Organization (1993b, p. 31).
26. Morton Goldberg and Jesse Feder in World Intellectual Property Organization (1993b, p. 43).
27. Bruce York and Arthur Levine in World Intellectual Property Organization (1993b, p. 131).
28. Bruce York and Arthur Levine in World Intellectual Property Organization (1993b, p. 133).

was poised to undergo revolutionary change in its distribution methods: "Everything capable of being reduced to zeros and ones, whether literary text, audio or audio-visual signals, or other information, can be delivered to the home without manufacturing costs or environmental waste. . . . Industries that have produced and manufactured cultural goods will become service rather than goods providers." Electronic delivery will one day replace existing retail marketing systems for phonograms but only if appropriate technical and legal means of antipiracy are established.[29]

A representative of the Hungarian author's society posited that decoding and decrypting of digitized works ought be banned. A copyright scholar from Germany's Max Planck Institute commented that digitization was blurring traditional product distinctions among computer programs, databases, and audio-visual works. In the process it was blurring traditional legal distinctions between authorship and adaptation.[30] Recalling the history of the author's rights institution in France and Germany, he explained that personality was receding because of digitization and networking, which was affording many human and computer contributions to a finished expression product, and speculated that economic rights were becoming evermore central.[31]

A Cambridge University copyright scholar explained that new agreements amending the Berne Convention would need to accomodate the divergences that had developed between the British imperial copyright institution and the American institution.[32] The imperial copyright system was institutionalized in 1911 throughout fifty-one territories, sixteen colonies, South Africa, and Israel as well as in England, Scotland, Wales, and Ireland. An important difference is the definition of *work,* which is categorized and discrete (film, music, literary) in the imperial tradition but toward which the United States takes a more holistic approach. Multimedia products would need carefully drafted treaty language.

A representative from the French film industry commented that producers were very concerned about the physical loss of control of their film works due to digitization and networking and that in intellectual property

29. Jason Berman and Nicholas Garnett in World Intellectual Property Organization (1993b, pp. 93, 107–10).
30. Peter Gyertyanfy and Thomas Dreier in World Intellectual Property Organization (1993b, pp. 163, 197).
31. Thomas Dreier in World Intellectual Property Organization (1994b, pp. 53–57).
32. William Cornish in World Intellectual Property Organization (1994b, pp. 82–85).

law the principle of remuneration for private copying must secure their substantial investments.[33] A representative of the International Federation of the Phonographic Industry, noting that his industry saw itself as being in the networking phase of the digital revolution, recommended a legal and technical strategy for dealing with digital challenges: copyright reform and information management systems composed of SID codes and encryption standards.[34] Publishing in France, explained a French attorney, typically assigns through contract total control over distribution of a literary work under the rationale that the "publisher takes the risk of publishing the work, so . . . he should be able to offset the initial investment with other forms of exploitation, made possible by the existence of that initial risk."[35] But French courts have determined that such modifications to literary works as the addition of a preface and extensive cuts in the text are breaches of the author's rights. How should the institutions evolve regarding electronic rights? Performance in France, explained a French actor, typically rewards a performer by remuneration through collective societies that were institutionalized during the old era of physical performance. Given digitized and distributed performances, how ought the system be reinstitutionalized?[36]

A Finnish copyright authority explained that the copy machine had introduced a tremendous technological challenge in scientific, technical, and medical journal publishing. The challenge assumed greater economic consequence in the 1980s as libraries faced tighter budgets but growing demand for articles in science, engineering, and medicine.[37] Interlibrary loan proliferated to the consternation of the main journal publishers Reed Elsevier and Springer-Verlag, so a solution was found through levies on copying equipment, paybacks to copyright associations, increased journal prices, less expensive distribution through CD-ROM, and acceptance of interlibrary loan. The principles could be applied to electronic distribution because "there is rather general agreement that the displaying or viewing of protected material on a screen ought to be subject to copyright. The protection can be constituted . . . by considering a display to be a copy and the act consequently subject to the right of reproduction."

The conflict between U.S copyright's emphasis on the economic rights of the risk-taking producer or distributor and Europe's emphasis on the

33. Pascal Rogard in World Intellectual Property Organization (1994b, pp. 91–94).
34. Nicholas Garnett in World Intellectual Property Organization (1994b, pp. 100–12).
35. Hubert Tilliet in World Intellectual Property Organization (1994b, pp. 133–35).
36. Francois Parrot in World Intellectual Property Organization (1994b, p. 161).
37. Tarja Koskinen in World Intellectual Property Organization (1994b, pp. 180–87).

expressive rights of the author or director was proclaimed by a Belgian screenwriter: "it is . . . ridiculous to claim that the creator of *Citizen Kane* was RKO, Inc., in 1943, and the Turner Corporation in 1994."[38] (Turner, the new owner of a library of old films, had colorized some classics, to the consternation of film buffs.) "Europe," he concluded, "is the only place in the world where men have been able to combine economic progress with social and cultural progress," an enviable position it owes to its moral rights institution. The Turner colorization brightly contrasted the differences between laws in the United States and Europe: moral rights of creators in Europe would have made Turner's action illegal despite the corporation's ownership of copyrights. A Stanford law professor offered the counterpoint: "Every serious creator wants to communicate his work to as large an audience as his vision can command. Copyright and author's right create the shelter of privacy that authors need, and give publishers and other risk-taking intermediaries the economic protection they need, to make this hoped-for communication between author and audience a reality."[39] The creator loses control as a trade-off to wider and more remunerative distribution.

A professor from Belgium recounted the steps the European Commission had taken to reform the law related to literary and artistic works.[40] The Maastricht Treaty inserts the word *culture* into the Treaty of Rome, thereby definitively inserting moral rights into the EU literary and artistic rights agenda. Three green papers in the 1980s presented a policy strategy for a cable and satellite television common market, discussed the growing piracy problem, and emphasized artistic and moral rights and the role of expression in the cultures of Europe. A 1990 report, "Broadcasting and Copyright in the Internal Market," led to the circulation of a proposed directive, while a 1991 "Follow-Up to the Green Paper" detailed a work program for European policy harmonization. A directive was issued in 1992 to harmonize law regarding databases, including special provisions from the Scandinavians to prevent poaching of data from databases in addition to regular copyrights covering original arrangement of databases. The work was summarized in the 1993 directive, "Coordination of Certain Rules Concerning Copyright and Rights Related to Copyright Applicable to Satellite Broadcasting and Cable Retransmission."

38. Joao Correa in World Intellectual Property Organization (1994b, p. 197).
39. Paul Goldstein in World Intellectual Property Organization (1994b, p. 261).
40. Frank Gotzen in World Intellectual Property Organization (1994b, pp. 239–56).

Science, technology, and medical librarians are increasingly "access providers" not "archivists": "Just in time rather than just in case."[41] A representative of the French Ministry of National Education and Culture noted that, employing digital compression technologies invented by Thomson, the ministry was scanning and digitizing art and literary works and that digital media would permit easier use by millions of people.[42] The assistant director of WIPO for copyright norm creation attempted to define controversies and summarize the issues. First, multimedia products were clearly already covered by the Berne Convention. Second, "the borderlines among the right of reproduction, the right of distribution, and the right of communication to the public are getting ever more blurred" and may simply be stated in fact if not in law as "digital delivery." Finally, "technical means, such as copy-protection and copy-management systems, smart cards, digital subcodes, identification numbers and the like, may be more frequently applied."[43] Similarly, at the Mexico City conference, he said,

"Multimedia" is an expression which needs definition if we deal with it; as a category of works it may be "multi" but not "media," "digital superhighways" will be digital but they will not function as highways; the "information society" and the "Global Information Infrastructure" may exist but, from the viewpoint of copyright, what is important is not the "infrastructure" and what is truly involved is not just "information"; "cyberspace" is a catchy expression, but it would be misleading to believe that works are just floating in it like in space.[44]

Treaty language that could find broad support among Berne Convention members would confer the right of distribution on digital transmissions; treaty language that would likely have difficulty getting broad support would confer the right to authorize digital transmissions. He sensed there was consensus that "the introduction and application of . . . technical means [copy protection, copy management devices, encryption, and indentification] should preferably be left to the interested rights owners." However, "efficient sanctions may have to be prescribed against those who manufacture, import or distribute unauthorized devices the only or main purpose of

41. Jon Baumgarten in World Intellectual Property Organization (1993b, p. 65).
42. Andre Lange in World Intellectual Property Organization (1993b, pp. 227–29).
43. Mihaly Ficsor in World Intellectual Property Organization (1994b, pp. 209–19).
44. Mihaly Ficsor in World Intellectual Property Organization (1995a, pp. 369, 378).

which is to defeat or circumvent copy-protection, copy-management or encryption systems. . . ."

At the Mexico City conference in May 1995 the commissioner of the U.S. Patent and Trademark Office called for digital transmission to be defined as an exclusive right of distribution. He also asked for "provisions to prohibit decoders and anticopy prevention devices and services," pointed out that the digital audio issue had been resolved to include royalties on blank recording media and recorders, and stated that some further consideration of "providing for a *sui generis* unfair extraction right to supplement copyright protection may prove to be useful."[45] The European Commission representative stated that the EU Action Program announced in 1994 mirrored the U.S. position: digital transmission should be a reproduction right, databases are copyrightable "by reason of selection or arrangement" of data, and a fifteen-year sui generis right was provided against "unauthorized extraction and reutilization of the entire or a substantial part of the database."[46] The Japanese representative stated that his government's "Multimedia Report" rejected the view that copyrights should be weakened to spur the development of multimedia expression products.[47] The Mexico City conference indicated that there was considerable consensus among government representatives regarding the essentials of a new copyright treaty but that national institutional differences in concepts and language still posed a challenge to drafting one.

At the October 1995 Naples conference, the WIPO assistant director general captured the essence of the issues:

Digital transmissions are like a kind of psychological test for those who deal with copyright. If a copyright Sigmund Freud asks you to lie down on his divan and speak about digital transmissions, to tell him what you think digital transmission is, what kinds of rights may be involved, he will be able to tell you who you are, from which country you are, what your profession is, what your interests are, and what problems you have. If you say: "I think that digital transmission is just distribution of copies and phonorecords," the copyright Sigmund Freud will be able to tell you that you are probably a producer of phonograms and probably from the United States of America. If you say you consider that digital transmission is just communication to

45. Bruce Lehman in World Intellectual Property Organization (1995a, pp. 79–80).
46. Paul Vandoren in World Intellectual Property Organization (1995a, pp. 85–100).
47. Kaoru Okamoto in World Intellectual Property Organization (1995a, pp. 105–09).

the public—communication to the public even if the transmission is not in real time—he will be able to tell you that you are probably a representative of a performing rights society of authors. If you say that digital transmission is rental, he will be able to tell you that you have just read the Green Paper of the European Commission and you are under its influence.[48]

The Lehman report, he noted, had offered "a very innovative solution" to the problem of defining reproduction: "The economic impact of such 'distribution by transmission' is really the same as that of distribution of tangible copies." But "at the international level, this solution may not be acceptable for many countries. . . . It cannot be the only approach because, in the national laws of many countries, the notion of distribution is closely linked to the distribution of tangible copies." He concluded that, nevertheless, most agree that such a right should be codified, thereby implying that language should be carefully drafted to achieve the spirit if not the text.

The Committee of Experts, the representatives of the national governments that were party to the Berne Convention, met in May 1996 in Geneva to move toward consensus so that treaties could be concluded by the end of the year. Observers who were not members of the committee included representatives from international governmental organizations such as the United Nations Educational, Scientific, and Cultural Organization (UNESCO) and the International Labor Organization (ILO) and such nongovernmental organizations as the American Bar Association, Association of Commercial Television in Europe, Business Software Alliance, Computer and Communications Industry Association, Ibero–Latin American Federation of Performers, Information Industry Association, International Federation of the Phonographic Industry, Japan Electronic Industry Development Association, National Association of Broadcasters, and Software Publishers Association. Representatives of the on-line service providers did not attend.[49] They apparently did not yet realize that their interests were at stake. By the end of the meeting, most governments expressed their optimism that treaties addressing copyright and performers' rights would be concluded in December. Many governments held the view that a database

---

48. Mihaly Ficsor in World Intellectual Property Organization (1995, p. 135).

49. "Committee of Experts on a Possible Instrument for the Protection of the Rights Performers and Producers of Phonograms, Sixth Session," and "Committee of Experts on a Possible Protocol to the Berne Convention, Seventh Session," May 22–23, 1996, Geneva: World Intellectual Property Organization.

agreement would be premature, and a December treaty was unlikely despite the advocacy of the USPTO and European Commission.

In December 1996 a three-week-long diplomatic conference resulted in two international agreements, the WIPO Copyright Treaty and the WIPO Performances and Phonograms Treaty. The Copyright Treaty amends the Berne Convention; the Performances and Phonograms Treaty amends the International Convention for the Protection of Performers, Producers of Phonograms and Broadcasting Organizations (the so-called Rome Convention).[50] Adopted by the state representatives on December 20, the treaties will not come into force as a matter of international law until thirty governments have formally acceded to them, which by agreement must occur by December 31, 1997.

The preamble to the copyright agreement states that the contracting parties desire to "develop and maintain the protection of the rights of authors in their literary and artistic works" because they recognize the "profound impact of the development and convergence of information and communication technologies on the creation and use of literary and artistic works." It goes on to recognize the "need to maintain a balance between the rights of authors and the larger public interest, particularly education, research and access to information, as reflected in the Berne Convention."[51]

Article 2 reinforces continuity with the traditional scope of the copyright institution that "copyright protection extends to expressions and not to ideas, procedures, methods of operation or mathematical concepts as such." Articles 4 and 5, however, extend Berne Convention protections to computer programs and databases. On databases, article 5 states that the "protection does not extend to the data or the material itself," but databases are protectable by "reason of the selection or arrangement of their contents," which constitutes "intellectual creations." Articles 6, 7, and 8 extend to authors exclusive rights regarding distribution, rental, and communication to the public.

The language of article 12 is of considerable consequence both for what is said and for what is not. The "Obligations concerning Rights Management Information" states that contracting parties

50. "WIPO Performances and Phonograms Treaty," CRNR/DC/96, Geneva: World Intellectual Property Organization.

51. "WIPO Copyright Treaty," CRNR/DC/94, Geneva: World Intellectual Property Organization. http://www.wipo.int/eng/diplconf/distrib/94dc.htm

shall provide adequate and effective legal remedies against any person knowingly performing any of the following acts knowing, or with respect to civil remedies having reasonable grounds to know, that it will induce, enable, facilitate or conceal an infringement of any right covered by this Treaty or the Berne Convention: (1) to remove or alter any electronic rights management information without authority; (2) to distribute, import for distribution, broadcast or communicate to the public, without authority, works or copies of works knowing that electronic rights management information has been removed or altered without authority.

Electronic rights management information, the article states,

means information which identifies the work, the author of the work, the owner of any right in the work, or information about the terms and conditions of use of the work, and any numbers or codes that represent such information, when any of these items of information is attached to a copy of a work or appears in connection with the communication of a work to the public.

The treaty does not ban digital audio or video machines, Internet connection devices, or any other consumer electronics hardware that may now or might in the future be used to commit piracy. In diplomacy that mirrored the VCR court battle of the 1980s in the United States, the U.S. government delegation urged language that would ban devices having a substantial purpose to infringe, but the Japanese and Asian governments opposed.[52] Furthermore, the treaty does not define transitory copies of copyrighted works in computer memory as "copyright-significant acts," which was proposed by the U.S. government delegation but opposed by the U.S. communication, computer, library, and scientific interests that were well represented in Geneva during the negotiations.[53] These language differences will have a significant effect on the future development of electronic communication and electronic commerce. The proposed language meant that a copyrighted work would have to have been paid for using e-cash systems at the time of calling up a copyrighted expression on-line; otherwise infringement would have occurred. The adopted language means that identification codes and encryption will be used to permit access on line to

---

52. Browning (1997, p.186).
53. Samuelson (1997, p. 64).

copyrighted works but will prevent copying of expressions; e-cash systems will be designed to demand payment for downloading or other use of the information.

The preamble to the Performances and Phonograms Treaty states that the contracting parties desire to "develop and maintain the protection of the rights of performers and producers of phonograms" because they recognize the "profound impact of the development and convergence of information and communication technologies on the production and use of performances and phonograms." Yet the contracting parties also recognize the "need to maintain a balance between the rights of performers and producers of phonograms and the larger public interest, particularly education, research and access to information."

After defining *performers, phonogram, fixation, producer of a phonogram*, and *publication*, article 2 defines *broadcasting* as the "transmission by wireless means for public reception of sounds or of images and sounds or of the representations thereof" and includes transmission by satellite and transmission of encrypted signals as broadcasts. It defines *communication to the public* as the "transmission to the public by any medium, otherwise than by broadcasting, of sounds of a performance or the sounds or the representations of sounds fixed in a phonogram." This language explicitly puts digital transmission within the meaning of the rights of performers as it relates to broadcasting and phonogram production. Article 4 provides that each contracting party shall provide national treatment to the nationals of other contracting parties.

Article 5 provides that performers have moral rights independent of economic rights "even after the transfer of those rights" as regards "live aural performances or performances fixed in phonograms," including the "right to claim to be identified as the performer of his performances" and to "object to any distortion, mutilation or other modification of his performances that would be prejudicial to his reputation." It is noteworthy that the second right is qualified through the language: "object" rather than stronger language such as "prevent any distortion." Article 6 provides that performers "enjoy the exclusive right of authorizing, as regards their performances: (1) the broadcasting and communication to the public of their unfixed performances except where the performance is already a broadcast performance; and (2) the fixation of their unfixed performances." Article 7 provides performers with the exclusive right to authorize reproduction of their performances; article 8 provides exclusive right of distribution to performers; and article 9 provides exclusive rental rights to performers.

Producers of phonograms, article 11 states, enjoy the "exclusive right of authorizing the direct or indirect reproduction of their phonograms." Article 12 states that they enjoy "exclusive right of authorizing the making available to the public of the original and copies of their phonograms through sale or other transfer of ownership," but contracting parties may limit this right to first sales. Article 13 provides that producers enjoy rights regarding commercial rental of the original and copies of their phonograms (which means that they can prevent rentals if they wish). Article 13 also provides a grandfather clause: provided that there is "equitable remuneration" for producers and that commercial rental is "not giving rise to the material impairment of the exclusive rights of reproduction," existing phonogram rental systems may be maintained. Article 14 provides broad language aimed at dealing with distribution through such communication means at the Internet: "Producers of phonograms shall enjoy the exclusive right of authorizing the making available to the public of their phonograms, by wire or wireless means, in such a way that members of the public may access them from a place and at a time individually chosen by them." Thus, the final text leaves the fixation status of "ephemeral" copies and the liability issues to be decided within national legal jurisdictions or in some subsequent international copyright agreement. The outcome was as predicted more than a year before at the Naples conference by the assistant director general of the WIPO Secretariat.

The first actions to test the U.S. law of copyright-product distribution and the Internet (but actions that will influence the evolution of the international treaty law) were filed in June 1997 by eight major music producers (A&M, Capitol, Island, Maverick, MCA, PolyGram, Sony, and Warner).[54] They charged that three nonlicensed Internet sites had each copied one hundred or more full-length sound recordings to a computer server connected to the Internet and made them illegally available to consumers. "A fledgling industry in pirated copies of sound recordings thus is emerging on the Internet." They cited their annual worldwide losses from conventional piracy and stated the urgency of the situation: "With the explosive growth of the Internet, these figures may be dwarfed by on-line piracy unless

---

54. *A&M Records et al. v. Internet Site Known as Fresh Kutz,* U.S. District Court, Southern District of California, June 1997; *MCA Records et al. v. Internet Site Known as FTP://PARSOFT.COM/MP3s/,* U.S. District Court, Northern District of Texas, June 1997; and *Sony Music Entertainment Inc. v. Internet Site Known as FTP://208.197.0.28/,* U.S. District Court, Southern District of New York, June 1997.

privacy is deterred by the courts, applying well-established principles of copyright law to infringing on-line conduct." The companies seek an injunction and damages to deter on-line piracy.

The 1996 Geneva conference did not provide databases with the protocol to the Berne Convention that was especially desired by the delegations of the European Union and the United States: precise language for a protocol acceptable to all members could not be found. Both the EU and U.S. delegations contended that the copyright institution offered insufficient incentives and that special intellectual property protection was needed. Neither the copyright law in the United States nor in the EU member states went beyond offering protection for the "selection and arrangement" of information, thus leaving the information itself unprotected. (In 1992 the U.S. Supreme Court had ruled in *Feist Publications* v. *Rural Telephone Service* that copyright protected "original" works but not works produced by the "sweat of the brow"—thus the white pages of a telephone directory could not be copyrighted unless something more creative than mere alphabetic listing was offered.)[55] Springer-Verlag, Reed Elsevier, and others pursued their goal with policymakers in Brussels; in Washington the lobbyist was the Information Industry Association (although some of its members, such as Dun & Bradstreet, opposed special protections). All the interested parties were using new technologies to gather, organize, and make available information for commercial and financial use. The Information Industry Association pointed out that database software was lowering the barriers for entry into the information business and thus increasing the number of stakeholders in strong protections for their investment in gathering and organizing information. The association advocated sui generis protection to be institutionalized by congressional statute and by U.S. executive negotiation within the WIPO Berne Convention Diplomatic Conference.[56]

Opponents of sui generis database protection contend that lower court decisions emphasize that databases showing originality receive copyright protection and that the level of originality need not be high. A statement submitted on behalf of the Association of Research Libraries, American Library Association, American Association of Law Libraries, Medical Library Association, and Special Libraries Association opposed such protection because "the progress of knowledge is furthered by the reuse of

55. Gorman (1992).
56. Information Industry Association (1995).

information in other works."[57] They argued that the proposed special protection tilted too far toward protecting the economic interests of database creators and impeding access to information. The library associations were discredited in this contention, however, because their loose practices with respect to photocopying and interlibrary loan of science and technology research articles had raised the complaints of the same U.S. and European publishers that were urging that the substance of databases be protected.

Politically more persuasive statements consistent with the library associations' position came from the Biotechnology Industry Organization, On-Line Banking Association, and Dun & Bradstreet.[58] The biotechnology companies were busily digitizing human genome research, so-called bioinformatics, and these databases possessed enormous commercial potential. Yet biotech interests argued that amending the Berne convention to strengthen their copyrights was premature. The on-line bankers also contended that the special database protection was premature. Dunn and Bradstreet summarized the position of all three by emphasizing that creators of databases were also users of information gathered by others; that institutional means in addition to copyright, such as licensing and contract, were available for database protection; that no examples of commercially important database piracy had yet been put forward; and that many of the European states had not then implemented—and likely would not implement—the commission directive regarding special protection of databases (a harmonization rationale offered by U.S. supporters). It concluded that there was no reason for haste to achieve a December 1996 agreement. But the U.S. delegation led by the Patent and Trademark Office determined that the limitations of database copyright and the European directive to harmonize EU laws in favor of special protection for databases recommended that the U.S. position at the WIPO diplomatic conference support special protection through an amendment to the Berne convention.

The European Union had submitted a draft text calling for new special intellectual property protection for databases in November 1995, then a revised text in January 1996. The U.S. government submitted its own draft protocol language in May 1996. The drafts agreed that "the legal protection set forth in this [instrument] concerns databases in any form" and that

57. Statement of Prudence Adler, Association of Research Libraries, Washington, November 1996.

58. Statements of Biotechnology Industry Organization, On-Line Banking Association, and Dun & Bradstreet, Washington, November 1996.

"Contracting Parties shall protect substantial investments in databases."[59] However, there were some significant differences. The United States proposed that "contracting parties shall protect all databases that represent a substantial investment in the collection, assembly, verification, organization, or presentation of the database contents, whether or not such database is made commercially available to . . . the public." The European Union proposed leaner language: "such protection shall apply irrespective of the eligibility of the contents of the database for protection by copyright." The United States proposed a twenty-five-year term for the protection; the European Union a fifteen-year term. Because many governments at the conference opposed both proposals as premature and insufficiently considered, the Berne convention members agreed to continue negotiations during 1997.

Global Electronic Commerce and Internet Domain Name Institutionalization

The explosive growth of the Internet and especially its commercialization as the World Wide Web created a need for reform of the registration system for Internet domain names, the routing addresses of communications, for example, "georgetown.edu."[60] Top-level domain (TLD) names, unlike individual addresses, exist as categories of addresses such as ".com" and ".gov," as well as an address for each country. The first problem confronted by the existing registration system is the intersection of domain names with trademarks. Under trademark law the same name can be registered as a trademark by different owners—ones in different industry sectors or different countries—but an Internet domain name must be unique, thus creating the potential for disputes between entities that desire the same name. In addition, the need for unique names has been growing rapidly, but ".com" is the only international top-level name available to companies and individuals. A third problem is the institutionalization of domain name registration. A single registration authority in the United States—Network

---

59. "Committee on Experts on a Possible Protocol to the Berne Convention: Proposal Submitted by the European Community and Its Member States," BCP/CE/VI/13, Geneva: World Intellectual Property Organization, January 31, 1996; and "Committee on Experts on a Possible Protocol to the Berne Convention: Proposal of the United States of America on *Sui Generis* Protection of Databases," BCP/CE/VII/2, Geneva: World Intellectual Property Organization, May 20, 1996.

60. World Intellectual Property Organization (1995c).

Solutions Inc. in Herndon, Virginia—assigns domain names for a $100 fee. This system, established by the National Science Foundation when the Internet was a communication system used by researchers and academics, is scheduled to end in 1998 when the NSF–Network Solutions contract expires. Related to the first problem is that Network Solutions has in the past been sued over disputes regarding name registrations.

To reinstitutionalize domain name registration, the nongovernmental Internet Society was established in January 1992. The society is an eleven-member international ad hoc committee composed of one representative from the World Intellectual Property Organization, one from the International Telecommunications Union, one from the National Science Foundation, three attorneys in private practice, a Japanese academic, and four representatives from the Internet community.[61] The committee established a process to discuss, seek international public comment, recommend, and institutionalize a reformed domain name system by summer 1997. The goals for a new system were that it would

—entitle every owner of a valid trademark registration to a unique domain name that contains the trademark without alteration;

—allow registration of domain names corresponding to identical trademarks by different owners of that trademark (for example, in different goods and services);

—allow the most efficient registration procedures possible;

—stop rampant piracy without resorting to extensive multiple litigation;

—avoid the need for policing all other TLDs;

—avoid legal liability of registries in the context of trademark domain name disputes; and

—take into consideration the needs of noncommercial domain name owners.

In February 1997, after receiving some 4,000 comments from interested parties, the committee circulated a draft plan for public comment.[62] New generic top-level domain names will be established if the proposal is adopted. These include

.firm for businesses or firms;

.store for businesses offering goods to purchase;

.web for entities emphasizing activities relating to the World Wide Web;

.arts for entities emphasizing cultural and entertainment activities;

---

61. World Intellectual Property Organization (1997).
62. http://www.isoc.org/infosvc/forum/970220forum.txt.

.*rec* for entities emphasizing recreation and entertainment;
.*info* for entities providing information services; and
.*nom* for individuals desiring personal nomenclature.
The committee recommended national top-level domain names be established to correspond with the International Standard Organization 3166 country code, so that, for example, Switzerland would use .*ch* nomenclature, Japan would use .*jp,* and the United States would use .*us.*

The committee proposed that in place of the single registration firm in Virginia, twenty-eight firms be established, four competing in each of seven world regions. It also recommended that an independent, nonprofit Council of Registrars (CORE) be established in Geneva under the nonprofit organization laws of Switzerland to oversee the registration system. The proposal establishes criteria for selecting registration firms. They must be located in countries that are either members of the Paris Convention for the Protection of Industrial Property or the World Trade Organization, present a business or marketing plan, comply with standard accounting practices, and have liability insurance, adequate capitalization, experienced staff, customer service measures, reliable on-line access capabilities, robust backup procedures, disaster recovery plans, and management expertise. The registrars selected would sign a Memorandum of Understanding regarding operation of registration sites and pay fees to CORE. They would be subject to CORE oversight, and the entire system would be subject to the oversight of the Top-Level Domain Name Policy Oversight Committee, a group with representation in staggered terms from the International Telecommunications Union, International Organization for Standards, World Intellectual Property Organization, and several nongovernmental Internet and trademark organizations. Disputes regarding domain names would be settled through mediation offered by the Arbitration and Mediation Center of the World Intellectual Property Organization.

The proposals were not adopted in 1997 because the Ad Hoc Committee's activity was slowed when its legitimacy and process were questioned.[63] Critics, including Network Solutions, charged that a nongovernmental organization, not a national government, had put reforming the system on the international agenda and established the committee charged with bringing it about (and bringing the Network Solutions monopoly to an end). The committee included limited official government representation (a

63. Quick (1997).

representative from the National Science Foundation), and the representatives of international governmental organizations were said to be participating in personal, not official, capacities. The committee had also established a timetable that allowed only a month for the public to comment on matters crucial to the future of global electronic communication and commerce.

But neither the United States nor any other government had expressed interest in active involvement. The Internet Society had presciently identified a nascent international policy problem and established a committee with a representatives from the creator of the Internet (the NSF), international public servants (WIPO and International Telecommunication Union, and Internet interests and Internet-specialist attorneys. It had adopted a transparent process, offered opportunity for public comment, and designed a system that would internationalize name registration, create more differentiation in names, and provide dispute settlement provisions—and it had done so on a timetable that would have put everything in place in time for the expiration of the NSF–Network Solutions contract. In late 1997 it appears that the general outline of the proposal from the committee, renamed the Interim Policy Oversight Committee, will ultimately be adopted, although there will probably be more government representation in decisionmaking.

The attempted reform of domain name registration illustrates the challenges posed by the Internet. Although the U.S. government established the medium, it has grown rapidly without government aid. Users are finding themselves in conflict and governments are struggling to institutionalize new structures, processes, rules, and dispute-settlement procedures, all in an era when government is discredited by many citizens (especially members of the "Net culture") as the chief social and economic problem. International governmental organizations have become important brokers in the attempt to achieve international cooperation.

With its National Information Infrastructure initiative, U.S. executive branch officials have sponsored public hearings and working groups to help devise new policy in this difficult milieu. This activity has generated acrimony and disagreement among copyright interests concerned about piracy, networking computing and communication interests concerned about electronic commerce, and communication services and hardware makers concerned about liability. In the 1990s an all-electronic era began to dawn in which digitized, networked, integrated communication media with large flat panel screens was envisioned as displaying encrypted news and entertainment, video mail, and myriad personal services under protection of copyright with acknowledgment of fair use. But the reality in Washington has been one of nervous representatives of nervous company CEOs struggling to create winning business strategies in a turbulent, uncertain environment. If there are shared interests and a shared vision of the future, the policymaking process in Washington did not uncover it.

As the future of copyright, interactive communication, and electronic commerce became an issue, Geneva again became the setting of international negotiations, this time over copyrights and this time at the World Intellectual Property Organization rather than the GATT/WTO. The future of electronic commerce will be shaped by the institutional change established there, as well as by continued technological development, standard setting, and business strategies regarding the World Wide Web. The agreements completed in December 1996—the Copyright Treaty amendment to the Berne Convention and the Performances and Phonograms Treaty amendment to the Rome Convention—aim to preserve the intent of the intellectual property policy of conferring exclusive rights of authorship and distribution while maintaining the public's access to information and expression. The new technologies make the balance tricky to achieve.

The 1996 copyright negotiations differed substantially from the TRIPS negotiations. The WIPO-based negotiations were more open than those at the GATT Uruguay Round. In the WIPO forum some 150 national governments were represented in the conference rooms; representatives from nongovernmental organizations sat in the back rows of the auditorium. The TRIPS negotiations had been cloaked in secrecy, with a few government delegations negotiating privately and nongovernmental organizations banished to hotels and restaurants. The negotiations also differed because U.S. government negotiators did not go to the copyright talks with the unified support of business interests and nongovernmental organizations as they had in the TRIPS negotiations. The U.S. patent commissioner led a delegation composed of representatives from the Copyright Office, the Commerce Department, and the State Department. The delegation had the support of the copyright industries—film, music, publishing, and information—but not of the communications and network computing companies (newly institutionalized as the Global Internet Project at the Information Technology Association of America), the consumer electronics companies, or the librarians and scientists. Thus the interest-group advocacy on copyright matters moved from Washington to Geneva, with the curious spectacle that the targets for lobbying were neither representatives of Congress nor the president but the delegates from developing countries. The enemy of Washington lobbyists in the 1980s, one-nation, one-vote decisionmaking at WIPO, became their friend in the 1990s.

The copyright interests, institutionalized to deal with the Berne and Rome Conventions and any reform of their rules, were long engaged and sure of their goals. The computer and communication interests arrived on the copyright scene much later. Many of the representatives I interviewed cited the NII–Lehman report process as the catalyst for active learning about copyright and commented that it signaled to them that old expectations about which policy issues mattered and which did not were obsolete. Digital convergence would require heightened vigilance toward Washington policymaking: corporate headquarters could provide insight into overall business strategies, but in the 1990s Washington became the primary source for learning about the implications of technological change for policy and of policy for competition in many converging industry sectors.

The rationale for trade-related intellectual property negotiations within the GATT forum had been to use linkage bargaining to overcome opposition to patent treaty reforms among developing countries. Linkage bargaining was not possible at the 1996 copyright conferences because the agenda was the reform of the Berne and Rome Conventions, yet agreements were nevertheless achieved because the conflict to be resolved was copyright interests versus communications and computer interests rather than industrialized versus developing countries. Thus several years of WIPO informational and public-comment conferences established international consensus sufficient for deft diplomacy and draftsmanship. The issues were, of course, far from permanently settled. The information revolution continues to bring extraordinary challenges to the international intellectual property institutions.

NINE

Knowledge Diplomacy

KNOWLEDGE DIPLOMACY is being conducted in the 1990s to meet the economic, political, and social needs created by fundamental change in the world political economy. The cold war is over and the North-South relationship is no longer basically conflictual. The weight of world economic activity is shifting toward intellectual property-based products and knowledge-oriented services. New communication and information technologies are establishing new organizational capabilities and strategic imperatives for multinational business enterprises. In terms of trade, knowledge diplomacy will largely supplant industrial diplomacy, whose agenda has largely been realized, and will provide the agenda for international trade policy cooperation well into the next century. Knowledge diplomacy calls for the further institutionalization of service trade liberalization; the deep integration of the harmonization of product and service regulations and standards; the liberalization of policies regarding information so that truly global information markets can emerge; and the adaptation for the information age of intellectual property institutions regarding patent, trade secret, and copyright for life.

Knowledge diplomacy is being conducted with participation from nearly all the world's states. But states' interests and goals differ widely because of variations in level of wealth, economic structure, technological capability, governmental form, and cultural tradition. Universality thus complicates the negotiation of international economic agreements. Achieving agreement, as this book has shown, will depend on the institutional capabilities of specialized international governmental organizations that can provide function-specific diplomacy and of the World Trade Organization's linkage-bargain, trade-related diplomacy.

A Changing World Political Economy

Industrial diplomacy was conducted during the cold war between the Soviet Union and its communist bloc and the United States with its allied industrialized democracies. The Soviet Union established the Council of Mutual Economic Assistance for barter-based trade within the communist political economy, and economic relations with the West were limited. In the 1980s the economies of the CMEA crumbled, leading to the delegitimization of their economic strategies and the breakup of the Soviet bloc political economy. During the 1990s the Eastern bloc and Asian communist countries have been shifting from state-led command economies to market-based economies and have been joining the international governmental institutions established by the industrial democracies.

Meanwhile, decolonization during the 1960s and 1970s had led to manifold increases in the number of sovereign states. The economic policies of these new states frequently diverged from the economic policy norms of the industrial democracies, although economic relations were modest with the communist economies of the CMEA. Asserting their interests, the poor countries of the third world declared a New International Economic Order in the UN General Assembly and UN Conference on Trade and Development, establishing commodity cartels and calling for more favorable terms of trade. But debt crises delegitimized these strategies of self-reliance in many developing countries, while the success of Korea, Taiwan, and Singapore showed that economic engagement with the industrialized countries could produce strong growth. Many developing countries have been altering their economic policy strategies to achieve more market openness toward the industrialized economies.

Although the world political economy has become less polarized and more integrated in the 1990s, the economic characteristics of countries differ widely. Sixty-four countries have GNPs of less than $765 per capita; sixty-seven are between $765 and $3,035; thirty between $3,036 and $9,385; and fifty-one greater than $9,386.[1] But income diversity only be-

---

1. World Bank (1997a, inside cover).

gins to suggest potential conflicts of economic and political interest. Agriculture as a share of GDP is 6 percent in Argentina, 28 percent in Nigeria, and nonexistent in Singapore.[2] Trade ranges from 15 percent of GDP in Brazil to 194 percent in Malaysia. At the time the GATT Uruguay Round was concluding, mean tariffs were 11 percent in Brazil, 36 percent in China, 11 percent in Hungary, 56 percent in India, 14 percent in Malaysia, and 20 percent in South Africa.[3] There are 25 personal computers for every 1,000 people in Argentina, 3 in Egypt, 39 in Hungary, 1 in India, 121 in Korea, and 328 in the United States.[4] These wide variations in economy mean equally scattered interests of polity.

The Changing Trade Product Mix

The value to the U.S. economy of trade in goods based on intellectual property rights was significant by the 1980s, and policymakers, until then generally uninformed about intellectual property–based production, began to understand that the value added in these products is the knowledge that goes into them, not the physical manufacturing processes. Foreign economic policymakers were beginning to recognize that manufacturing's contribution to the wealth of industrialized economies was shrinking. In 1980, the year after the conclusion of the GATT Tokyo Round, manufacturing represented 23 percent of world production, while services had expanded to 53 percent (manufacturing was contributing an increasing share of wealth in developing economies, where it was displacing agriculture).[5] By the end of the GATT Uruguay Round in 1994, manufacturing represented 21 percent of world production and services 63 percent.

In the United States the transformation was even more pronounced: financial, telecommunication, transportation, and professional services were coming to lead the economy. Because these services are usually knowledge and technology intensive, U.S. producers were among the most competitive in the world. However, few American service providers had attempted international business operations, and thus few were organized to carry them out. By the early 1980s American Express, Citicorp, AIG, and

2. World Bank (1997a, pp. 14–17).
3. World Bank (1997a, pp. 252–54).
4. World Bank (1997a, pp. 284–86).
5. World Bank (1997b, p. 237).

other financial services companies forged international business strategies, but many foreign governments had created strong barriers to market entry: providers of professional services faced certification barriers, and transportation service providers faced bilaterally negotiated quotas in air transportation and multilaterally negotiated quotas in ocean liner agreements. None of the GATT rules regarding nondiscrimination and transparency in trade policies applied to services, because the GATT agreement was limited to trade in goods.

Thus, these service providers urged the Office of the U.S. Trade Representative to add liberalization of trade in services to the Uruguay Round agenda. Negotiations toward a General Agreement on Trade in Services (GATS) were initiated in 1986. At the time, the United States enjoyed a trade surplus in services of $5 billion, and the surplus and the value of exports would grow every year thereafter: in 1995 the surplus was $68 billion on $210 billion in services exports.[6] With knowledge-based services and intellectual property goods dominating world trade production, the economics underlying knowledge diplomacy were taking shape.

New Communication Technologies

The GATS agenda on liberalizing impediments to services was premised on changes in communication resulting from regulatory and technological changes in the United States. In 1982 when a U.S. federal court demanded that AT&T divest its regional Bell operating companies, the company was left with its research operation (Bell Labs), equipment manufacturing operation (Western Electric), and long-distance telephony service inside the United States. It needed a new corporate strategy. Alhough federal regulators had forced it out of the international telephony service business early in the century (selling the business to ITT), AT&T decided to reenter the international market. That meant challenging and overcoming the barriers imposed by foreign governments, which generally owned telephony service as a public monopoly. AT&T was thus aligning itself with American Express, AIG, and other financial services providers with the common interest in liberalizing restrictions on international services.

---

6. International Trade Commission (1997, pp. 2–4).

Changes in communication technology were, however, pushing communication providers and financial services companies together for reasons of business rather than of advocacy. Telephony service had revolutionized twentieth-century communication and been fundamental to the industrial age, but it was becoming capable of much more—value-added networks (VANs). These included new communication services: facsimile transmission, data distribution and interchange, database access, voice mail, and electronic mail. The telephone was merging with the computer, and the computer had itself become a communication device though the Internet. For financial service providers, moving information was what their business was all about. An American Express cardholder could pay for dinner only if AMEX would approve the credit quickly, and that required a VAN. In the United States this kind of network was encouraged by the standardization of networks that promoted competition among service providers. Financial service providers could thus choose among communication providers in the United States, and they wanted the same kinds of service capabilities in the rest of the world. But communication policies in other countries were not welcoming, so the GATS intiative would entail knowledge diplomacy of long duration and tedious process and would draw participation from the membership and the Secretariats of the International Telecommunications Union and the International Organization for Standards.

By the mid-1990s, network computing and communication were offering new capabilities to all. Interactive communication now includes audio, video, and data, and the data may be described as intelligent because software computing affords speedy manipulation, processing, and analysis before transmittal. For example, an information technology manufacturer that assembles a final product in Malaysia from components made by itself and suppliers in the United States, Korea, and Thailand can create not only an intraorganizational network but interorganizational networks to promote efficient manufacturing. Network computing and communication offer opportunities for the global organization and management, but not without the knowlege diplomacy that is bringing the regulatory change and standardization needed to allow it to happen.

New Strategies for Multinational Enterprises

When telephony was the primary means of international interactive communication, the units of a multinational enterprise functioned more or less independently of each other and headquarters. Information simply moved too slowly to organize and manage more centrally. But network computing and audio, video, and data interactive communication have allowed truly global management strategies. Managers at headquarters and throughout globally located operations can provide information to each other that allows globally integrated decisionmaking.

But although network computing and fiber optic cables may deliver processed information, they cannot manage knowledge. Managing a multinational enterprise involves practices premised on the collective learning of the organization and conducted through mastery of cultural differences and nationally distinct ways of thinking about markets, businesses, and social life. Managing a multinational enterprise also involves a knowledge of political differences and countries' different ways of regulating the flow of information. These businesses require knowledge diplomacy by their governments to reduce barriers to the free flow of the information vital to their global endeavors. As in the era of industrial diplomacy, these enterprises strongly influence the international trade policy agenda, and it is their objectives that guide the demands they place on policymakers. Global knowledge management as a strategic organizing principle of multinational enterprises provides an important context for the conduct of knowledge diplomacy.

The International Trade Regime and Knowledge Diplomacy

World War II planners of the industrial diplomacy that would produce GATT and the international trade regime were guided by comparative-advantage trade theory and committed to reducing trade barriers among states to encourage economic growth and the efficient use of resources. To achieve these goals, the planners established five principles for GATT: reduction of trade barriers, policy nondiscrimination, policy transparency, law-based cooperation, and good faith conflict resolution. The tariff reductions carried out under GATT article 2 in the multilateral trade negotiations and the prohibition against quantitative restraints in article 11 reduced trade barriers. Article 1, the most-favored-nation provision (that with certain exceptions any trade benefit conferred on one member must be conferred on all), article 3, the national treatment provision (that foreign firms must be treated no less favorably than domestic firms), and the articles restricting export subsidies are representative of the commitment to nondiscrimination. The article 10 obligation to make trade policies and regulations open to foreign citizens and policymakers codifies the transparency principle. The principle of a law-based regime was carried out through the GATT treaty itself and subsequent formalized agreements achieved under auspices of the regime. The GATT treaty specifies procedures for settling disputes between contracting member states through consultation or more formal adjudicatory means that were later refined, most importantly by the Dispute Settlement Understanding agreement achieved at the Uruguay Round.

The industrial diplomacy program has been largely successful. Tariffs, quantitative restraints, and other trade barriers are much reduced, generally in a way that does not discriminate among trading partners. Customs rules and procedures have been made transparent to importers. Import licensing has been reduced and typically made transparent where it still exists. Several hundred disputes between contracting member states have been amicably settled under GATT/WTO auspices. The need to place primary emphasis on such elements of industrial diplomacy has therefore passed.

The emphasis must now be on knowledge diplomacy with its ambitious new international trade policy agenda of deep integration. The reduction of trade barriers and improvements in the transparency of trade policies must now reach beyond border trade measures to national product regulations and standards, because it is these differences that distort competition in world markets. The first such extension within the GATT regime was the sanitary and phytosanitary standards agreement regarding animal and food products that was achieved during the Uruguay Round. But further extension of rule making regarding product regulations and standards under auspices of the World Trade Organization is controversial. Ought pharmaceutical and chemical products standards be harmonized? Should food labeling practices be harmonized? Opponents of increased regulation contend that it takes the WTO away from its principle of getting government out of the business of market intervention. Other opponents contend that regulatory harmonization takes the WTO too far beyond its traditional emphasis on tariff and quota reduction.

Supporters of the WTO's regulation and harmonization initiatives contend that competing national regulations and standards are substantial barriers to trade. Global knowledge management by multinational enterprises requires information gathering about differing national policies regarding the delivery of local goods and services, but reducing the costs of product and service delivery and providing to consumers better products and services requires harmonization of the various national regulations and standards. These supporters contend that the trade regime must adapt to meet new challenges or lose its relevance. They cite the 1979 decision of the European Court of Justice in *Cassis de Dijon* that the 1957 Treaty of Rome establishing the European Economic Communities legitimizes issues of product regulation and standards as a concern of trade policy when it states in article 30, "Quantitative restrictions on imports and *all measures having equivalent effect* shall . . . be prohibited between Member States" (emphasis added). *Cassis de Dijon* and subsequent decisions involving pasta and bottling established a program of mutual recognition of regulations and standards, and the so-called EC92 initiative established the more extensive and difficult-to-achieve program of harmonizing regulations and standards of countries in the European Union through the implementation by the member governments of some 300 directives established by the European Commission in Brussels.[7]

Nevertheless, even proponents of harmonization are unsure which matters ought be addressed by the WTO's forum for rule creation rather than by the International Organization for Standards, World Health Organization, International Telecommunications Union, Food and Agriculture Organization, or other international governmental organizations (IGOs). Should information and communication standards be established within the WTO or the ITU? Should pharmaceutical product efficacy and safety regulations be established within the WTO or the WHO? This book emphasizes that the specialized IGOs are better positioned to provide the expert knowledge and function-specific diplomacy while the WTO is better positioned to provide the occasionally needed linkage-bargain diplomacy.

Knowledge diplomacy also confronts the challenge of providing multinational enterprises with the opportunity for free movement of information in the world political economy. As it stands, some governments regulate the flow of information to protect societal values, preserve cultural values, or maintain political authority. For example, France imposes quotas on imports of foreign films and China prevents imports of information products. Restrictions on information, films, music, and literature have never before been placed on the agenda of an international institution for the purpose of liberalizing them. Although the UN Educational, Scientific, and Cultural Organization (UNESCO) was a forum for the third world's New World Information Order, the initiative was aimed not at liberalizing access to

---

7. See Hufbauer (1990).

information but at righting a perceived North-South imbalance in control over information by preventing Western-owned media intersts from gaining access to developing countries. The New World Information Order agenda equally served the causes of authoritarian governments in developing countries.

The precise agenda for liberalizing access to information has not been created, but one is taking shape in an international context of democratic transitions within developing countries and the formerly communist countries. Authoritarian and oligarchic political regimes in eastern Europe, Asia, Latin America, and Africa are in transition toward competitive party politics and limited republican government. The knowledge diplomacy program of liberalizing information markets promotes this democratizing trend by institutionalizing within these countries the principles of free expression of ideas and rights of news and information-providing services to establish themselves.

Making International Intellectual Property Law for the Next Century

The Agreement on Trade-Related Intellectual Property Rights (TRIPS) takes basic standards of intellectual property protection to almost all countries of the world by globalizing the intellectual property treaties of the industrial era. However, the TRIPS initiative did not address the policy challenges imposed on intellectual property law by information and communication technologies that are revolutionizing business activity, government service, and social life. The 1996 World Intellectual Property Organization (WIPO) treaties on copyrights and performance rights only begin to address these challenges. Competitive opportunities within many industries will be shaped by contemporary policy choices regarding the scope of protections offered to intellectual property by the institutions of patent, trade secret, and copyright.

Although the TRIPS agreement explicitly extends copyright protections to computer software programs, it offers no details on the scope of the protections or the delineation between fair use and infringement. Similarly, the finer points of software patenting receive no comment in the TRIPS agreement or in the WIPO-administered Paris Convention. These issues have been in the 1990s the subject of much controversy in the United States, the world's leader in software innovation and expression. The future of software competition and the benefits to society will be determined by the policy choices made by the governments of the world at Geneva as well as within their own capitals.

Information is the primary product of the world economy, and the intellectual property policy toward it is controversial because new technologies open unprecented capabilities in generating and managing it. Debate and controversy aimed at striking the right balances between protection of and access to information have been heated in the industrial democracies in the 1990s. Institutionalizing the right scope of intellectual property protection for information strikes at the core of the contemporary economics of capitalism and the politics of democracy in this information age. Scientists and technologists seek from government the policies that would provide incentives for their investment into creating new information and knowledge, but also policies that would ensure competitive access to new information and knowledge. Librarians aim to preserve their roles as public disseminators of information and knowledge without fundamentally changing the economics of their activities. Citizens seek more information, presented more usefully and at lower cost. The governments of the world are challenged to make policies that achieve all these outcomes through the creation of the right mix of policies.

The TRIPS agreement calls on policymakers to return to the negotiation table after a five-year hiatus to discuss the intellectual property policy challenges introduced by biotechnology. U.S. policy regarding the patentability of bioengineered plants and animals continues to be controversial despite nearly thirty years of policy development within the courts, Congress, and the executive branch. Because new technologies are making the opportunities of bioengineering no longer fantastic, establishing the proper scopes of patent protection for bioengineered innovations is a seminal challenge for the world's policymakers. Biotechnology is by its very nature about information: the identification and manipulation of sequence information encoded into DNA. Thus, encouraging the dissemination of biotechnological information while providing appropriate incentives of exclusive protection is a matter of importance to future research, development, and commercialization with important effects on health care, food production, and environmental cleanup applications. Striking the right balances is yet again the challenge of intellectual property lawmaking.

The new knowledge diplomacy is being conducted in a context of cooperation on international trade policy with nearly universal state participation. Universality complicates the political economy of the negotiation of international agreements because no two countries have the same pressures and goals. And the goals of knowledge diplomacy are ambitious, which further complicates negotiations and trade arrangements. Together the two conditions ensure that function-specific diplomacy will be conducted alongside the linkage-bargain, trade-related diplomacy that produced TRIPS, the first agreement of the new knowledge diplomacy.

Reference List

THIS LIST is divided into four parts to group books and articles on similar subjects. The groups are "Intellectual Property Law and Policy," "Business Competition and Management," "Organizations and Learning," and "International and Comparative Political Economy." Newspaper and newsmagazine articles without attribution and memos and other minor writings are cited in full in the footnotes and are not repeated here.

Intellectual Property Law and Policy

Acharya, Rohini. 1991. "Patenting of Biotechnology: GATT and the Erosion of the World's Biodiversity." *Journal of World Trade* 25:71–87.

Alford, William. 1995. *To Steal a Book Is an Elegant Violation*. Harvard University Press.

Arter and Hadden. 1996. *Special 301 Comments on Video Game Piracy*. Washington (February).

Baldwin, Neil. 1995. *Edison: Inventing the Century*. Hyperion.

Band, Jonathan, and Masanobu Katoh. 1995. *Interfaces on Trial: Intellectual Property and Interoperability in the Global Software Industry*. Boulder, Colo.: Westview Press.

Barons, Lisa. 1991. "Amending Section 337 to Obtain GATT Consistency and Retain Border Protection." *Law and Policy in International Business* 22:289–331.

Beath, John. 1990. "Innovation, Intellectual Property Rights and the Uruguay Round." *World Economy* 13:411–26.

Beier, David W., and Emery Simon. 1996. "Cures and Treatments for Serious Unmet Medical Needs: The Role of Patents to Stimulate and Reward Innovation." Washington.

Benko, Robert P. 1987. *Protecting Intellectual Property Rights Issues and Controversies*. Washington: American Enterprise Institute.

Bogsch, Arpad. 1992. *The First Twenty-Five Years of the World Intellectual Property Organization, from 1967 to 1992*. Geneva: World Intellectual Property Organization.

———. 1995. *The First Twenty-Five Years of the Patent Cooperation Treaty, 1970–1995*. Geneva: World Intellectual Property Organization.

Boyle, James. 1996. *Shamans, Software, and Spleens: Law and the Construction of the Information Society*. Harvard University Press.

Brand, Ronald A. 1990. "Private Parties and GATT Dispute Resolution: Implications of the Panel Report on Section 337 of the US Tariff Act of 1930." *Journal of World Trade Law* 24 (June):5–30.

Breyer, Stephen. 1970. "The Uneasy Case for Copyright: A Study of Copyright in Books, Photocopies, and Computer Programs." *Harvard Law Review* 84:281–351.

Brown, Carole Ganz, and Francis W. Rushing. 1990. *Intellectual Property Rights in Science Technology and Economic Performance*. Boulder, Colo.: Westview Press.

Browning, John. 1997. "Africa 1, Hollywood 0." *Wired* 5 (March):61–64, 185–88.

Bugbee, Bruce W. 1967. *Genesis of American Patent and Copyright Law*. Washington: Public Affairs Press.

Business Software Alliance. Various years. *Special 301 Recommendations*. Washington.

Caves, Richard E., Michael D. Winston, and Mark A. Hurwitz. 1991. "Patent Expiration, Entry, and Competition in the U.S. Pharmaceutical Industry." *Brookings Papers on Economic Activity: Microeconomics 1991:* 1–65.

Chemical Manufacturers Association. 1995. *U.S. Chemical Industry Statistical Handbook*. Washington.

Choate, Robert A., William H. Francis, and Robert C. Collins. 1987. *Cases and Materials on Patent Law: Including Trade Secrets, Copyrights, Trademarks*. 3d ed. St. Paul, Minn.: West Publishing.

Chun-Tsung. 1991. "Protection of Intellectual Property between the US and East Asian Newly Industrializing Countries." Center for Politics and Policy, Claremont Graduate School.

Clapes, Anthony Lawrence. 1993. *Softwars: The Legal Battles for Control of the Global Software Industry.* Westport, Conn.: Quorum Books.

Coleman, Patrick. 1997. "U.S. Trade in Intangible Intellectual Property: Royalties and Licensing Fees." *Industry, Trade, and Technology Review* (April):23–31.

Conner, Kathleen R., and Richard P. Rumelt. 1991. "Software Piracy: An Analysis of Protection Strategies." *Management Science* 37:125–39.

Cornish, W. R. 1997. "Scope and Interpretation of Patent Claims under Article 69 of the EPC." International Intellectual Property Law and Policy Conference, Fordham University Law School. April.

Coyne, Randall. 1991. "Rights of Reproduction and the Provision of Library Services." *University of Arkansas at Little Rock Law Journal* 13:485–505.

Curesky, Karen M. 1989. "International Patent Harmonization through WIPO: An Analysis of the US Proposal to Adopt a "First-to-File" Patent System." *Law and Policy in International Business* 2:289–308.

Dam, Kenneth W. 1994. "The Economic Underpinnings of Patent Law." *Journal of Legal Studies* 23:247–71.

Damich, Edward J. 1988. "The Right of Personality: A Common-Law Basis for the Protection of the Moral Rights of Authors." *Georgia Law Review* 23:1–96.

Daughtrey, S. Carran. 1994. "Reverse Engineering of Software for Interoperability and Analysis." *Vanderbilt Law Review* 47:145–87.

Deardorff, Alan V. 1992a. "Should Patent Protection Be Extended to All Developing Countries?" *World Economy* 13:497–508.

———. 1992b. "Welfare Effects of Global Patent Protection." *Economica* 233:35–51.

Diwan, Ishac, and Dani Rodrik. 1991. "Patents, Appropriate Technology, and North-South Trade." *Journal of International Economics* 30:27–47.

Draft Final Act Embodying the Results of the Uruguay Round of Multilateral Trade Negotiations, 20 December 1991. 1992. Buffalo, N.Y.: William S. Hein.

Dunner, Donald R., and J. Michael Jakes. 1993. "The Equitable Doctrine of Equivalents." *Journal of the Patent and Trademark Office Society* 75:857–73.

Duvall, Donald Knox. 1990. *Federal Unfair Competition Actions: Practice and Procedure Under Section 337 of the Tariff Act of 1930.* Clark Boardman.

Eisenberg, Rebecca. 1987. "Proprietary Rights and the Norms of Science in Biotechnology Research." *Yale Law Journal* 97:179–231.

——. 1989. "Patents and the Progress of Science: Exclusive Rights and Experimental Use." *University of Chicago Law Review* 56:1017–86.

Engelsman, E. C., and A. F. J. van Raan. 1994. "A Patent-Based Cartography of Technology." *Research Policy* 23:1–26.

Feinberg, Robert M. 1988. "Intellectual Property, Injury, and International Trade." *Journal of World Trade Law* 22 (April):45–56.

Finlayson, Grant E. 1987. "Rethinking the Overlapping Jurisdictions of Section 337 and the U.S. Courts." *Journal of World Trade Law* 21 (April):41–63.

Friedman, David D., William M. Landes, and Richard A. Posner. 1991. "Some Economics of Trade Secret Law." *Journal of Economic Perspectives* 5:61–72.

Friedman, Edward, Paul Pickowicz, and Mark Selden. 1991. *Chinese Village, Socialist State.* Yale University Press.

Gadbaw, R. Michael. 1989. "Intellectual Property and International Trade: Merger or Marriage of Convenience?" *Vanderbilt Journal of Transnational Law* 22:223–42.

Gadbaw, R. Michael, and Timothy Richards, eds. 1988. *Intellectual Property Rights: Global Consensus, Global Conflict?* Boulder, Colo.: Westview Press.

Gallini, Nancy T. 1992. "Patent Policy and Costly Imitation," *RAND Journal of Economics* 23 (Spring):52–63.

Gibbens, R. D. 1989. "The Moral Rights of Artists and the Copyright Act Amendments." *Canadian Business Law Journal* 15:441–70.

Ginsburg, Jane C. 1990. "Creation and Commercial Value: Copyright Protection of Works of Information." *Columbia Law Review* 90:1865–1938.

——. 1993. "Copyright Without Walls?: Speculations on Literary Property in the Library of the Future." *Representations* 42:53–73.

Goodman, Jeffrey S. 1984. "The Policy Implications of Granting Patent Protection to Computer Software: An Economic Analysis." *Vanderbilt Law Review* 37:147–81.

Gorman, Robert A. 1992. "The Feist Case: Reflections on a Pathbreaking Copyright Decision." *Rutgers Computer and Technology Law Journal* 18:73–172.

Goyder, D. G. 1993. *EC Competition Law.* Oxford University Press.

Greenfield, Michael S. 1992. "Recombinant DNA Technology: A Science Stuggling with the Patent Law." *Stanford Law Review* 44:1051–94.

Hardy, I. T. 1988. "An Economic Understanding of Copyright Law's Work-Made-for-Hire Doctrine." *Columbia-VLA Journal of Law and the Arts* 12:181–227.

Ho, Samuel P. S., and Ralph W. Huenemann. 1984. *China's Open Door Policy: The Quest for Foreign Technology and Capital.* University of British Columbia Press.

Information Industry Association. 1995. "Database Protection: An Industry Perspective on the Issues." Washington, August.

Information Infrastructure Task Force. 1995. "Intellectual Property and the National Information Infrastructure: The Report of the Working Group on Intellectual Property Rights." Department of Commerce.

Information Technology Association of America. 1995. "Intellectual Property Protection in Cyberspace: Towards a New Consensus." Washington.

International Intellectual Property Alliance. Various years. *Special 301 Recommendations.* Washington.

———. 1985a. *Piracy of U.S. Copyrighted Works in Ten Selected Countries.* Washington.

———. 1985b. "U.S. Government Trade Policy: Views of the Copyright Industry." Washington.

———. 1989. *Trade Losses Due to Piracy and Other Market Access Barriers Affecting the U.S. Copyright Industries.* Washington, April.

———. 1995. *Estimates of 1995 U.S Trade Losses Due to Foreign Policy and Levels of Piracy.* Washington.

Johnson, William R. 1985. "The Economics of Copying." *Journal of Political Economy* 93 (February):158–74.

Jordan, Dawn. 1988. "Software Piracy: The United States Needs to Utilize the Protection Provided by the Berne Convention in the Pacific Rim." *Emory Journal of International Dispute Resolution* 3:133–56.

Joyce, Craig, and others. 1995. *Copyright Law,* 3d ed. Matthew Bender.

Kastenmeier, Robert W., and David Beier. 1989. "International Trade and Intellectual Property: Promise, Risks, and Reality." *Vanderbilt Journal of Transnational Law* 22:285–307.

Kaufer, Erich. 1989. *The Economics of the Patent System.* Chur, Switzerland: Harwood Academic Publishers.

Kiely, Tom. 1991. "Life Patents Go Global." *Technology Review* 94:21–22.

Kitch, Edmund W. 1977. "The Nature and Function of the Patent System." *Journal of Law and Economics* 20 (October):265–90.

———. 1980. "The Law and Economics of Rights in Valuable Information." *Journal of Legal Studies* 9:683–723.

Klett, Daniel. 1986. "The U.S. Tariff Act: Section 337 Off-Shore Assembly and the 'Domestic Industry.'" *Journal of World Trade Law* 20:294–312.

Kravetz, Paul I. 1992. "Copyright Protection of Screen Displays after *Lotus Development Corporation v. Paperback Software*." *DePaul Business Law Journal* 4:485–518.

Kotabe, Masaaki. 1992. "A Comparative Study of U.S. and Japanese Patent Systems." *Journal of International Business Studies* 23:147–68.

Lambelet, Dorian. 1987. "Internationalizing the Copyright Code: An Analysis of Legislative Proposals Seeking Adherence to the Berne Convention." *Georgetown Law Journal* 76:467–505.

Landes, William M., and Richard A. Posner. 1989. "An Economic Analysis of Copyright Law." *Journal of Legal Studies* 18:325–63.

Lardner, James. 1987a. "Annals of Law: The BetamaCase–I." *New Yorker* (April 6):45–71.

———. 1987b. "Annals of Law, The BetamaCase–II." *New Yorker* (April 13):60–81.

Latman, Alan. 1990. "'Probative Similarity' as Proof of Copying: Toward Dispelling Some Myths in Copyright Infringement." *Columbia Law Review* 90 (June):1187–1214.

Lent, John A. 1990. *The Asian Film Industry*. University of Texas Press.

Liebovich, Mark. 1998. "IBM Leads World in U.S. Patents for 4th Year in a Row." *Washington Post* (January 12):A10.

Litman, Jessica D. 1987. "Copyright, Compromise and Legislative History." *Cornell Law Review* 72:857–904.

———. 1989. "Copyright Legislation and Technological Change." *Oregon Law Review* 68:275–361.

Mansfield, Edwin. 1986. "Patents and Innovation: An Empirical Study." *Management Science* 32:173–81.

———. 1995. "Intellectual Property Protection, Direct Investment, and Technology Transfer: Germany, Japan, and the United States," discussion paper 27. Washington: International Finance Corporation, World Bank.

Maskus, Keith E. 1990. "Normative Concerns in the International Protection of Intellectual Property Rights." *World Economy* 13:387–410.

Meinhardt, Peter. 1946. *Inventions, Patents, and Monopoly*. London: Stevens and Sons.

Merges, Robert P. 1994. "Intellectual Property Rights and Bargaining Breakdown: The Case of Blocking Patents." *Tennessee Law Review* 62 (Fall):75–106.

Merges, Robert P., and Richard R. Nelson. 1990. "On the CompleEconomics of Patent Scope." *Columbia Law Review* 90 (May):839–916.

———. 1994. "On Limiting or Encouraging Rivalry in Technical Progress: The Effect of Patent Scope Decisions." *Journal of Economic Behavior and Organization* 25 (September):1–24.

Miller, Arthur H., and Michael H. Davis. 1990. *Intellectual Property: Patents, Trademarks, and Copyright in a Nutshell*, 2d ed. St. Paul, Minn.: West Publishing.

Miller, Arthur R. 1993. "Copyright Protection for Computer Programs, Databases, and Computer-Generated Works: Is Anything New Since CONTU?" *Harvard Law Review* 106:978–1073.

Mutti, John. 1993. "Intellectual Property Protection in the United States under Section 337." *World Economy* 16 (May):339–57.

Mutti, John, and Bernard Yeung. 1996. "Section 337 and the Protection of Intellectual Property in the United States: The Complainants and the Impact." *Review of Economics and Statistics* 78 (August):510–20.

Narin, Francis, Elliot Noma, and Ross Perry. 1987. "Patents as Indicators of Corporate Technological Strength." *Research Policy* 16:143–55.

Nelson, Gary. 1996. "The Sufficiency of Copyright Protection in the Video Electronic Game Industry: Comparing the United States with the European Union." *Law and Policy in International Business* 27:805–24.

Newman, Andrew S. 1989. "The Amendments to Section 337: Increased Protection for Intellectual Property Rights." *Law and Policy in International Business* 20:571–88.

Oddi, A. Samuel. 1989. "Contributory Copyright Infringement: The Tort and Technological Tensions." *Notre Dame Law Review* 64:47–105.

Ordover, Janus A. 1991. "A Patent System for Both Diffusion and Exclusion." *Journal of Economic Perspectives* 5 (Winter):43–60.

Organization for Economic Cooperation and Development. 1987. *International Technology Licensing: Survey Results*. Paris.

———. 1989. *Competition Policy and Intellectual Property Rights*. Paris.

Paine, Lynn Sharpe. 1991. "Trade Secrets and the Justification of Intellectual Property: A Comment on Hettinger." *Philosophy and Public Affairs* 20 (Summer):247–63.

Palmeter, N. David. 1984. "The U.S. International Trade Commission at Common Law: Unfair Competition, Trademark, and Section 337 of the Tariff Act." *Journal of World Trade Law* 18:497–511.

Pescatore, Pierre, William J. Davey, and Andreas F. Lowenfeld. Annual. *Handbook of WTO/GATT Dispute Settlement*. Irvington-on-Hudson, N.Y.: Transnational Publishers.

Pharmaceutical Research and Manufacturers of America. 1997. *Industry Profile 1997*. Washington.

———. Various years. *Submission for the "Special 301" Report on Intellectual Property Barriers*. Washington.

Pisano, Gary. 1991. "Manufacturing, Firm Boundaries, and the Protection of Intellectual Property." Harvard Business School.

Posner, Steve. 1991. "Can a Computer Language Be Copyrighted? The State of Confusion in Computer Copyright Law." *Computer/Law Journal* 11:97–130.

Prager, Frank D. 1944. "A History of Intellectual Property from 1545 to 1787." *Journal of the Patent Office Society* 26 (November):711–60.

Primo Braga, Carlos A. 1995a. "The Economic Justification for the Grant of Intellectual Property Rights: Patterns of Convergence and Conflict." Public Policy and Global Technological Integration Symposium, Kent College of Law, Illinois Institute of Technology. October.

———. 1995b. "Trade-Related Intellectual Property Issues: The Uruguay Round Agreement and Its Economic Implications." In Will Martin and L. Alan Winters, eds., *The Uruguay Round and the Developing Economies*, 381–911. Washington: World Bank.

Quick, Rebecca. 1997. "On-line: Internet Addresses Spark Storm in Cyberspace." *Wall Street Journal* (April 29):B1.

Rader, Randall. 1997. "The Markman Era." International Intellectual Property Law and Policy Conference, Fordham University School of Law. April.

Rapp, Richart T., and Richard P. Rozek. 1990. "Benefits and Costs of Intellectual Property Protection in Developing Countries." *Journal of World Trade* 24:75–102.

Raskind, Leo J. 1985. "Reverse Engineering, Unfair Competition, and Fair Use." *Minnesotal Law Review* 70 (December):385–415.

Reichman, J. H. 1989. "Intellectual Property in International Trade: Opportunities and Risks of a GATT Connection," *Vanderbilt Journal of Transnational Law* 22:747–891.

Richardson, Martin. 1991. "Intellectual Property Rights: An International Economics Perspective." *Review of Industrial Organization* 6:247–67.

Robinson, William C. 1890. *Law of Patents for Useful Inventions.* Boston: Little, Brown.

Rose, Lance. 1995. *Netlaw: Your Rights in the Online World.* McGraw-Hill.

Ryan, Michael P., and Justine Bednarik. 1995. "Drugs, Books, and Videos: U.S.-Korea Trade Dispute over Intellectual Property Rights." *Georgetown Cases in International Business Strategy.* Georgetown University Institute for the Study of Diplomacy.

Samuelson, Pamela. 1996. "The Copyright Grab." *Wired* 6 (January).

———. "Big Media Beaten Back." 1997. *Wired* 5 (March):61–64, 178–84.

Samuelson, Pamela, and others. 1994. "A Manifesto Concerning the Legal Protection of Computer Programs." *Columbia Law Review* 94:2308–2431.

Santoro, Michael A., and Lynn Sharp Paine. 1995. *Pfizer: Global Protection of Intellectual Property.* Harvard Business School Cases. Harvard Business School.

Schaumberg, Tom M. 1982. "Section 337 of the Tariff Act of 1930 as an Antitrust Remedy." *Antitrust Bulletin* 27:51–81.

Schulman, Seth. 1991. "Life Patents Go Global." *Technology Review* 94:21–22.

Schwartz, Bryan A. 1995. "The Fate of Section 337 Litigation after the Uruguay Round Agreements Act." *Law and Policy in International Business* 27 (Fall):1–32.

Sell, Susan K. 1995. "Intellectual Property Protection and Antitrust in the Developing World: Crisis, Coercion, and Choice." *International Organization* 49:315–50.

Sherwood, Robert M. 1997a. "Intellectual Property Systems and Investment Stimulation: The Rating of Systems in Eighteen Developing Countries." *IDEA* 37 (Winter):261–370.

———. 1997b. "The TRIPS Agreement: Implications for Developing Countries." *IDEA* 37 (Spring):491–544.

Sherwood, Robert M., and Carlos A. Primo Braga. 1996. "Intellectual Property, Trade and Economic Development: A Road Map for the FTAA Negotiations." North-South Agenda Papers 21. University of Miami, Florida.

Siwek, Stephen E., and Gale Mosteller. 1996. *Copyright Industries in the U.S. Economy: The 1996 Report.* Washington: Economists, Inc., prepared for the International Intellectual Property Alliance.

Smith, Patrick. 1989. *Introduction to Patent Law and Practice: The Basic Concepts.* Geneva: World Intellectual Property Organization.

Sokoloff, Kenneth L. 1988. "Inventive Activity in Early Industrial America: Evidence from Patent Records, 1790–1846," *Journal of Economic History* 48 (December):813–50.

Soma, John T., and B. F. Smith. 1989. "Software Trends: Who's Getting How Many of What? 1978 to 1987." *Journal of the Patent and Trademark Organization Society* 71:415–32.

Software Publishers Association. *1996 "Special 301" Review–Policies and Practices of Foreign Countries Regarding Intellectual Property Rights.* Washington.

Strayer, Joseph R., and Dana C. Munro. 1970. *The Middle Ages, 395–1500,* 5th ed. Appleton-Century-Crofts.

Subramanian, Arvind. 1990. "TRIPs and the Paradigm of GATT: A Tropical, Temperate View." *World Economy* 13:509–21.

———. 1991. "The International Economics of Intellectual Property Right Protection: A Welfare-Theoretic Trade Policy Analysis." *World Development* 19 (August):945–56.

Suchman, Marc C. 1989. "Invention and Ritual: Notes on the Interrelation of Magic and Intellectual Property in Preliterate Societies," *Columbia Law Review* 89:1264–94.

Swamy, M. R. K. 1993. "Are Super 301 Provisions of the US Omnibus Trade and Competitiveness Act of 1988 Gainful to Developing Countries? A Financial Management Analysis." *Journal of Financial Management and Analysis* 6:59–65.

Tanouye, Elsye, Steven Lipin, and Stephen D. Moore. 1996. "In Big Drug Merger, Sando and Ceba-Geigy Plan to Join Forces." *Wall Street Journal,* March 7: A1.

Thomas, John R. 1996. "Litigation beyond the Technological Frontier: Comparative Approaches to Multinational Patent Enforcement." *Law and Policy in International Business* 27 (Winter):277–352.

Tong, Quesong, and J. Davidson Frame. 1994. "Measuring National Technological Performance with Patent Claims Data." *Research Policy* 23:133–41.

Toren, Peter J. G. 1994. "The Prosecution of Trade Secrets Thefts under Federal Law." *Pepperdine Law Review* 22:59–98.

U.S. International Trade Commission. 1997. *Recent Trends in U.S. Services Trade*. Washington.

U.S. Trade Representative. 1990. *1990 Trade Estimate Report on Foreign Trade Barriers*. Washington.

———. 1989. "'Special 301' on Intellectual Property." Washington.

———. 1996. "USTR Announces Two Decisions: Title VII and 'Special 301.'" Press Release. Washington (April).

Velasco, Julian. 1994. "The Copyrightability of Nonliteral Elements of Computer Programs." *Columbia Law Review* 94:242–92.

Wiley, John Shepard Jr. 1991. "Copyright at the School of Patent." *University of Chicago Law Review* 58 (Winter):119–85.

Wolfhard, Eric. 1991. "International Trade in Intellectual Property: The Emerging GATT Regime." *University of Toronto Faculty of Law Review* 49:106–51.

World Bank. 1997a. *World Development Indicators*. Washington.

———. 1997b. *World Development Report 1997*. Washington.

World Intellectual Property Organization. Various years. *Activities*. Geneva.

———. Various years. *Industrial Property Statistics*. Geneva.

———. 1989. *Introduction to Patent Law and Practice: The Basic Concepts, A WIPO Training Manual*. Geneva.

———. 1990. *Asian and Pacific Regional Training Course on Copyright Trials*. Geneva.

———. 1991. *WIPO Worldwide Symposium on the Intellectual Property Aspects of Artificial Intelligence*. Geneva.

———. 1992. *Guide to Licensing of Biotechnology*. Geneva.

———. 1993a. *Background Reading Material on the Intellectual Property System of China*. Geneva.

———. 1993b. *WIPO Worldwide Symposium on the Impact of Digital Technology on Copyright and Neighboring Rights*. Geneva.

———. 1994a. *WIPO World Forum on the Arbitration of Intellectual Property Disputes*. Geneva.

———. 1994b. *WIPO Worldwide Symposium on the Future of Copyright and Neighboring Rights*. Geneva.

———. 1995a. *WIPO Worldwide Symposium on Copyright in the Global Information Infrastructure*. Geneva.

———. 1995b. *WIPO Worldwide Forum on the Protection of Intellectual Creations in the Information Society*. Geneva.

———. 1995c. "Meeting of Consultants on Trademarks and Internet Domain Names," TDN/MC/I/1. Geneva.

———. 1995d. "States Party to the Convention Establishing the World Intellectual Property Organization and/or the Other Treaties Administered by WIPO." Geneva.

———. 1997. "Final Report of the International Ad Hoc Committee: Recommendations for Administration and Management of TLDs." Geneva.

World Trade Organization. 1994. *The Results of the Uruguay Round of Multilateral Trade Negotiations: The Legal Texts.* Geneva.

Wright, William R. 1991. "Litigation as a Mechanism for Inefficiency in Software Copyright Law." *UCLA Law Review* 39:397–437.

Yen, Alfred C. 1990. "Restoring the Natural Law: Copyright as Labor and Possession." *Ohio State Law Journal* 51:517–59.

Yorke, Brian A. 1984. "Pharmaceutical Patent Protection." *Medicinal Research Reviews* 4:25–46.

Zeitler, William A. 1987. "A Preventative Approach to Import-Related Disputes: Antidumping, Countervailing Duty, and Section 337 Investigations." *Harvard International Law Review* 28:69–105.

Business Competition and Management

Abernathy, William J., and Kim B. Clark. 1985. "Innovation: Mapping the Winds of Creative Destruction." *Research Policy* 14:3–22.

Abernathy, William J., and Phillip L. Townsend. 1975. "Technology, Productivity, and Process Change." *Technological Forecasting and Social Change* 7:379–96.

Abernathy, William J., and James M. Utterback. 1978. "Patterns of Innovation in Technology. *Technology Review* 80 (7):40–47.

Aftalion, Fred. 1991. *A History of the International Chemical Industry.* University of Pennsylvania Press.

Aharoni, Yair. 1966. *The Foreign Investment Decision Process.* Harvard Graduate School of Business Administration.

American Chemical Society. 1994. *Current Trends in Chemical Technology, Business, and Employment.* Washington.

Baines, William. 1993. *Biotechnology from A to Z.* Oxford University Press.

Baldwin, Neil. 1995. *Edison: Inventing the Century.* Hyperion.

Ballance, Robert, Janos Pogany, and Helmut Forstner. 1992. *The World's Pharmaceutical Industries: An International Perspective on Innovation, Competition and Policy.* Lyme, N.H.: Edward Elgar.

Beltz, Cynthia. 1994. *Financing Entrepreneurs.* Washington: American Enterprise Institute.

Bradley, Stephen P., Jerry A. Hausman, and Richard L. Nolan, eds. 1993. *Globalization, Technology, and Competition: The Fusion of Computers and Telecommunications in the 1990s.* Harvard Business School Press.

Brennan, Mary, and Janice Long. 1994. "Facts and Figures for Chemical R&D." *Chemical and Engineering News* (August 22):2.

Brockman, John. 1996. *Digerati: Encounters with the Cyber Elite.* San Francisco: Hardwired.

Burgelman, Robert A., Modesto A. Maidique, and Steven C. Wheelwright. 1996. *Strategic Management of Technology and Innovation*, 2d ed. Burr Ridge, Ill.: Irwin.

Burnett, Robert. 1996. *The Global Jukebox: The International Music Industry.* Routledge.

Caves, Richard E. 1996. *Multinational Enterprise and Economic Analysis.* Cambridge University Press.

Clifton, Mark. 1988. "Patent Drugs Abuse." *Far Eastern Economic Review* (June 30):48.

Cottrell, Tom. 1994. "Fragmented Standards and the Development of Japan's Microcomputer Software Industry." *Research Policy* 23:143–74.

Cusumano, Michael A., and Detelin Elenkov. 1994. "Linking International Technology Transfer with Strategy and Management: A Literature Commentary." *Research Policy* 23:195–215.

Cusumano, Michael A., and Richard W. Selby. 1995. *Microsoft Secrets: How the World's Most Powerful Software Company Creates Technology, Shapes Markets, and Manages People.* Free Press.

Dosi, Giovanni. 1982. "Technological Paradigms and Technological Trajectories." *Research Policy* 11:147–62.

Dreifus, Claudia. 1996. "The Cyber-Maxims of Esther Dyson." *New York Times Magazine* (July 7): 16–18.

Dunning, John H. 1994. "Multinational Enterprises and the Globalization of Innovatory Capacity." *Research Policy* 23:67–88.

Dyer, Jeffrey H., and William G. Ouchi. 1993. "Japanese Style Partnerships: Giving Companies a Competitive Edge." *Sloan Management Review* 35:51–63.

Feigenbaum, Edward A. 1995. "Where's the 'Walkman' in Japan's Software Future?" In Leebaert, ed., *Future of Software,* 215–26.

Foster, Richard N. 1971. "Organize for Technology Transfer." *Harvard Business Review* 49 (November-December):110–19.

Friar, John, and Mel Horwitch. 1985. "The Emergence of Technology Strategy: A New Dimension of Strategic Management." *Technology in Society* 7:143–78.

Ganot, Israel M., and Michael J. Enright. 1995. *Hoechst and Biotechnology,* Harvard Business School Cases. Harvard Business School.

Garrette, Bernard, and Bertrand Quelin. 1994. "An Empirical Study of Hybrid Forms of Governance Structure: The Case of the Telecommunications Equipment Industry." *Research Policy* 23:395–412.

Garud, Raghu. 1994. "Cooperative and Competitive Behaviors during the Process of Creative Destruction." *Research Policy* 23:385–94.

Gilpin, Robert. 1981. *War and Change in World Politics.* Cambridge University Press.

———. 1987. *The Political Economy of International Relations.* Princeton University Press.

Goldberg, Ray, Osman Mardin, and Hans-Peter Biemann. 1986. *Amgen,* Harvard Business School Cases. Harvard Business School Press.

Grandstand, O., L. Hakanson, and S. Sjolander. 1993. "Internationalization of R&D: A Survey of Some Recent Research." *Research Policy* 22:413–30.

Håkanson, L., and R. Nobel. 1993a. "Determinants of Foreign R&D in Swedish Multinationals." *Research Policy* 22:397–412.

———. 1993b. "Foreign Research and Development in Swedish Multinationals." *Research Policy* 22:373–96.

Hamel, Gary, Yves Doz, and C. K. Prahalad. 1989. "Collaborate with Your Competitors—and Win." *Harvard Business Review* 67(1):133–39.

Hamel, Gary, and C. K. Prahalad. 1985. "Do You Really Have a Global Strategy?" *Harvard Business Review* 63(4):149–58.

———. 1989. "Strategic Intent." *Harvard Business Review* 67:63–76.

———. 1993. "Strategy as Stretch and Leverage." *Harvard Business Review* 71 (February):75–84.

Hamilton, William F., and others. 1990. "Patterns of Strategic Choice in Emerging Firms: Positioning for Innovation in Biotechnology." *California Management Review* 32:73–85.

Häusler, J., H. W. Hohn, and S. Lütz. 1994. "Contingencies of Innovative Networks: A Case Study of Successful Interfirm R&D Collaboration." *Research Policy* 23:47–66.

Hicks, D., and others. 1994. "Japanese Corporations, Scientific Research and Globalization." *Research Policy* 23:375–84.

International Trade Commission. 1991. *Global Competitiveness of U.S. Advanced Technology Manufacturing Industries: Pharmaceuticals.* Washington.

Johnson, William R. Jr. 1995. "Anything, Anytime, Anywhere: The Future of Networking." In Leebaert, ed. *Future of Software.* 150–75.

Kaitin, Kenneth I., Natalie R. Bryant, and Louis Lasagna. 1993. "The Role of the Research-Based Pharmaceutical Industry in Medical Progress in the United States." *Health Care Policy* 33:412–17.

Keen, Peter G. W. 1995. *Every Manager's Guide to Information Technology.* Harvard Business School Press.

Kenney, Martin, and Richard Florida. 1994. "The Organization and Geography of Japanese R&D: Results from a Survey of Japanese Electronics and Biotechnology Firms." *Research Policy* 23:305–23.

Khazam, J., and David Mowery. 1994. "The Commercialization of RISC: Strategies for the Creation of Dominant Designs." *Research Policy* 23:89–102.

Kim, Linsu. 1980. "Stages of Development of Industrial Technology in a Developing Country: A Model." *Research Policy* 9:254–77.

———. 1997. *Imitation to Innovation: The Dynamics of Korea's Techological Learning.* Harvard Business School Press.

Kline, Stephen J., and Nathan Rosenberg. 1986. "An Overview of Innovation." In Landau and Rosenberg, eds., *Positive Sum Strategy,* 275–305. Washington: National Academy Press.

Kogut, Bruce, and Udo Zander. 1992. "Knowledge of the Firm, Combinative Capabilities, and the Replication of Technology." *Organization Science* 3 (August):383–97.

———. 1993. "Knowledge of the Firm and the Evolutionary Theory of the Multinational Corporation." *Journal of International Business Studies* 24:625–45.

Koszarski, Richard. 1990. *An Evening's Entertainment: The Age of the Silent Feature Picture, 1915–1928.* University of California Press.

Kotabe, Massaki. 1996. "Emerging Role of Technology Licensing in the Development of Global Product Strategy: Conceptual Framework and Research Propositions." *Journal of Marketing* 60:73–88.

Leebaert, Derek, ed. 1995. *The Future of Software.* MIT Press.

———. 1991. *Technology 2001: The Future of Computing and Communications.* MIT Press.

Levins, Richard C., and others. 1987. "Appropriating the Returns from Industrial Research and Development." *Brookings Papers on Economic Activity* (3):783.

Louis, Deborah K., and L. Alexander Morrow. 1995. "The Prairie School: The Future of Workgroup Computing." In Leebaert, ed., *Future of Software,* 105–26.

Malone, Michael S. 1995. *The Microprocessor: A Biography.* Santa Clara, Calif.: TELOS.

Malone, Thomas W., and John F. Rockart. 1993. "How Will Information Technology Reshape Organizations? Computers as Coordination Technology." In Bradley, Stephen P., Jerry A. Hausman, and Richard L. Nolan, *Globalization, Technology, and Competition: The Fusion of Computers and Telecommunications in the 1990s,* 37–56. Harvard Business School Press.

Maney, Kevin. 1995. *Megamedia Shakeout: The Inside Story of the Leaders and the Losers in the Exploding Communications Industry.* John Wiley.

McFetridge, Donald, ed. 1991. *Foreign Investment, Technology, and Economic Growth.* University of Calgary Press.

Methé, David T. 1991. *Technological Competition in Global Industries: Marketing and Planning Strategies for American Industry.* Quorum Books.

Meyer, Marc H., and Edward B. Roberts. 1988. "Focusing Product Technology for Corporate Growth." *Sloan Management Review* 29 (Summer):7–16.

Miller, Roger. 1994. "Global R&D Networks and Large-Scale Innovations: The Case of the Automobile Industry." *Research Policy* 23:27–46.

Moran, Theodore H. 1985. "International Political Risk Assessment, Corporate Planning, and Strategies to Offset Political Risk." In Moran, ed., *Multinational Corporations: The Political Economy of Foreign Direct Investment,* 107–18. Lexington, Mass.: D. C. Heath.

Mowery, David C., ed. 1996. *The International Computer Software Industry Association: A Comparative Study of Industry Evolution and Structure.* Oxford University Press.

Mowery, David, and Nathan Rosenberg. 1989. *Technology and the Pursuit of Economic Growth.* Cambridge Univesity Press.

National Research Council. 1992. *Critical Technologies: The Role of Chemistry and Chemical Engineering.* Washington: National Academy Press.

Negroponte, Nicholas. 1995. *Being Digital.* Alfred A. Knopf.

Nelson, Richard R., and Sidney G. Winter. 1982. *The Evolutionary Theory of Economic Change.* Harvard University Press.

Ordover, JanusA., and Robert D. Willig. 1985. "Antitrust for High-Technology Industries: Assessing Research Joint Ventures and Mergers." *Journal of Law and Economics* 28:311–33.

Ouchi, William G., and Michele Kremen Bolton. 1988. "The Logic of Joint Research and Development." *California Management Review* 30:9–33.

Oxley, Joanne. 1997. "Intellectual Property Protection and International Strategic Alliances." University of Michigan School of Business Administration.

Packard, David. 1995. *The HP Way: How Bill Hewlett and I Built Our Company.* Harper.

Pavitt, Keith. 1990. "What We Know about the Strategic Management of Technology." *California Management Review* 32:17–26.

Pharmaceutical Research and Manufacturers of America. 1997. "Industry Profile 1997." Washington.

———. 1996–97. *Annual Report, 1996/97.* Washington.

———. 1996. *"Special 301" Report on Intellectual Property Barriers.* Washington.

Porter, Michael E. 1980. *Competitive Strategy: Techniques for Analyzing Industries and Competitors.* Free Press.

———. 1990. *The Competitive Advantage of Nations.* Free Press.

Prahalad, C. K., and Gary Hamel. 1990. "The Core Competence of the Corporation." *Harvard Business Review* 68 (6):79–91.

Price Waterhouse, LLP. 1996. *1996/97 Software Business Practices Survey.* Boston.

Pucik, Vladimir. 1988. "Strategic Alliances, Organizational Learning, and Competitive Advantage: The HRM Agenda." *Human Resource Management* 27:77–93.

Quinn, James Brian. 1985. "Managing Innovation: Controlled Chaos." *Harvard Business Review* 63 (5):73–84.

Root, Franklin R. 1994. *Entry Strategies for International Markets.* Lexington, Mass.: D. C. Heath.

Rosenbloom, Richard S., and Michael A. Cusumano. 1987. "Technological Pioneering and Competitive Advantage: The Birth of the VCR Industry." *California Management Review* 29:51–71.

Sahal, Devendra. 1985. "Technological Guideposts and Innovation Avenues." *Research Policy* 14:61–82.

Samuels, Richard J. 1994. "Pathways of Technological Diffusion in Japan." *Sloan Management Review* 35 (Spring):21–34.

Sanjek, Russell. 1996. *Pennies from Heaven: The American Popular Music Business in the Twentieth Century.* Da Capo Press.

Scherer, F. M. 1992. *International High-Technology Competition.* Harvard University Press.

Sullivan, Erin B. 1993. *People's Republic of China: Special Topic Report– Industrial Sector Analysis.* Beijing.

Tanaka, Masami. 1989. "Japanese-Style Evaluation Systems for R&D Projects: The MITI Experience." *Research Policy* 18:361–78.

Teece, David J. 1987. *The Competitive Challenge: Strategies for Industrial Innovation and Revival.* Cambridge, Mass.: Ballinger.

———. 1987. "Profiting from Technological Innovation: Implications for Integration, Collaboration, Licensing, and Public Policy." *Research Policy* 15:285–305.

Teisberg, Elizabeth, and Sharon Rossi. 1992. *Biotechnology Strategies in 1992.* Harvard Business School Cases. Harvard Business School Press.

Teitelman, Robert. 1994. *Profits of Science: The American Marriage of Business and Technology.* Basic Books.

Utterback, James M., and Fernando F. Suarez. 1993. "Innovation, Competition, and Industry Structure." *Research Policy* 22:1–21.

Vagelos, P. Roy. 1991. "Are Prescription Drug Prices High?" *Science* 252 (5):3–7.

Vogel, Harold L. 1994. *Entertainment Industry Economics: A Guide for Financial Analysis,* 3d ed. Cambridge University Press.

Walsh, Vivien. 1984. "Invention and Innovation in the Chemical Industry: Demand Pull or Discovery Push?" *Research Policy* 13:211–34.

Wasko, Janet. 1994. *Hollywood in the Information Age.* University of Texas Press.

Werth, Barry. 1994. *The Billion-Dollar Molecule: One Company's Quest for the Perfect Drug*. Simon and Schuster.

Westerman, Mariet. 1996. *A Worldly Art: The Dutch Republic, 1585–1718*. Harry N. Abrams.

Wexler, Joyce Piell. 1997. *Who Paid for Modernism? Art, Money, and the Fiction of Conrad, Joyce, and Lawrence*. University of Arkansas Press.

Wheaton, James J. 1986. "Generic Competition and Pharmaceutical Innovation: The Drug Price Competition and Patent Term Restoration Act of 1984." *Catholic University Law Review* 35:433–87.

Zachary, G. Pascal. 1994. *Show-Stopper: The Breakneck Race to Create Windows NT and the Next Generation at Microsoft*. Free Press.

Organizations and Learning

Bandura, Albert. 1986. *Social Foundations of Thought and Action: A Social Cognitive Theory*. Englewood Cliffs, N.J.: Prentice-Hall.

Corno, L., and R. E. Snow. 1986. "Adapting Teaching to Individual Differences among Learners." in M. Wittrock, ed., *Handbook of Research on Teaching*. Macmillan.

Guskin, Alan E., and Michael A. Bassis. 1985. "Leadership Style and Institutional Renewal." *New Directions for Higher Education* 12:13–22.

Kim, Daniel H. 1993. "The Link between Individual and Organizational Learning." *Sloan Management Review* 35:37–50

Levitt, Barbara, and James G. March. 1988. "Organizational Learning," *Annual Review of Sociology* 14:319–40.

Litwin, George H., and Robert A. Stringer Jr. 1968 *Motivation and Organizational Climate*. Harvard University Press.

March, James G., and Johan P. Olsen. 1989. *Rediscovering Institutions: The Organizational Basis of Politics*. Free Press.

Mohr, Lawrence. 1969 "Determinants of Innovation in Organizations." *American Political Science Review* 63:111–26.

Olson, Mancur. 1965. *The Logic of Collective Action: Public Goods and the Theory of Groups*. Harvard University Press.

Pintrich, Paul, and others. 1986. "Instructional Psychology." *Annual Review of Psychology* 37:611–51.

Pucik, Vladimir. 1988. "Strategic Alliances, Organizational Learning, and Competitive Advantage: The HRM Agenda." *Human Resource Management* 27 (Spring):77–93.

Pucik, Vladimir, Noel M. Tichy, and Carole K. Barnett, eds. 1992. *Globalizing Management: Creating and Leading the Competitive Organization.* John Wiley.

Reiter, Dan. 1994. "Learning, Realism, and Alliances: The Weight of the Shadow of the Past." *World Politics* 46 (July):490–526.

Schein, Edgar H. 1984. "Coming to a New Awareness of Organizational Culture." *Sloan Management Review* 25:3–16.

———. 1993. "How Can Organizations Learn Faster? The Challenge of Entering the Green Room." *Sloan Management Review* 34:85–92.

Simon, Herbert A. 1991a. "Bounded Rationality and Organized Learning." *Organization Science* 2 (February):125–34.

———. 1991b. "Organizations and Markets." *Journal of Economic Perspectives* 5:25–44.

von Hippel, Eric. 1987. "Cooperation between Rivals: Informal Know-How Trading." *Research Policy* 16:291–302.

Wilensky, Harold L. 1967. *Organizational Intelligence: Knowledge and Policy in Government and Industry.* Basic Books.

Wilkins, Alan L., and William G. Ouchi. 1983. "Efficient Cultures: Exploring the Relationship between Culture and Organizational Performance." *Administrative Science Quarterly* 28:468–81.

Wilson, Dick. 1992. "Benefits and Beggars: The GSP Is Complicated, Unpredictable, and Controlled Esssentialy by Importers." *Far Eastern Economic Review*, March 19:44.

Wilson, James Q. 1995. *Political Organizations.* Princeton University Press.

International and Comparative Political Economy

Adas, Michael. 1989. *Machines as the Measure of Men: Science, Technology, and Ideologies of Western Dominance.* Cornell University Press.

Aggarwal, Vinod K. 1985. *Liberal Protectionism: The International Politics of Organized Textile Trade.* University of California Press.

Aggarwal, Vinod K., Robert O. Keohane, and David B. Yoffie. 1987. "The Dynamics of Negotiated Protectionism." *American Political Science Review* 81:345–66.

Amsden, Alice. 1989. *Asia's Next Giant: South Korea and Late Industrialization.* Oxford University Press.

Anchordoguy, Marie. 1988. "Mastering the Market: Japanese Government Targeting of the Computer Industry." *International Organization* 42:509–44.

Ayres, Robert L. 1983. *Banking on the Poor: The World Bank and World Poverty.* MIT Press.

Baldwin, Neil. 1995. *Edison: Inventing the Century.* Hyperion.

Balmer, Brian, and Margaret Sharp. 1993. "The Battle for Biotechnology: Scientific and Technological Paradigms and the Management of Biotechnology in Britain in the 1980s." *Research Policy* 22:463–78.

Bauer, Raymond A., Ithiel de Sola Pool, and Lewis Anthony Dexter. 1972. *American Business and Public Policy: The Politics of Foreign Trade,* 2d ed. Chicago: Aldine-Atherton.

Bayard, Thomas O., and Kimberly Ann Elliott. 1994. *Reciprocity and Retaliation in U.S. Trade Policy.* Washington: Institute for International Economics.

Bedini, Silvio A. 1990. *Thomas Jefferson: Statesman of Science.* Macmillan.

Bennett, Douglas C., and Kenneth E. Sharpe. 1985. *Transnational Corporations versus the State: The Political Economy of the Mexican Auto Industry.* Princeton University Press.

Bernheim, B. Douglas, and J. B. Shoven. 1992. "Comparing the Cost of Capital in the United States and Japan." In Nathan Rosenberg and others, eds., *Technology and the Wealth of Nations,* 151–74. Stanford University Press.

Bhattacharya, Anindya K. 1976. "The Influence of the International Secretariat: UNCTAD and Generalized Tariff Preferences." *International Organization* 30:76–90.

Biersteker, Thomas J. 1987. *Multinationals, the State, and Control of the Nigerian Economy.* Princeton University Press.

———. 1990. "Reducing the Role of the State in the Economy: A Conceptual Exploration of IMF and World Bank Prescriptions." *International Studies Quarterly* 34:477–92.

Birnbaum, Philip H. 1984. "The Choice of Strategic Alternatives under Increasing Regulation in High Technology Companies." *Academy of Management Journal* 27:489–510.

Boskin, Michael J., and Lawrence J. Lau. 1992. "Capital, Technology, and Economic Growth." In Nathan Rosenberg and others, eds., *Technology and the Wealth of Nations,* 17–56. Stanford University Press.

Brander, James A. 1988. "Rationales for Strategic Trade and Industrial Policy." In Paul Krugman, ed., *Strategic Trade Policy and the New International Economics*, 23–46. MIT Press.

Branscomb, Lewis M., ed. 1993. *Empowering Technology: Implementating a U.S. Strategy* MIT Press.

Brownlie, Ian. 1990. *Principles of Public International Law*. Oxford University Press.

Busch, Lawrence, and others. 1991. *Plants, Power, and Profit: Social, Economic, and Ethical Consequences of the New Biotechnologies*. Cambridge, Mass.: Basil Blackwell.

Calder, Kent E. 1993. *Strategic Capitalism: Private Business and Public Purpose in Japanese Industrial Finance*. Princeton University Press.

Callan, Benedicte. 1995. "Who Gains from Genes? A Study of National Innovation Strategies in the Globalizing Biotechnology Markets." PhD dissertation, University of California at Berkeley.

Cardwell, Donald. 1995. *The Norton History of Technology*. Norton.

Chamberlin, E. R. 1965. *Everyday Life in Renaissance Times*. Putnam.

Cheng, Tun-jen. 1990. "Political Regimes and Development Strategies: South Korea and Taiwan." In Gary Gereffi and Donald L. Wymon, eds., *Manufacturing Miracles: Paths of Industrialization in Latin America and East Asia*. Princeton University Press.

Clark, Kim B., Robert H. Hayes, and Christopher Lorenz. 1985. *The Uneasy Alliance: Managing the Productivity-Technology Dilemma*. Harvard Business School Press.

Cline, William R., ed. 1983. *Trade Policy in the 1980s*. Washington: Institute for International Economics.

Cohen, H. Floris. 1994. *The Scientific Revolution: A Historical Inquiry*. University of Chicago Press.

Cohen, Stephen S., and John Zysman. 1987. *Manufacturing Matters: The Myth of the Post-Industrial Economy*. Basic Books.

Collier, David, and James Mahoney. 1996. "Insights and Pitfalls: Selection Bias in Qualitative Research." *World Politics* 49 (1):56–91.

Commisso, Ellen. 1986. "State Structures, Political Processes, and Collective Choice in CMEA States." *International Organization* 40:195–238.

Committee on Ways and Means, U.S. House of Representatives. 1989. *Overview and Compilation of U.S. Trade Statutes*. Government Printing Office.

Conybeare, John A. C. 1990. "International Organization and the Theory of Property Rights." *International Organization* 34:307–34.

Cook-Deegan, Robert. 1994. *The Gene Wars: Science, Politics, and the Human Genome*. Norton.

Cox, Robert W., and others. 1973. *The Anatomy of Influence: Decision Making in International Organization*. Yale University Press.

Crawford, Beverly, and Stefanie Lenway. 1985. "Decision Modes and International Regime Change: Western Collaboration on East-West Trade." *World Politics* 37:375–402.

Curzon, Gerard. 1965. *Multilateral Commercial Diplomacy: The General Agreement on Tariffs and Trade and Its Impact on National Commercial Policies and Techniques*. Praeger.

Cutahar, Michael Zammit, ed. 1984. *UNCTAD and the South-North Dialogue: The First Twenty Years*. Pergamon.

Dakolias, Maria. 1995. "A Strategy for Judicial Reform: The Experience in Latin America." *Virginia Journal of International Law* 36:167–232.

Dam, Kenneth W. 1970. *The GATT: Law and International Economic Organization*. University of Chicago Press.

Deardorff, Alan. 1984. "Testing Trade Theories and Predicting Trade Flows." In R.W. Jones and Peter Kenen, eds., *Handbook of International Economics,* 467–517. Cambridge University Press.

Derian, Jean-Claude. 1990. *America's Struggle for Leadership in Technology*. MIT Press.

Destler, I. M. 1992. *American Trade Politics*. Washington: Institute for International Economics.

Dexter, Lewis Anthony, ed. 1970. *Elite and Specialized Interviewing*. Northwestern University Press.

Deyo, Frederic C., ed. 1987. *The Political Economy of the New Asian Industrialism*. Cornell University Press.

Diamond, Larry, Juan J. Linz, and Seymour Martin Lipset, eds. 1995. *Politics in Developing Countries: Comparing Experiences with Democracy*. Boulder, Colo.: Lynne Rienner.

Dornbusch, Rudiger, and F. Leslie C. H. Helmers, eds. 1988. *The Open Economy: Tools for Policymakers in Developing Countries*. Oxford University Press for the World Bank.

Drake, William J. 1995. *The New Information Infrastructure: Strategies for US Policy*. New York: Twentieth Century Fund Press.

Eggertsson, Thrainn. 1990. *Economic Behavior and Institutions*. Cambridge University Press.

Encarnation, Dennis J. 1989. *Dislodging the Multinationals: India's Strategy in Comparative Perspective*. Cornell University Press.

Evans, Gail. 1994. "Intellectual Property as a Trade Issue: The Making of the Agreementf on Trade-Related Aspects of Intellectual Property Rights." *World Competition* 1:137–80.

Evans, Peter. 1979. *Dependent Development: The Alliance of Multinational, State, and Local Capital in Brazil*. Princeton University Press.

———. 1995. *Embedded Autonomy: States and Industrial Transformation*. Princeton University Press.

Evanson, Robert E., and Gustav Ranis. 1990. *Science and Technology: Lessons for Development Policy*. Boulder, Colo.: Westview Press.

Fagerberg, J. 1987. "A Technology Gap Approach to Why Growth Rates Differ." *Research Policy* 16:87–99.

Finlayson, Jock A., and Mark W. Zacher. 1983. "The GATT and the Regulation of Trade Barriers: Regime Dynamics and Functions." In Stephen D. Krasner, ed., *International Regimes*, 273–314. Cornell University Press.

———. 1990. *Managing International Markets: Developing Countries and the Commodity Trade Regime*. Columbia University Press.

Flamm, Kenneth. 1988. *Creating the Computer: Government, Industry, and High Technology*. Brookings.

———. 1996. *Mismanaged Trade: Strategic Policy and the Semiconductor Industry*. Brookings.

Frenkel, Jacob A., and Morris Goldstein, eds. 1991. *International Financial Policy*. Washington: International Monetary Fund.

Friman, H. Richard. 1993. "Side Payments versus Security Cards: Domestic Bargaining Tactics in International Economic Negotiations." *International Organization* 47 (Summer):387–410.

Gaddis, John Lewis. 1982. *Strategies of Containment: A Critical Appraisal of Postwar American National Security Policy*. Oxford University Press.

Garrett, Geoffrey, and Peter Lange. 1995. "Internationalism, Institutions, and Political Change." *International Organization* 49:627–56.

Garritsen de Vries, Margaret. 1987. *Balance of Payments Adjustment, 1945 to 1986*. Washington: International Monetary Fund.

George, Alexander. 1979. "Case Studies and Theory Development: The Method of Structured, Focused Comparison." In Paul G. Lauren, ed., *Diplomacy: New Approaches in History, Theory, and Policy*, 43–68. Free Press.

Gilpin, Robert. 1975. *U.S. Power and the Multinational Corporation: The Political Economy of Foreign Direct Investment*. Basic Books.

———. 1987. *The Political Economy of International Relations*. Princeton University Press.

Goodman, John, and Louis Pauly. 1993. "The Obsolescence of Capital Controls? Economic Management in an Age of Global Markets." *World Politics*, 46:50–82.

Goodman, Louis W. 1987. *Small Nations, Giant Firms*. Holmes & Meier.

Graham, Otis L. Jr. 1992. *Losing Time: The Industrial Policy Debate*. Harvard University Press.

Grossman, Gene, and Elhanan Helpman. 1991. *Innovation and Growth in the Global Economy*. MIT Press.

Guisinger, Stephen. 1986. "Host-Country Policies to Attract and Control Foreign Investment." In Theodore H. Moran, ed., *Investing in Development: New Roles of Private Capital*, 157–72. New Brunswick, N.J.: Transaction Books.

Haas, Ernst B. 1964. *Beyond the Nation State: Functionalism and International Organization* Stanford University Press.

———. 1990. *When Knowledge Is Power: Three Models of Change in International Organizations*. University of California Press.

Haas, Peter M. 1989. "Do Regimes Matter? Epistemic Communities and Mediterranean Pollution Control." *International Organization* 43 (Summer):386–87.

———. 1992. "Banning Chlorofluorocarbons: Epistemic Community Efforts to Protect Stratospheric Ozone," *International Organization* 46 (Winter):187–224.

Haggard, Stephan. 1992. *Pathways from the Periphery: The Politics of Growth in the Newly Industrialized Countries*. Princeton University Press.

———. 1995. *Developing Nations and the Politics of Global Integration*. Brookings.

Haggard, Stephan, and Robert Kaufman. 1995. *The Political Economy of Democratic Transitions*. Princeton University Press.

Haggard, Stephan, and Beth Simmons. 1987. "Theories of International Regimes." *International Organization* 41 (Summer):491–517.

Harris, Marth Caldwell, and Gordon E. Moore, eds. 1992. *Linking Trade and Technology Policies: An International Comparison of the Policies of Industrialized Nations*. Washington: National Academy Press.

Heiduk, Gunter, and Kozo Yamamura, eds. 1990. *Technological Competition and Interdependence: The Search for Policy in the United States, West Germany, and Japan*. University of Washington Press.

Henkin, Louis, and others. 1980. *International Law: Cases and Materials.* St. Paul, Minn.: West Publishing.

Hoekman, Bernard M. 1989. "Determining the Need for Issue Linkages in Multilateral Trade Negotiations." *International Organization* 43 (Autumn):693–714.

Hudec, Robert E. 1987. *Developing Countries in the GATT Legal System.* Brookfield, Vt.: Gower Publishing.

——. 1993. *Enforcing International Trade Law: The Evolution of the Modern GATT Legal System.* Salem, N.H.: Butterworth.

Hufbauer, Gary C. 1984. *Subsidies in International Trade.* Washington: Institute for International Economics.

——, ed. 1990. *Europe 1992: An American Perspective.* Brookings.

Hufbauer, Gary C., and Jeffrey J. Schott. 1985. *Trading for Growth: The Next Round of Trade Negotiations.* Washington: Institute for International Economics.

Huff, Toby E. 1993. *The Rise of Early Modern Science: Islam, China, and the West.* Cambridge University Press.

Huntington, Samuel P. 1968. *Political Order in Changing Societies.* Yale University Press.

International Intellectual Property Alliance. Various years. *Special 301 Recommendations.* Washington.

International Trade Commission. 1997. *Recent Trends in U.S. Services Trade.* Washington.

Islam, Shafiqul, and Michael Mandelbaum. 1993. *Making Markets: Economic Transformation in Eastern Europe and the Post-Soviet States.* New York: Council on Foreign Relations.

Jackson, John H. 1980. "The Birth of the GATT-MTN System: A Constitutional Appraisal." *Law and Policy in International Business* 12:21–58.

Jackson, John H., Jean-Victor Louis, and Mitsuo Matsushita. 1984. *Implementing the Tokyo Round: National Constitutions and International Economic Rules.* University of Michigan Press.

Jackson, Robert H. 1990. *Quasi-States: Sovereignty, International Relations and the Third World.* Cambridge University Press.

Jacobson, Harold K. 1984. *Networks of Interdependence: International Organizations and the Global Political System,* 2d ed. Knopf.

Jacobson, Harold K., and Eric Stein. 1966. *Diplomats, Scientists, and Politicians: The United States and the Nuclear Test Ban Negotiations.* University of Michigan Press.

Jansen, Dorothea. 1994. "National Research Systems and Change: The Reaction of the British and German Research Systems to the Discovery of High-Technology Superconductors." *Research Policy* 23:357–74.

Jasanoff, Sheila. 1985. "Technological Innovation in a Corporatist State: The Case of Biotechnology in the Federal Republic of Germany." *Research Policy* 14:23–38.

Johnson, Chalmers. 1982. *MITI and the Japanese Miracle*. Stanford University Press.

———. 1986. "The Nonsocialist NICs: East Asia." *International Organization* 40:557–66.

Jorde, Thomas M., and David J. Teece, eds. 1992. *Antitrust, Innovation, and Competitiveness*. Oxford University Press.

Kahler, Miles, ed. 1986. *The Politics of International Debt*. Cornell University Press.

———. 1995. *International Institutions and the Political Economy of Integration*. Brookings.

Kelly, J. M. 1992. *A Short History of Western Legal Theory*. Oxford University Press.

Keohane, Robert O. 1984. *After Hegemony: Cooperation and Discord in the World Political Economy*. Princeton University Press.

Keohane, Robert O., and Joseph S. Nye. 1977. *Power and Interdependence: World Politics in Transition*. Boston: Little, Brown.

Kindleberger, Charles P. 1973. *The World in Depression, 1929–1939*. University of California Press.

Kingdon, John W. 1984. *Agendas, Alternatives, and Public Policies*. Boston: Little, Brown.

———. 1989. *Congressmen's Voting Decisions*. University of Michigan Press.

Kitschelt, Herbert. 1991. "Industrial Governance Structures, Innovation Strategies, and the Case of Japan: Sectoral or Cross-National Comparative Analysis." *International Organization* 45:453–94.

Kobrin, Stephen J. 1987. "Testing the Bargaining Hypothesis in the Manufacturing Sector in Developing Countries." *International Organization* 41:609–38.

Kogut, Bruce. 1991. "Country Capabilities and the Permeability of Borders." *Strategic Management Journal* 12:33–47.

Kornai, Janos. 1990. "Socialist Transformation and Privatization: Shifting from a Socialist System." *East European Politics and Societies* 4:255–304.

Krasner, Stephen D. 1974. "Oil Is the Exception." *Foreign Policy* 14:64–85.

——. 1976. "State Power and the Structure of International Trade." *World Politics* 28:317–47.

——. 1978. *Defending the National Interest: Raw Materials Investments and U.S. Foreign Policy*. Princeton University Press.

——. 1983a. *International Regimes*. Cornell University Press.

——. 1983b. "Structural Causes and Regime Consequences: Regimes as Intervening Variables." In Krasner, ed., *International Regimes*, 1–22.

——. 1985. *Structural Conflict: The Third World against Global Liberalism*. University of California Press.

Krueger, Anne O. 1995. *Trade Policies and Developing Nations*. Brookings.

Kuehn, Thomas J., and Alan L. Porter, eds. 1991. *Science, Technology, and National Policy*. Cornell University Press.

Kwitny, Jonathan. 1984. *Endless Enemies: The Making of an Unfriendly World*. Congdon & Weed.

Landes, David S. 1969. *The Unbound Prometheus: Technological Change and Industrial Development in Western Europe from 1750 to the Present*. Cambridge University Press.

Landau, Martin, and Nathan Rosenberg, eds. 1986. *Positive Sum Strategy*. Washington: National Academy Press.

Lardy, Nicholas. 1992. *Foreign Trade and Economic Reform in China, 1978–1990*. Cambridge University Press.

Lawrence, Robert Z. 1996. *Regionalism, Multilateralism, and Deeper Integration*. Brookings.

Lewis, John P. 1991. "Some Consequences of Giantism: The Case of India." *World Politics* 43:367–89.

——. 1995. *India's Political Economy: Governance and Reform*. Oxford University Press.

Lindblom, Charles E. 1977. *Politics and Markets: The World's Political Economic Systems*. Basic Books.

Lipson, Charles. 1985. *Standing Guard: Protecting Foreign Capital in the Nineteenth and Twentieth Centuries*. University of California Press.

Martin, Cathie Jo. 1995. "Nature or Nurture? Sources of Firm Preferences for National Health Reform." *American Political Science Review* 89:898–913.

Mardon, Russell. 1990. "The State and the Effective Control of Foreign Capital: The Case of South Korea." *World Politics* 43:111–38.

Marresse, Michael. 1986. "CMEA: Effective but Cumbersome Political Economy." *International Organization* 40:287–328.

McKenna, Regis, Michael Borrus, and Stephen Cohen. 1984. "Industrial Policy and International Competition in High Technology." *California Management Review* 26:15–32.

Miller, Donald L. 1996. *City of the Century: The Epic of Chicago and the Making of America.* Simon and Schuster.

Milner, Helen V. 1988. *Resisting Protectionism: Global Industries and the Politics of International Trade.* Princeton University Press.

Milner, Helen V., and David B. Yoffie. "Between Free Trade and Protectionism: Strategic Trade Policy and a Theory of Corporate Trade Demands." *International Organization* 43:239–73.

Mitrany, David. 1966. *A Working Peace System: An Argument for the Functional Development of International Organization.* Chicago: Quadrangle Books.

Montinola, Gabriella, and others. 1995. "Federalism, Chinese Style: The Political Basis for Economic Success in China." *World Politics* 48:50–81.

Moran, Theodore H., ed. 1985. *Multinational Corporations: The Political Economy of Foreign Direct Investment.* Lexington, Mass.: D. C. Heath.

Mowery, David C., and Nathan Rosenberg, eds. 1989. *Technology and the Pursuit of Economic Growth.* Cambridge University Press.

Murtha, Thomas P. 1991. "Surviving Industrial Targeting: State Credibility and Public Policy Contingencies in Multinational Subcontracting." *Journal of Law, Economics, and Organization* 7:117–43.

National Research Council and The World Bank. 1995. *Marshaling Technology for Development.* Washington: National Academy Press.

National Science Board. 1996. *Science and Engineering Indicators 1996.* Washington: National Science Foundation.

Nelson, Joan M., ed. 1990. *Economic Crisis and Policy Choice: The Politics of Adjustment in the Third World.* Princeton University Press.

Nelson, Richard R., ed. 1993. *National Innovation Systems.* Oxford University Press.

North, Douglass C. 1990. *Institutions, Institutional Change, and Economic Performance.* Cambridge University Press.

Okimoto, Daniel I. 1989. *Between MITI and the Market: Japanese Industrial Policy for High Technology*. Stanford University Press.

Organization for Economic Cooperation and Development. 1987. *International Technology Licensing: Survey Results*. Paris.

———. 1987. *The Internationalization of Software and Computer Services*. Paris.

Ostry, Sylvia, and Richard R. Nelson. 1995. *Techno-Nationalism and Techno-Globalism: Conflict and Cooperation*. Brookings.

Oye, Kenneth A. 1992. *Economic Discrimination and Political Exchange: World Political Ecoomy in the 1930s and 1980s*. Princeton University Press.

Pearson, Margaret M. 1991. *Joint Ventures in the People's Republic of China*. Princeton University Press.

Preeg, Ernest H. 1970. *Traders and Diplomats: An Analysis of the Kennedy Round of Negotiations under the General Agreement on Tariffs and Trade*. Brookings.

Putnam, Robert D. 1988. "Diplomacy and Domestic Politics: The Logic of Two-Level Games." *International Organization* 42:427–60.

Przeworski, Adam. 1991. *Democracy and the Market: Political and Economic Reforms in Eastern Europe and Latin America*. Cambridge University Press.

Ramsey, Robert. 1984. "UCTAD's Failures: The Rich Get Richer." *International Organization* 38:387–97.

Rosenberg, Nathan, Ralph Landau, and David C. Mowery, eds. 1992. *Technology and the Wealth of Nations*. Stanford University Press.

Rosenberg, Nathan, and Richard R. Nelson. 1994. "American Universities and Technical Advance in Industry" *Research Policy* 23:323–48.

Rothstein, Robert L. 1984. "Regime-Creation by a Coalition of the Weak: Lessons from the NIEO and the Integrated Program for Commodities." *International Studies Quarterly* 28:307–28.

Rubin, Seymour J., and Thomas R. Graham, eds. 1984. *Managing Trade Relations in the 1980s: Issues Involved in the GATT Ministerial Meeting of 1982*. Totowa, N.J.: Rowman & Allanheld.

Ryan, Michael P. 1994. "Industrial Policy: Theory and Concepts." In Gunnar K. Sletmo and Gavin Boyd, eds., *Pacific Industrial Policies*, 1–26. Boulder, Colo.: Westview Press.

———. 1995a. *Playing by the Rules: American Trade Power and Diplomacy in the Pacific* Georgetown University Press.

——. 1995b. "USTR's Implementation of 301 Policy in the Pacific." *International Studies Quarterly* 39 (September):333–50.

Sandholtz, Wayne. 1993. "Institutions and Collective Action: The New Telecommunications in Western Europe." *World Politics* 45:242–70.

Scherer, F. M. 1992. *International High-Technology Competition.* Harvard University Press.

——. 1994. *Competition Policies for an Integrated World Economy.* Brookings.

Schon, Donald. 1981. "The National Climate for Technological Innovation." In Thomas J. Kuehn and Alan L. Porter, *Science, Technology, and National Policy,* 148–60. Cornell University Press.

Schoppa, Leonard J. 1993. "Two-Level Games and Bargaining Outcomes: Why Gaiatsu Succeeds in Japan in Some Cases but Not Others." *International Organization* 47 (Summer):353–86.

Scott, James C. 1972. *Comparative Political Corruption.* Englewood Cliffs, N.J.: Prentice-Hall.

Sebenius, James K. 1983. "Negotiation Arithmetic: Adding and Subtracting Issues and Parties." *International Organization* 37:281–316.

Shihata, Ibrahim F. I. 1991. *The World Bank in a Changing World.* Boston: Martinus Nijhoff.

Shirk, Susan. 1993. *The Political Logic of Economic Reform in China.* University of California Press.

Sklar, Martin J. 1992. *The United States as a Developing Country: Studies in U.S. History in the Progressive Era and the 1920s.* Cambridge University Press.

Skolnikoff, Eugene B. 1993. *The Elusive Transformation: Science, Technology, and the Evolution of International Politics.* Princeton University Press.

Snyder, Jack. 1984-85. "Richness, Rigor, and Relevance in the Study of Soviet Foreign Policy" 9:89–108.

Tollison, Robert, and Thonternational SecurityImas Willett. 1989. "An Economic Theory of Mutually Advantageous Issue Linkages in International Negotiations." *International Organization* 43:425–49.

Tyson, Laura D'Andrea. 1992. *Who's Bashing Whom? Trade Conflict in High-Technology Industries.* Washington: Institute for International Economics.

United Nations Commission on Transnational Corporations. 1989. *New Issues in the Uruguay Round of Multilateral Trade Negotiations,* E.90.II.A.15. New York.

——. 1990. *The Determinants of Foreign Direct Investment: A Survey of Evidence,* E.92.II.A.2. New York.

United Nations Conference on Trade and Development. 1986. "Periodic Report 1986: Policies, Laws, and Regulations on Transfer, Application, and Development of Technology," TD/B/C.6/133. Geneva.

Wade, Robert. 1990. *Governing the Market: Economic Theory and the Role of Government in East Asian Industrialization.* Princeton University Press.

Walker, Jack L. Jr. 1991. *Mobilizing Interest Groups in America: Patrons, Professions, and Social Movements.* University of Michigan Press.

Wallace, Cynthia Day. 1992. "Foreign Direct Investment in the Third World." In Cynthia Day Wallace, ed., *Foreign Direct Investment in the 1990s.* Washington: Center for Strategic and International Studies.

Williamson, John, ed. 1983. *IMF Conditionality.* Washington: Institute for International Economics.

Winham, Gilbert R. 1980. "Robert Strauss, MTN, and the Control of Faction." *Journal of World Trade* 14:377–97.

——. 1986. *International Trade and the Tokyo Round Negotiation.* Princeton University Press.

Wolfers, Arnold. 1962. *Discord and Collaboration: Essays on International Politics.* Johns Hopkins University Press.

Young, Oran R. 1983. "Regime Dynamics: The Rise and Fall of International Regimes." In Stephen Krasner, ed., *International Regimes,* 93–114. Cornell University Press.

Index

A&M Records, 182
Advisory Committee on Trade
  Policy and Negotiation (ACTPN),
  10, 68, 69, 105
Agreement on Trade-Related
  Aspects of Intellectual Property
  Rights. *See* TRIPS
AIG, 193–94
Akzo, 45
American Association of Law
  Libraries, 183
American Association of Publishers,
  70
American Express, 193–94, 195
American Film Marketing
  Association, 70
American Library Association, 163,
  183
America Online, 163, 164–65
Animals: transgenic, 113, 200
Appropriability problem, 5, 22, 26
Argentina, 87, 108
Arnstein, Ira, 59
Arnstein v. *Porter*, 59
Artificial intelligence, 135
Artworks, visual: copyright for, 55;
  digitized, 176
Asia: economic policies, 151; U.S.
  imports from, 44. *See also specific
  countries*

Association of Research Libraries,
  183
AT&T, 194
Audio Home Recording Act, 168
Audio tape recorders, 61; digital,
  168–69
Australia, 88
Author's rights, 48, 55, 56, 63–65,
  101–02, 119–20, 173, 174
AZT, 78

Banks: on-line services, 184
Bell Atlantic, 163, 164
Berne Convention for the Protection
  of Literary and Artistic Works,
  100–02, 131; administration, 126;
  amendment by WIPO Copyright
  Treaty, 179–81, 183, 189;
  application to multimedia
  products, 176; Chinese accession
  to, 81; incorporation in NAFTA,
  119; incorporation in TRIPS, 109;
  membership, 102; proposed
  reforms, 68, 105, 109, 159,
  176–77, 178–79; U.S. accession
  to, 50
Bilateral diplomacy: U.S. and
  developing countries, 11, 70, 71,
  73–79, 86–88; U.S. and Japan, 39
Bioengineering industry, 31, 184, 200

235